Glimpses into My Own Black Box

OTHER BOOKS
BY GEORGE W. STOCKING, JR.

Race, Culture, and Evolution: Essays in the History of Anthropology

Victorian Anthropology

The Ethnographer's Magic and Other Essays in the History of Anthropology

After Tylor: British Social Anthropology, 1888–1951

Delimiting Anthropology: Occasional Essays and Reflections

Glimpses into My Own Black Box

An Exercise in Self-Deconstruction

GEORGE W. STOCKING, JR.

THE UNIVERSITY OF WISCONSIN PRESS

The University of Wisconsin Press
1930 Monroe Street, 3rd Floor
Madison, Wisconsin 53711-2059
uwpress.wisc.edu

3 Henrietta Street
London WCE 8LU, England
eurospanbookstore.com

1   3   5   4   2

Printed in the United States of America

Library of Congress Cataloging-in-Publication Data
Stocking, George W., 1928–
Glimpses into my own black box: an exercise in self-deconstruction /
George W. Stocking.
    p.   cm.—(History of anthropology)
Includes bibliographical references and index.
ISBN 978-0-299-24984-7 (pbk.: alk. paper)
ISBN 978-0-299-24983-0 (e-book)
    1. Stocking, George W., 1928–
    2. Anthropologists—United States—Biography.
    I. Title.   II. Series: History of anthropology; v. 12.
GN21.S785S76   2010
    301.092—dc22
        [B]
    2010012966

This book is dedicated to the women who have engendered so many of the "rich complexities" of my life, whose contributions are manifest in the text, but not systematically explicated—including my mother, my sisters, both of my wives, my sisters-in-law, my daughters, my grand-daughters, as well as numerous teachers, students, research assistants, departmental secretaries, and editors of this and other books—going back in time to the nine Greek muses, including especially Clio, the muse of history, as well as Margaret Mead, who might be a likely candidate if there were a tenth muse for anthropology—all the way back to Pandora, whose curiosity led her to open the first "Black Box."

Contents

Epilogue

Illustrations

Given the autobiographical nature of this book, the illustrations focus on events, situations, and people important in my own life, and with a few exceptions were garnered from photographs in my possession when the production process was already underway. Taken together, they form a kind of "family album" of my life. Unfortunately, there are major episodes that remain undocumented, either because suitable illustrations do not exist or due to the difficulty of obtaining them in the time available. Among the excluded are my trade union activities, my membership in the Communist Party, my experience of "race relations," and the solitary processes of my historical research. With the exception of the initial grouping of illustrations of FBI documents, the rest of the pictures have been placed in close relation to relevant passages in the narrative, as indicated in the listing below.

Glimpses into My Own Black Box

Prologue

My Life under Surveillance

For seven years during the McCarthy era, from 1949 to 1956, I was a member of the Communist Party—roughly, from the time its leaders were indicted under the Smith Act, through the period when it was semi-legal and eventually outlawed, until it began to fall apart in the aftermath of the Khrushchev "revelations." It was not a propitious time to be a Communist, and we were well aware that the Federal Bureau of Investigation might at any moment be watching or listening. We took for granted that certain phones might be tapped, and our comings and goings observed. My in-laws' summer house at Sandwich on Cape Cod, which was often visited by party friends and sympathizers, was at times obviously "staked out," and when we drove away, we were sometimes aware of being followed. At one point, the neighboring summer house of another radical family was broken into in a search for "incriminating" documents; all the time, of course, the FBI was adding entries into its own bureaucratic hoard of incriminating records. In 1989, when I was entering the age of reminiscence, I took advantage of the Freedom of Information Act to request my FBI file, along with that of my father. This, in the hope that these might supplement and jog my memory—which even in the best of times functioned like a sieve, with passing experience leaving residues that might expand if given appropriate stimulation—visual, conversational, or more often, from a methodological point of view, textual.

After a lapse of over a year, I received a package of photocopies four inches thick. My father's file was a series of security checks for government jobs, starting in the fall of 1940, when he joined the Advisory Commission to the Council of National Defense. It included numerous testimonials from citizens of Clarendon, Texas, where my grandfather had set up medical practice in 1885. Although there were occasional comments on the Stocking family's anti-Trinitarian religious views and their preference for the life of the mind rather than the business world, all of them affirmed the family's patriotic Americanism. In 1947, the only blot on my father's record was his membership in the University of Texas chapter of the American Committee for Democracy and Intellectual Freedom, chaired nationally by Franz Boas but cited by the House Un-American Activities Committee in 1942 as a Communist front organization. In 1951 and later, however, it was my own affiliations and activities that caused him problems. However, despite the fact that my membership in the party had by then been on several occasions a painful issue between the two of us, he did not mention it to the FBI, nor did he mention to me the fact that that they had interviewed him.[1]

Given the numerous countervailing attestations by his friends and colleagues of my father's hatred of Communist totalitarianism and his support of the "free enterprise system," it is unlikely that he lost any appointment on my account. However, much of the material in his file relating to me was blacked out, and that was even truer of my own file, from which whole pages were "withheld entirely," for various coded reasons (most frequently, b7d: "could reasonably be expected to disclose the identity of a confidential source"). The same code categories accounted for other blacked-out passage of less than a page—on many of which there were only a few words left legible. Following up the first stage of the slow appeal procedure, I later obtained another half inch or so of photocopies—at which point I gave up pursuing the matter.

Despite all that black marking, my file did provide a kind of grid for memory, beginning just after the disappointment of Henry Wallace's performance in the presidential election of 1948. Several items summarized from the Harvard *Crimson* ("Unknown Assailants Attack HYD [Harvard Youth for Democracy] Pamphlet Distributor") evoked the traumatic recollection of a rainy night when I was roughed up and

---

1. Several years ago, my brother Myron told me that the FBI had also questioned him about my activities when he was beginning his service as a doctor in the U.S. Navy in the mid-1950s.

knocked to the ground by three Harvard students in an entry to Wigglesworth Hall, where I was slipping under doorways a leaflet announcing a meeting to be addressed by the district organizer of the Communist Party. According to the FBI summary of the *Crimson* account, I planned to file an assault complaint with Dean Benda [*sic*], and I do vaguely recall a meeting in Wilbur Bender's office. A week later, the *Crimson* carried an article saying that three Wallace clubs at the university (undergraduate, graduate, and law) were joining together to form the Young Progressives of Harvard, whose spokesman called for "university-wide protests against the Fascist-like beating of George Stocking."

Surviving from the blackout of informant-based information were references to some of my more public political activities over the next several years: picketing at Boston Garden in March 1949, when Winston Churchill, three years after his "Iron Curtain" speech, addressed an MIT convocation; picketing at the Massachusetts State House that May, protesting a proposed amendment of the state "blasphemy" laws to include "the doctrines of atheistic Communism"; my arrest the following December for "blocking free foot passage" while handing out leaflets at a Roxbury department store that refused to hire "Negroes"—for which six of us spent part of a night in jail and were later tried and found innocent, when measurements of the store entrance indicated that the police must have been lying in testifying that no one could enter; being observed in April 1950 riding in the truck that set up sound equipment for a meeting in the garment district announcing a May Day celebration; selling the *Daily Worker* a few days later in front of the textile union convention; being seen at a national meeting of the Labor Youth League in New York in 1950; and marching in a State House vigil on the eve of the execution of Julius and Ethel Rosenberg in June 1953. Unrecorded in my file were a talk I gave over a Fall River, Massachusetts, radio station under a pseudonym as representative of the Communist Party, or midnight expeditions into the Boston garment district to post flyers against the Korean War, or a district convention of the United Packinghouse Workers when, on the same issue, I lost my cool and blurted out "to hell with the United States government"—to the outrage of most delegates and the horror of my comrades. Indeed, there was nothing in my file about my trade union activities, though it scrupulously noted every change of residence or employment (confirmed by "pretext telephone calls")—most strikingly in May of 1954, when J. Edgar Hoover himself notified the Inspector General of the Air Force that I had gone to work at the Springfield plant of American Bosch, which he identified as a "key facility." This, perhaps in consequence of my having been re-garded, at the outbreak of the Korean War, as a serious enough security risk to merit "priority consideration" if subjects with "index cards" were to be "apprehended in case of war with the USSR."

On three occasions, I was interviewed by the FBI. The first time was in August 1956, in Springfield, Massachusetts. The file indicates that I had that year been "Acting Section Organizer for the Communist Party" (a factoid about as reliable as the description of me as 150 pounds and blue-eyed—when I then weighed forty pounds more, and my eyes have always been brown). According to an informant, I had become "disillusioned" as "a result of the anti-Stalin line of the Commu-nist Party," and was apparently therefore considered likely to be coop-erative. However, when two agents engaged me in brief conversation on the front porch of our house on Greene Street, they reported that "Stocking stated he would refuse to answer questions regarding his membership," and that they terminated the interview "when it was ob-vious that further endeavors to solicit his cooperation would be with-out results." The second time was in December 1961, in Berkeley, Cali-fornia, when I was described as polite but uncooperative; two months later a planned re-interview was canceled, because my employment as professor "might well cause embarrassment to the Bureau"—and I was put on the "reserve index." My last encounter with the FBI was in the fall of 1967, after I had accompanied other academics from the Univer-sity of Pennsylvania to Washington to join a demonstration in front of the Department of Justice—part of a national anti–Vietnam War draft resistance campaign in which thousands of participants were eventu-ally accused of draft offenses. At the age of thirty-eight, turning in my draft card seemed only a slightly anxious symbolic gesture; but two weeks later there was a brief telephone interrogation by the FBI, in which I was recorded as having "nothing whatsoever to say to the FBI about anything"—and then having hung up the phone.

What amazed me on reading the unblacked-out portions of my file was that "a case had been opened" for each of 350 academics who on that occasion turned in their cards—with "indices searched," regional offices involved (in my case five), relatives and employers consulted, local selective service boards and prosecuting attorneys contacted. This follow-up continued for another year and a half, until my local board in Nashville, Tennessee, decided not to declare me delinquent, and the prosecuting attorney, after consultation with the Department of Justice, decided not to pursue the case because I was overage. Multiply by 350 the bureaucratic effort expended on one person, and that figure by the thousands who must have had "cases opened" during the Cold War and Vietnam periods, and one has a poignantly personal sense of just how large and costly a venture the search for subversives and dissenters was. And how costly it continues still to be, if one includes the Kafka clerks who pore over masses of documents line by line, blacking out words, phrases, sentences, paragraphs, and whole pages, pausing momentarily to consider which of the deletion codes should be noted in the margin—this, decades after the events that generated all that paper.[2]

What follows is another sheaf of paper, a self-reflexive "essay" that may allow glimpses into the "black box" out of which my historiography has been generated. As originally drafted in a much shorter version more than ten years ago, it was intended to serve as the introduction to a volume of essays on "anthropology yesterday," and it therefore emphasized formative experiences in my own life between 1945 and 1972. As now presented, it has been extended in time and divided into three parts. "Autobiographical Recollections" is a selective narrative account of the life events that shaped my work as an historian, which has recently been supplemented by the insertion of two new sections covering earlier phases of my life. "Historiographical Reflections" is a retrospective analytic interpretation of major methodological and substantive themes in the work shaped by that life. The third part, "Octogenarian Afterthoughts: 'Fragments Shored against My Ruins,'" was first drafted in 2008 and 2009, and in its present form covers events through the beginning of 2010.

In my more self-critical moments, the resulting essay/monograph seems self-indulgently long, occasionally repetitive, and presumptuously egoistic. I console myself with the observation that "Glimpses into My Own Black Box," when searched for on the Internet, did not match any documents. While I cannot claim to have examined more than a small fraction of works that might be included within the general rubric of that title, there may nevertheless be some general historiographical

2. Although in this essay I have not systematically cited all secondary sources, readers interested in the problems of accessing FBI materials may consult Diamond (1992) or Price (2004). In general, published sources will be cited in a modified version of the anthropological parenthetic form (author's name and date of publication), with the full title and place of publication provided in the References Cited section. Since many of these refer to my own work, their authorship in the text itself will be indicated simply by GS.

interest in an attempt that is more frankly autobiographical and systematically self-critical than others with which I am familiar.

In the process, I have drawn on surviving professional and personal documents, conversations with friends, various published materials, and several extended reminiscent interviews (notably those taped by my students Matti Bunzl and Ira Bashkow). However, my never fully reliable and now fading memory has also been a major source. And if I have revealed much of what seems relevant in my own personality and life experience to the way in which I have written history, there is still within my black box much that will remain obscure, whether by accident or design. Others, I am sure, might remember (or reconstruct) events differently. Indeed, this interplay of various sources has made me acutely conscious of processes of amnesia, repression, distortion, invention, and archetypification in the retrospective and regenerative dance of memory and personal history—which must always take place in a present moment. Let the reader beware.[3]

When this book was first drafted nearly fifteen years ago, the manuscript was only sixty pages long, and I had no definite plans for publication. Six months ago I bit the bullet and the publication process is now in its final stages. In those six months I have made many changes, some of them quite substantial, and having just read the final page proofs, I am sure that given "world enough and time" there would be many more (cf. A. Marvel c. 1650). But at this late stage—only weeks before the book has been scheduled to be published—the best I can do is augment my cautionary comments for prospective readers. This text is not an "easy read," even for those familiar with my work over the past half century. Its difficulty may be more sharply felt by those who come from other scholarly fields, or as members of more recent anthropological cohorts—including "post-colonial" generations trained after 1960, as well as the post-"information revolution" generation of the 1990s, many of whom might prefer a quick reference to Wikipedia rather than working their way through a text that is at many points dense and repetitive. This text, however, is not a Wikipedia article but an attempt (with many "linkages") to cast light into "my own black

---

3. During the period when they might have been relevant, I was unable to take full advantage of my professional papers, now being deposited in the Special Collections Research Center at the University of Chicago. Although there is a preliminary listing of the major portion of them, my ability to consult these materials has been limited by late-life mobility problems, as well as construction going on in the Center.

box" and to suggest why these "glimpses" have been recorded in a particular way. As the table of contents indicates, there are three major "parts," each of them written from a different perspective at a different moment of my life, each representing a different "take" on my career as an historian of anthropology. So, also, the rather lengthy illustration captions and footnotes—as well as the index prepared by Blythe Woolston—may be thought of as additional "takes," as augmentations of the text itself. With this in mind, I hope that prospective readers will find the time spent reading the book worth the effort.

Documenting Surveillance

The documents included here have been selected to tell the story of my surveillance by the FBI, and represent only a small sample of the total number of relevant documents I obtained under the Freedom of Information Act. Among the documents not included here are several from as early as 1940, when my father had his first background check for federal employment. The present sequence begins in 1950, when the FBI put me on the list of those to be arrested in the event of war with the USSR. The next document is the first page of a fifteen-page dossier describing both my public activities prior to that date as well as information gathered from informants within the party, whose names are blacked out.

The document following this is a four-page "Interrogatory for George Ward Stocking," the record of an interview with my father about his own past associations with groups later deemed "un-American" as well as his reaction to my membership in the Communist Party. The seven remaining documents are all from the period after I had left the party but continued to be under some form of surveillance, which after a series of failed attempts to interview me, consisted almost entirely of simply noting my changes of address and employment in various cities through the years, down to my current residence in Chicago. The sequence of documents included here ends with one from 1984, the occasion of which was not indicated, but was perhaps related to my having traveled to the Soviet Union and to Japan during that year. In contrast to the tendency to think of the FBI as a structure, it is worth noting the document suggesting that continued surveillance of me after I had taken up my position at a state university might cause "embarrassment to the bureau," which implies that local units worried that general concerns of the bureau might impact adversely on their ability to function locally. Finally, although the FBI on several different occasions referred to my eyes as blue, they have always been brown.

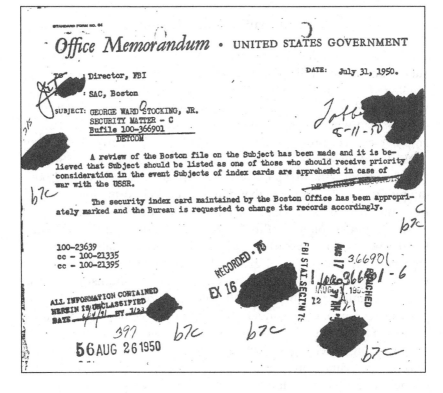

STANDARD FORM NO. 64

Office Memorandum • UNITED STATES GOVERNMENT

TO   : Director, FBI   DATE: July 31, 1950.

FROM   : SAC, Boston

SUBJECT: GEORGE WARD STOCKING, JR.
         SECURITY MATTER - C
         Bufile 100-366901
              DETCOM

          A review of the Boston file on the Subject has been made and it is be-
lieved that Subject should be listed as one of those who should receive priority
consideration in the event Subjects of index cards are apprehended in case of
war with the USSR.

          The security index card maintained by the Boston Office has been appropri-
ately marked and the Bureau is requested to change its records accordingly.

100-23639
cc - 100-21335
cc - 100-21395

RECORDED · 70
EX 16

ALL INFORMATION CONTAINED
HEREIN IS UNCLASSIFIED
DATE   BY

56 AUG 26 1950

Form No. 1
THIS CASE ORIGINATED AT   BOSTON   FILE NO. 100-23639 , 1ke

REPORT MADE AT	DATE WHEN MADE	PERIOD FOR	REPORT MADE BY
BOSTON	1/13/50	12/21/49;1/3, 4,5,6,9/50	67c

TITLE	CHARACTER OF CASE
GEORGE WARD STOCKING, JR.	SECURITY MATTER - C

SYNOPSIS OF FACTS:

Records, Harvard College, reflect subject born
December 8, 1926, at Berlin, Germany, of American
parentage. Attended Harvard College from May,
1945, until June, 1949, when he was graduated,
cum laude, with an A.B. in field of English.
Presently residing at 367 Massachusetts Avenue,
Boston, Mass., and employed as general worker for
United Parlor Furniture Company, 11 Webster
Avenue, Boston, Mass. Description of subject
set out in details. Subject closely affiliated
with Communist Party at Headquarters, Communist
Party, USA, District No. 1. Active with Communist
Party front organizations, John Reed Club, Young
Progressives of Massachusetts, and Labor Youth
League. Has furthered cause of Communist Party
through picketing activities. Signed nominating
petition for known Communist candidate in recent
Boston city elections.   in Communist Party
in Greater Boston area. No credit record. Subject
arrested by Boston Police 12/20/49 on charge of
obstructing foot passage, disposition still pend-

- P -

DETAILS:

This investigation was predicated upon information
made available by Confidential Informant   of
known reliability, that subject was an Associate
Editor of "YPM", monthly newspaper edited and published by the Young Progressives of Massachusetts.

APPROVED AND
FORWARDED: SPECIAL AGENT
                          IN CHARGE   DO NOT WRITE IN THESE SPACES

COPIES OF THIS REPORT   COPY IN FILE 100- 366901   RECORDED - 1
- Bureau
2 - Washington Field   INDEXED - 11
3 - Boston   JAN 16 1950

                                                            EX-78

COPIES DESTROYED
375   MAR 13 1963

INTERROGATORY FOR GEORGE WARD STOCKING

- - - - - - - - - - - -

1. Have you ever been a member of, affiliated with, or had any
connection with the Consumers National Federation? If so, please
relate the dates and circumstances; the nature and extent of your
interest and activities; your awareness, if any, of the alleged
Communist control, sympathies, and activities of the organization;
and what your attitude has been toward such alleged control, sympathies
and activities.

    I am not aware of the existence of the Consumers National Federati
I do not know what it is or what it stands for. Therefore, to the best
of my knowledge and belief, I have never been a member of it, affiliate
with it, or had any connection with it. I am a member of or a subscrib
to Consumer Reports, published monthly by Consumers Union, a non-profit
organization that investigates and advises its members on the comparati
merits of various consumers' goods. Whether Consumers Union has any
connection with the Consumers National Federation, I do not know. I ar
unaware of any alleged Communist control of Consumers Union or of any
sympathy on its part for Communism. At one time I was a member of or a
subscriber to the reports of Consumers Research, Inc., an agency simila
to Consumers Union. I am unaware of any alleged Communist control of
Consumers Research, Inc. or sympathy on its part for Communism. If the
Consumers National Federation is under Communist control or sympathetic
to the Communistic Party, I have no use or sympathy for it.

2. Have you ever been a member of, affiliated with, or had any connection with the American Committee for Democracy and Intellectual
Freedom? If so, please relate the dates and circumstances; the
nature and extent of your interest and activities; your awareness,
if any, of the alleged Communist control, sympathies, and
activities of the organization; and what your attitude has been tow
such alleged control, sympathies, and activities.

    To the best of my knowledge and belief, I was connected with the
American Committee for Democracy and Intellectual Freedom for several
weeks or perhaps months some 12 or 15 years ago. I am not sure of the
precise period because I have no materials in my files on it and I am
therefore speaking from memory. At the request of Professor
Wesley Clair Mitchell, distinguished economist of Columbia University
now deceased -- a man of unquestioned loyalty to the American democrati
system, I gave University of Texas faculty members an opportunity to
contribute funds to the Committee. A few responded, total contribution
including my own being perhaps $25. I associated myself with the organ
zation because I believe in democracy and intellectual freedom and beca
the distinguished names associated with the Committee lead me to believ
that its objectives corresponded with its name. Among those on its
executive committee, as I recall, were ████████████ of Princeton Universi
-- now retired -- Franz Boas -- now deceased -- noted anthropologist at
Columbia University, and as I have indicated, Wesley Mitchell. I dis-
associated myself from the organization after a short period because
it defended the rights of Communists to teach in the public schools of

b7c per FBI   Release per State Dept. and OPM
                         121-10970-47 Enclosure C

New York. Since then I have had nothing to do with it, and for the past decade I have been unaware of its existence. If it has continued to use my name in connection with its activities, it has done so without my knowledge or consent. I did not know at the time of my affiliation and I do not know now that it was Communist dominated or controlled and I would have had no sympathy with it if I had so known.

3. Have you ever been a member of, affiliated with, or had any connection with the National Federation for Constitutional Liberties? If so, please relate the dates and circumstances; the nature and extent of your interest and activities; your awareness, if any, of the alleged Communist control, sympathies, and activities of the organization; and what your attitude has been toward such alleged control, sympathies, and activities.

I am not familiar with the National Federation for Constitutional Liberties. I do not know what it is or what it stands for. To the best of my knowledge and belief I have never been a member of, affiliated with, or had any connection with it. If it is Communist controlled or sympathetic to the Communist program or activities, I have no use for it.

4. The reports contain considerable information regarding alleged Communist affiliations, activities, and sympathies of your son, George Ward Stocking, Jr., during recent years. He is reliably reported to have been an active member of the Communist Party as late as February, 1951, and testimony and information before the Board indicates that his membership and activities have continued until the present time. Please state fully for the Board's consideration your knowledge, if any, of the alleged Communist sympathies and activities of your son; your attitude toward such alleged sympathies and activities; the nature and extent of the relationship and association presently existing between you and your son; and any other comments you desire to make regarding the matter.

I became aware of the Communist affiliation of my son, George Ward Stocking, Jr., during the Christmas holidays of 1949. The revelation came as a shock to me. Communism is an ideology foreign to our home, one that he picked up among his associates at Harvard University when he was about 19 years old. My first reaction was one of anger and bitterness. I plead with him to see the error of his way and I told him that I would have no truck with Communism or Communists. I was visiting in Washington, D. C. at the time. After my return to Nashville I wrote him a letter setting forth more soberly and in detail (in words designed to convince him that I had some understanding of his problem) my position on the issues, and pleading with him to see the awful significance of his affiliation. It was not an easy letter to write and it was written only for him and his wife. But because you are entitled to know my thoughts on this matter, I am enclosing a copy of it.

Since December, 1949, I have seen little of my son and know nothing further of his affiliation or activities in the Communist Party. He has never been in my home since. Although the conflict in our political and economic beliefs constitutes an impassable gulf between us, I have not wished to sever all connections with him because I believe that his affiliation is largely a product of a youthful but deluded idealism and I have hoped that I might somehow be of some help to him in extricating him from the trap

Release per State Dept and CPM

into which he has fallen. Immediately before and after the
birth of his daughter in May of this year, he corresponded
with his mother more frequently and I saw him briefly on two
occasions this past summer. Although I did not on either
occasion discuss his party affiliation with him, I inferred
from a discussion I had with him about his future plans that
he may have abandoned his affiliation and that he might take
up the study of architecture as a profession. I indicated a
willingness to help him financially in educating himself for
a profession useful to a democratic society. Since then I
have not heard from him.

5. Are you now or have you ever been, a member of, affiliated with,
    or in sympathetic association with the Communist Party or any
    organization which is a front for, or controlled by the Communist
    Party? If so, explain fully.

    I am not now and never have been a member of, affiliated with,
    or in sympathetic association with the Communist Party or with
    any organization known to me to be a front for or controlled by
    the Communist Party.

6. Have you ever believed in or supported the ideologies of the
    Communist Party or any organization which is a front for or
    controlled by the Communist Party?

    I have never believed in nor supported the ideologies of the
    Communist Party nor any organization which I have known to be a
    front for or controlled by the Communist Party. I have no sympathy
    with the Communist ideology or the Communist program. I am
    opposed to totalitarianism in all its forms and even during World
    War II when many people were identifying Russia with the democra-
    cies, I saw little difference between the totalitarianism of
    Hitler and that of Stalin. I am a loyal supporter of the American
    Democracy and of my government which on several occasions in the
    past I have endeavored faithfully to serve in various governmental
    posts.
    I regard myself as an economic liberal, a firm believer in
    free enterprise and political democracy. Because I believe there
    is a causal relationship between the two, I view with distrust
    concentration of economic and political power -- at home and
    abroad. My views on these matters have been set forth in my
    writings during the past decade (See Cartels in Action; Cartels
    or Competition, particularly the last chapter; and Monopoly and
    Free Enterprise, again particularly the last chapter; -- all
    jointly authored by Myron Watkins and myself.)

7. Have you ever made a contribution of time, talent, or money to any activity known to you to be sponsored by or closely affiliated with the Communist Party?

    I have never contributed my time, talents, or money to any activity known by me to be sponsored by or closely affiliated with the Communist Party.

George W. Stocking
_____
Signature

October 10, 1951
_____
Date

Subscribed and sworn to before me this 10th day of October, 1951

Marie C. Horton
_____
Notary Public S.C.

Office Memorandum · UNITED STATES GOVERNMENT

TO : DIRECTOR, FBI (100-366901) DATE: August 14, 1956

FROM : SAC, BOSTON (100-23639)

SUBJECT: GEORGE WARD STOCKING, JR.
SM - C

SECURITY INFORMANT PROGRAM
BOSTON DIVISION

ALL INFORMATION CONTAINED
HEREIN IS UNCLASSIFIED
DATE ___ BY ___

ReBoslet dated July 3, 1956, and Bureau authority granted July 17, 1956.
Report of ~~[redacted]~~ dated August 14, 1956, at Boston.

On August 2, 1956, GEORGE WARD STOCKING, JR. was interviewed in the
vicinity of 44 Green Street, Springfield, Massachusetts, by Special
Agents ~~[redacted]~~ under secure circum-
stances.

Subject was observed leaving his automobile and was approached by the
interviewing Agents and an exchange of amenities was made. Subject
demanded to know the identity of the agents. At this point the Agents
identified themselves and advised him that they felt he was in a position
to furnish considerable assistance to the United States Government in its
investigation of subversive activities. STOCKING stated that he felt he
was aware of what the representatives of the FBI wanted of him and he
did not desire to afford such type of cooperation.

The Agents advised STOCKING that in view of Communist Party confusion
due to the report of the 20th Congress of the Soviet Union, that he
might be willing to discuss his knowledge of or activities in the Communist
Party. STOCKING, however, stated he would have to think over his problem
and resolve the questions for himself. He stated further that he did not
think that anyone should interfere with his political thinking. STOCKING
was then asked whether he would give any information concerning the fact
of his present membership in the Communist Party. STOCKING stated he
would refuse to answer questions regarding his membership and refused to
answer the question as to whether he believed that the Communist Party
was a criminal conspiracy rather than a bona fide political party.

The Agents pointed out to him that JOSEPH STALIN, the former dictator of
the Soviet Union, had been charged with many serious crimes against
humanity which he had committed in the name of Communism. It was also
pointed out to him that in view of the present charges against Communism
that it could not now be labelled as the vanguard of the working class.
Again STOCKING stated that he was not willing to discuss these matters
and he did not think he could give the type of cooperation that the FBI
would desire of him.

The Agents asked STOCKING to think the matter over and that in the event
he should have a change of mind he should feel free to call the FBI
office. STOCKING stated that he would consider the proposition but
pointed out that he did not feel that he would change his mind and that
he did not want the FBI to contact him.

The subject was courteous, affable and pleasant during the interview
and it was terminated when it was obvious that further endeavors to solicit
his cooperation would be without results.

No consideration is being given to a re-interview at this time in view
of subject's position that he did not want to be re-contacted by the FBI.
However, contact will be made with informants to determine the reaction
of the subject to the interview and should the information indicate a
possible change in the subject's position, re-interview will be considered
at that time.

FD-302 (Rev. 1-25-60)

FEDERAL BUREAU OF INVESTIGATION

Date _____ 12/22/61

      GEORGE WARD STOCKING, Jr., was contacted at his
residence, 1731 Milvia Street, Berkeley, California, and
asked if he would speak with agents. STOCKING stated that
his position has not changed since he was contacted approximately five years ago. He stated he feels that his personal
beliefs are an area where he is under no compulsion to discuss the matter and that he is not desirous of doing so.
He stated that he is a citizen loyal to his government although his ideas and thinking may differ in some respect from
other people. He stated he does not feel that the government
is necessarily right nor is there a position right on all
matters. STOCKING stated he does not feel that in his experience he has encountered anything which he could in any way
consider subversive and, therefore, he has no information
which he could impart in this particular field. He stated he
did not wish to discuss matters of other individuals or their
thinking and ideas which in some cases may have been mistaken
ideas. STOCKING further stated he feels he will probably be
contacted by agents again in the future and he feels his position will continue to remain the same even if contacted in the
future.

      STOCKING was asked to sum up his position, at which
time he stated, "Don't call me, I'll call you and don't sit
by the telephone waiting for it to ring".

      The following description of STOCKING was taken
from observation:

Race	White
Sex	Male
Age	33 (born 12/8/28)
Place of birth	Berlin, Germany
Height	6'
Weight	170 lbs.
Build	Slender
Hair	Blond to light brown, close cropped
Eyes	Blue
Complexion	Fair

On __12/19/61__ at __Berkeley, California__   File # __SF 100-46385__

by __SAs__ [redacted]   67C   Date dictated __12/20/61__

FD-305a (9-22-60)

1. ☐ Subject's name is being recommended for inclusion in Section ☐ A or ☐ B of the Reserve Index.

2. ☒ Subject's name is included in Section ☒ A or ☐ B of the Reserve Index.

3. ☐ The data appearing on the Reserve Index Card are current.

4. ☒ Changes on the Section A Reserve Index Card are necessary and Form FD-122a has been submitted to the Bureau.

5. ☒ A suitable photograph ☒ is ☐ is not available.

6. ☐ Careful consideration has been given to each source concealed and T symbols were utilized only in those instances where the identities of the sources must be concealed.

7. ☐ Subject is employed in a key facility and _____ is charged with security responsibility. Interested agencies are _____ .

8. ☐ This report is classified _____ because (state reason)

9. ☒ Subject was not reinterviewed because (state reason)
STOCKING was interviewed on 8/2/56 and refused to confirm or deny CP membership. He was reinterviewed on 12/20/61 and advised that he had no info to impart concerning security matters and declined to discuss his activities with Agents. This attitude coupled with his employment as a professor in a State university might well cause embarassment to the Bureau.

10. ☐ This case no longer meets the Section A Reserve Index criteria and a letter has been directed to the Bureau recommending cancellation of the Section A Reserve Index card.

11. ☒ This case has been re-evaluated in the light of the Reserve Index criteria and it continues to fall within such criteria because (state reason)
of STOCKING's previous responsible activity in the CP and various CP front organizations (ie: AYD,LYL, "Daily Worker, etc.) coupled with his present position as a professor at the University of California, Berkeley.

3*

FEDERAL BUREAU OF INVESTIGATION

Reporting Office	Office of Origin	Date	Investigative Period
SAN FRANCISCO	SAN FRANCISCO	12/27/61	12/19 - 20/61

TITLE OF CASE	Report made by		Typed By:
GEORGE WARD STOCKING, Jr.	SA ~~█████████~~ 67C		mrs
	CHARACTER OF CASE		
	SM - C		

Synopsis:

67C

REFERENCES: Report of SA ~~████████~~ 11/8/61, at San
Francisco.
Bureau letter to San Francisco, 11/20/61.

- P -

ALL INFORMATION CONTAINED
HEREIN IS UNCLASSIFIED
DATE ___ BY ___

ADMINISTRATIVE:

This case no longer meets Security Index criteria
and a letter has been directed to the Bureau recommending cancellation of the Security Index card.

LEAD:

SAN FRANCISCO

10/13/64 62
wodc/ab

At San Francisco, California

Will take appropriate administrative action upon re-
ceipt of advice from the Bureau.

Approved	Special Agent in Charge	Do not write in spaces below
Copies made:		

4 - Bureau (100-366901) (RM)

3 - San Francisco (100-46385)

100-366901-44   REC-12

4 DEC 29 1961

A*.
COVER PAGE

JAN 12 1962

FD-204 (Rev. 3-3-59)

UNITED STATES DEPARTMENT OF JUSTICE
FEDERAL BUREAU OF INVESTIGATION

Copy to: U. S. Attorney, Nashville, Tennessee

Report of: SA ▓▓▓▓▓▓▓▓▓▓▓▓▓▓▓▓▓▓▓▓▓▓ Office: MEMPHIS
Date: February 14, 1969

Field Office File #: Memphis 25-14424   *b7c*   Bureau File #: 25-562077

Title: GEORGE WARE STOCKING, JR.
SSN 40-20-28-778
PROTEST, WASHINGTON, D. C.
OCTOBER 20, 1967

Character: SELECTIVE SERVICE ACT, 1948

ALL INFORMATION CONTAINED
HEREIN IS UNCLASSIFIED
DATE ▓▓/▓/▓ BY ▓▓▓

Synopsis:

STOCKING one of several individuals who turned in Selective
Service Registration Certificate and Notice of Classification
issued by Local Board 20, Nashville, Tenn., to U. S. Department
of Justice, 10/20/67, by group engaged in protest activity
at Washington, D. C. AUSA, Nashville, Tenn., advised
instructions received from Department of Justice authorizing
prosecution be declined in this case due to registrant's age.

- C -

DETAILS:

AT NASHVILLE, TENNESSEE

STOCKING is one of several individuals who turned in
Selective Service Registration Certificate and Notice of
Classification issued by Local Board 20, Nashville, Tennessee,
to U. S. Department of Justice, October 20, 1967, by a group
engaged in protest activity at Washington, D. C.

On February 6, 1969, Assistant U. S. Attorney
ALFRED H. KNIGHT III, U. S. Court House, advised that he
received a letter from the U. S. Department of Justice on
February 3, 1969, authorizing him to decline prosecution of
STOCKING in this matter in view of the fact that the

OPTIONAL FORM NO. 10
MAY 1962 EDITION
GSA FPMR (41 CFR) 101-11.8

UNITED STATES GOVERNMENT

Memorandum

TO : DIRECTOR, FBI (100-366901)   DATE: 2/29/72

FROM : SAC, PHILADELPHIA (100-42693) (C)

SUBJECT: GEORGE WARD STOCKING, JR.
SM - C

Subject placed on RI-A on 2/9/62.

████████████████ and subscribes to "Daily Worker"
and "The Worker" 1952 through 1954; CP membership ████████

No overt activity noted in CP ████████████
therefore subject is being deleted from ADEX consideration
and is being removed from RI-A UACB.

ALL INFORMATION CONTAINED
HEREIN IS UNCLASSIFIED
DATE _____ BY _____

REC-103 100 - 366901 - 48

② - Bureau (RM)
1 - Philadelphia
(3)

15 MAR 3 1972

6 1 MAR 10 1972

Buy U.S. Savings Bonds Regularly on the Payroll Savings Plan

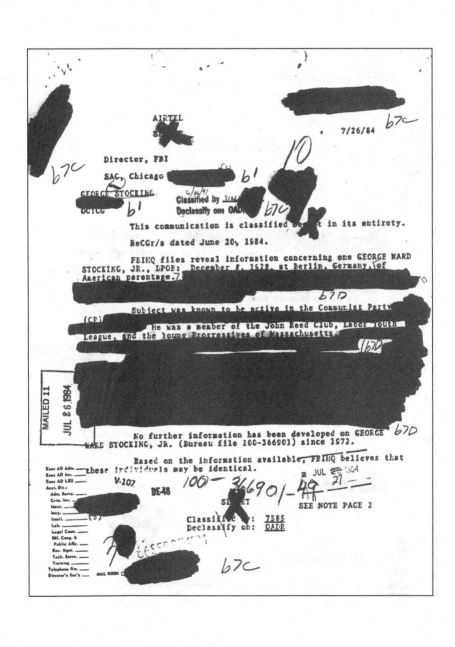

AIRTEL

7/26/84

Director, FBI

SAC, Chicago

GEORGE STOCKING
OC:CG

Classified by 7585
Declassify on: OADR

This communication is classified secret in its entirety.

ReCCr/s dated June 20, 1984.

FBIHQ files reveal information concerning one GEORGE WARD STOCKING, JR., DPOB: December 8, 1628, at Berlin, Germany, of American parentage.

Subject was known to be active in the Communist Party (CP). He was a member of the John Reed Club, Labor Youth League, and the Young Progressives of Massachusetts.

No further information has been developed on GEORGE WARD STOCKING, JR. (Bureau file 100-366901) since 1972.

Based on the information available, FBIHQ believes that these individuals may be identical.

2 JUL 27 1984

100-366901-49

SECRET

SEE NOTE PAGE 2

Classified by: 7585
Declassify on: OADR

MAILED 11
JUL 26 1984

V-107   DE-48

Exec AD Adm.
Exec AD Inv.
Exec AD LES
Asst. Dir.:
Adm. Servs.
Crim. Inv.
Ident.
Insp.
Intell.
Lab.
Legal Coun.
Off. Cong. &
Public Affs.
Rec. Mgnt.
Tech. Servs.
Training
Telephone Rm.
Director's Sec'y   MAIL ROOM

ONE

Autobiographical Recollections

From the Lincoln School to Harvard College

> Toward a world of peace eternal
> And a people strong and free,
> Toward a land of radiant beauty,
> Forward, sons of liberty.
>
> Never more shall earth be shaken
> By the tramp of marching men,
> Tools of war shall be forsaken,
> Wheels of peace shall turn, and then . . .
> [repeat first stanza]

Thus, if memory serves, ran the opening of the "Victory Cantata" (composed by two of my classmates) in which our voices joined at the graduation ceremony of the Horace Mann–Lincoln School in May of 1945. Victory in Europe had just been won, and the United Nations was in the process of formation in San Francisco. Although the sorrow over Franklin Roosevelt's death lingered, the hopes of Yalta were still bright, and the future had not yet been clouded by the atom bomb. Buoyed by the momentary prospect of a world at peace, our class stayed up all night celebrating the end of our high school days, and at the dawn of our new day we took the early morning ferry from Manhattan to Staten Island, returning to breakfast at a classmate's Park Avenue duplex—or so we might well have, since such posh venues had been the site of several class parties in the preceding year.

In contrast to my classmates, a number of whom had enjoyed Lincoln's Deweyite progressivism from the elementary grades, I had only been there for that one year, having arrived by a somewhat migratory route. Born in December 1928 in Berlin, Germany, where my father, a professor of economics at the University of Texas, had a leave of absence to study the German potash industry, I was my mother's much loved first-surviving child—my elder brother Hobart having died a week after his birth in November 1927. In the spirit of German child rearing, they placed me for several hours each cold winter day in a basket on a porch outside their apartment, and in the baby book she was keeping, my mother noted that my bowels were "'trained' at 5 wks." After a month in Paris for comparative study of potash issues, we sailed from Cherbourg to New York, where we spent a month with my mother's parents, and then set off by train to Austin, Texas, which I thought of as my "hometown" until 1944.

I went to elementary school in Austin until 1941, when my father went to work for the government, and although we lived in Arlington, Virginia, I graduated from Gordon Junior High School in Georgetown. After our return to Austin in the fall of 1942, I spent another term in junior high due to overcrowding at Austin High, which I assumed was the only high school in Austin, much later to realize that there must have been another, segregated one. When I entered Austin High early in 1943, a member of the football team who lived down the street—prodded, I suspect, by his academic parents—got me an invitation to join the Woodrow Wilsons, one of the four high school fraternities. Although I accepted, I have little recollection of its activities, other than the somewhat traumatic and degrading late-night initiation. I do remember having an unrequited crush on a fellow member of the school debating team who was later Miss Rheingold of 1949. But in general I recall feeling myself a social and physical misfit, a year or more younger and smaller than my classmates.

In the summer of 1944, our family moved to New York City, where my father was conducting research on monopolies and cartels, and I spent my last high school year at the Horace Mann–Lincoln School. My forty or so classmates were from privileged families—business, professional, academic—most of them liberal, many of them Jewish, several of them international, and a couple of them African American.[4] Although

---

4. From my 1960 doctoral dissertation on "American Social Scientists and Race Theory, 1890 to 1915" (1960a) to the publication of the "Black Box," my historiography

I was not able to match the "all A" record I had maintained in Austin, the intellectual environment was much more stimulating; I especially recall Miss Daringer, who carefully and critically read the two-hundred-word essays she assigned each week. While I was not a talented athlete, I did play as a substitute on the school basketball and baseball teams, in a league of comparable New York–area private schools. In contrast to my previous social backwardness my then noticeable Texas accent gave me a certain exotic cachet: in the course of the year I had a sequence of three "girl friends," with whom I danced (or better, swayed) to "Stardust" at those Park Avenue parties. By the time of our class reunion a half century later, I recalled the year at Lincoln as one of several formative *gemeinschaft* moments.

Outside of school there were other memorable cultural experiences. During the summer before we entered Lincoln, my younger brother Myron and I spent quite a bit of time in New York's many museums—a parentally acceptable activity that on several occasions we used as a cover for going to Hollywood double features. Once at Lincoln, it was more likely to be art films at the Thalia—although I recall also the Rockettes at Radio City, and Louis Prima, Benny Goodman, and other swing bands at venues around Times Square. Some oil painting lessons and a late spurt of intensive piano practice marked the end of my mother's aspirations for my cultural career[5]—though not of her hopes that I

---

has been unified by a concern with two large topics: changing assumptions about group identity, and changing methods of their study. During the extended period covered by my historical research (ca. 1700 to ca. 2000), as well as during the shorter period of my career, the terminology of group identity has gone through many changes, not only in popular and in scholarly usage but also in the self-designation of groups, where it is still a matter of debate—as a Web search will quickly confirm. This has been particularly at issue in the case of the group that has been a primary subject of my own research, now often referred to by the hyphenated phrase "African-American"—a term little used during the period of my research, when the non-pejorative terms in use among and about that group were more likely to have been "Colored," "Negro," or "Black," terms sometimes capitalized and sometimes not. Although often hyphenated today among African-Americans and other "ethnic" groups, hyphenation among those now called "Native Americans" would be both historically and semantically problematic. Without offering an exhaustive treatment of these problems, I would like to think of my own usage as "pragmatically historicist," which is simply to say that I have tried to use terminology appropriate in each particular case.

    5. In the late 1930s, I took art lessons and imagined that I might be a professional artist when I "grew up," and as late as the summer of 1944, after our arrival in New York,

might become an "hombre intellectual," as I had put it in a junior high school essay describing a summer in Saltillo, Mexico, where we had gone in 1943, in part to refresh the Spanish I had learned in 1932 when we all accompanied my father for his study of the Mexican oil industry, and in 1935 when my mother took us to Spain for six months. I recall also a brief but mind-expanding cultural encounter in the summer of 1944 down by the Hudson River near our West End Avenue apartment, when I talked for an hour with a young working-class Italian from Brooklyn, who for the first time in his life had taken the subway to Manhattan to get a view of the land to the west across the river. And later that summer there was an aborted three-day solo bicycle trip counterclockwise around the perimeter of New Jersey, which took me through areas of rural poverty in the northwest hills and then down the Delaware, until painful leg cramps after a hundred-mile day forced me to take the train from Trenton back to New York—where my father greeted me at the door after midnight by chiding me for not toughing it out.

Sometime during the fall of 1944, I realized that my Lincoln classmates were preparing applications for college, and that a number of them were applying to Harvard. So I applied there, and to no other school, on the assumption that if I were unsuccessful I could always go to the University of Texas. To my surprise, I was admitted, along with three others from my class—which I have since tended to explain by the fact that I could count for purposes of geographical distribution

---

I still harbored this notion. In the years since, the main outlet for my nonscholarly creative urges has been a series of needlepoint Christmas stockings made for my children and grandchildren. In addition, however, I have taken pleasure in a variety of creative pursuits—some of them utilitarian, some of them purely aesthetic, others a bit of both. In the 1960s, I converted a second-floor apartment into a "bachelor pad," in part by transforming an empty alcove into a decorative nook with an ivy-covered trellis and a pebbled floor with a large pottery bowl for goldfish—the better to impress interested lady friends. When Carol and I were at the Center for Advanced Study in Palo Alto, and later when we had guests to our summer place in Beverly Shores, I made several ventures into creative cooking. After we bought the Beverley Shores house in 1979, I put a lot of work into fixing it up, both inside and out, including substantial remodeling in two interior rooms, setting up a workshop in the basement, expanding a screened porch, leveling a large terrace, and putting in and later expanding a large garden—from which in one year I harvested five hundred roses and then tried with partial success to protect from the deer by putting up high wire fences. Later on, I specialized in "found objects" gathered in the woods, picked up on the beach, or rescued from the disposal bins in our apartment basement and transformed into useful furniture pieces or attractive wall decorations.

In February 1945 I was invited to participate in the "Youth Forum" program of Dorothy (Lerner) Gordon. Daughter of an American diplomat, Gordon was born in Russia in 1889 and from early childhood showed a remarkable musical talent. Starting in the early 1920s, she went on concert tours that were publicized on the local radio stations, but by 1930 she realized she could reach a much wider audience via commercial radio. In 1941 she became director of children's programs of the Office of War Information and in 1943 initiated a program of weekly discussions of current events sponsored by the *New York Times*, which from early 1945 were regularly broadcast on station WQXR. Although I have been unable to determine the topic of this particular discussion, I do know that the photograph was taken at the time of the Yalta conference in 1945, when I already had begun the transition from the Lincoln School to Harvard, which I entered that fall (Aron 2005).

as coming from Texas, and for quota purposes as being from New York City and not Jewish, unlike my three classmates. While I did not get a scholarship, and my going to a private university was unanticipated, my parents funded the venture—although I made some money that summer working in the mail room of *Life Magazine* in Rockefeller Center. I seem to recall celebrating V-J Day in Times Square on lunch hour, but it was a while before the full horror of the atom bomb hit home to me.

Pascal's Wager and Communist Politics at Harvard

During my first semester at Harvard I roomed in Kirkland House with a young man from Nacoochee, Georgia, whose father decades previously had studied philosophy at Harvard until a nervous breakdown forced his retirement from the modern world. My roommate had graduated from a one-room school and had never used a telephone before his bus trip up to Cambridge; his backwoods Marxism, which seemed to me a curiosity at the time, may have contributed subliminally to my later political awakening. In the fall of 1945, however, I was kept busy writing two-thousand-word essays every week for freshman composition—having failed, despite Miss Daringer's tutelage, to pass out of the requirement. Given close readings by a "section man" (who I later discovered was a well-known poet of the southern "agrarian" school), these efforts must have strengthened my appreciation of writing as a craft—although without weakening my predilection for long and complex sentences. As a member of the last Harvard freshman cohort required to take a semester of Latin, I recall being impressed when Professor Whatmough told us that he learned a new language every summer. But I don't recall much Latin—though it may have rubbed off in my somewhat Latinate written vocabulary and an obsession with the meaning of words (previously encouraged in my early adolescence by a book my father bought called *Thirty Days to a More Powerful Vocabulary*). After migrating to Dunster House to room with the lyricist of the "Victory Cantata," I followed in my father's footsteps and took the introductory course in economics, along with one entitled "Government Regulation of Industry"—which had been his life-long specialty. But I also sampled the wares of the recently established Department of Social Relations and seem to recall Clyde Kluckhohn telling an anecdote about serving rattlesnake canapés to guests in New Mexico, two out of three of whom threw up when told what they had consumed: "And that, gentlemen, is culture"—a force so powerful that it could govern even human physiological processes. I also recall one of my own experiences with culturally exotic foods, when as busboy in the Harvard faculty club I sometimes ate the horse meat steaks—a carry-over from wartime shortages—that patrons left on their plates barely touched.

By the third year, my oedipal energies sought a less directly competitive outlet, and I switched from Economics to English, which had been my mother's major at Barnard in the 1920s. I vaguely recall taking a course on American literature with F. O. Matthiessen, later active in the

Progressive Party, who jumped from a Boston hotel window in 1950, leaving behind a note of despair "at the state of the world"—and the magnificent book *American Renaissance*, which I was only later to appreciate. More vividly, I recall a lecture by Harry Levin, crafted so carefully that a concluding reference to a clock striking midnight coincided exactly with the noon chimes in the Harvard yard outside. And there were individual tutorial sessions with Albert Guerard, Jr., on twentieth-century literature—though what I best remember from my readings as an English major were the plays and prefaces of George Bernard Shaw, and his *Intelligent Woman's Guide to Socialism and Capitalism*. However, I was never a serious student: I worked hard enough in the fall to make the dean's list, but each year I was put on probation after goofing off in the spring. For the most part, what I retained from my formal education at Harvard was what "rubbed off" while my energies were devoted to the three *p*'s, in which I followed in the footsteps of my Lincoln School roommate, Leonard Ragozin (1997). The first was *pinball* (at Harry's Arcade Spa); the second was a high-stakes game of *poker*, with dire financial consequences, when I had to borrow $700 from my brother Myron to settle a losing bet to a higher four-of-a-kind; finally there was *politics*, which from the middle of my junior year took most of my time and energy.

Sometime in 1946, I had a religious crisis. My father, who had gone to camp meetings as a child, had lost his faith during World War I, when he could not fathom how the Deity could be simultaneously the Gott of Kaiser Wilhelm and the God of President Wilson; my mother, bred a German Lutheran, I knew simply as a feeling atheist—in contrast to my father's principled anti-dogmatic agnosticism. But in Texas and later in Tennessee they took on the protective color of Unitarianism, as my own later family briefly did when we moved to California in 1960—until our seven-year-old daughter Becky (who after reading the *Watchtower* had announced at age four that she wanted to be a Jehovah's Witness, and at six decided that she wanted to go to parochial school) rejected Unitarian Sunday school on the ground that they did not really believe in God, but only in evolution. My father's inherited Puritanism, however, was passed to me in infancy, when my parents, having boned up on the latest methods of child rearing, implemented John B. Watson's behaviorist technique for curing thumb sucking: standing behind the infant's crib—invisible, omniscient, and omnipotent—the father was to swat the infant's yearning thumb with a pencil whenever it moved mouthward. In the 1960s, when I appropriated my parents' marked-up copy of Watson's manual (1928:117) as a useful social science classic, I asked my father if he had actually done this; he replied, with some embarrassment, "only a couple of times—you learned quickly." Later, an essay on the Baptist background of Watson's behaviorism by my student Paul Creelan made me wonder whether this experience might have had something to do with my rigorous, if not God-fearing, Puritan conscience (see Creelan 1974). More formal religious experiences included several episodes of Sunday school in the 1930s and, after we moved to New York City, a brief, more serious phase, in which I composed prayers and even gave a sermon in the youth chapel of the Riverside Church.

"Something happened," however, while I was at Harvard. Perhaps it was a philosophy course I took with Raphael Demos (one of the few I recall with any specificity—though when it came to the final exam, I took an "absent"). I do vividly remember, however, what it felt like in the fall of 1946 to lie anxiously awake in my upper bunk bed in Dunster K-22, agonizing about God's existence and the possibility of an afterlife. After a few weeks, I refused Pascal's wager: though the reward be everlasting happiness and the penalty perdition, the chance for either seemed so small that I could no longer force myself to believe. I thought then that I had permanently abandoned religion, but in my junior year I accepted Pascal's wager by embracing a political faith.

Insofar as I have early political memories, they have mostly to do with wars. In the 1930s I recall newsreels of the Spanish Civil War. There are, however, more vivid recollections of World War II: the Pearl Harbor attack and Roosevelt's "infamy" speech; a friend in junior high who read to the class a poem ("High Flight") his brother in the RCAF had written before he was shot down; the silhouettes and models of warplanes; *Time Magazine* news-of-the-year quizzes I took with my father—to mention the ones that pop easily into mind. I had, however, strong pacifist inclinations and still preserve short junior high school essays with titles like "The Brutality of Modern Civilization" and "The Problem of Lasting Peace"—a topic on which I did research in 1944 as a member of the Austin High debate squad. In the aftermath of Hiroshima and Nagasaki, my pacifism began to take an apocalyptic turn: once I gave up the hope of life after death, I worried instead about the immediately pending end of all human existence. When Henry Wallace announced his candidacy in December 1947, I saw a chance to do something to forestall Armageddon, and by the beginning of 1948 I had become active in the Young Progressives of America (YPA).

It soon became evident to me that many of the most committed and hardest-working members of YPA were Communists. Rather than seeing this as domination, however, it seemed to me dedication: in the first instance, to world peace—and if beyond that lay socialism, it was a goal to which in a general Shavian way I was predisposed. But there were concerns that held me back: most notably, the Moscow trials of the 1930s, which I knew from Koestler's *Darkness at Noon*. But after reading a fellow-traveling book called *The Great Conspiracy: The Secret War against Soviet Russia* (Sayers and Kahn 1946) at the suggestion of the student friend who recruited me into the party, I was able to see accept Ivanov's "vivisectional" justification of "any means necessary" to the achievement of socialism: "should we shrink from sacrificing a few hundred thousand for the most promising experiment in history," when millions were "killed pointlessly" by disease and disaster, and by capitalist exploitation? Even Rubashov in the end yielded to the "logic" of party loyalty, to the extent of signing his own death warrant and acknowledging the historically necessary fiction that he had been "in the service of a hostile foreign power" (Koestler 1941:161–62, 239). Although I cannot recall this episode today without wincing, in the late spring of 1948 I dedicated myself to the great experiment.

For the next few months my main activity was working with even greater dedication in the Wallace campaign. During the summer of 1948, I attended the founding convention of the Progressive Party in Philadelphia, including a night-time "monster rally" in one of the major league baseball parks, at which Pete Seeger and Glen Taylor sang, and Congressman Vito Marcantonio gave a firebrand speech. But I spent most of the summer in New Bedford, Massachusetts, collecting signatures to get the Progressive Party on the state ballot. I roomed in the home of a Portuguese textile worker, a long-time Communist, and went out every day to knock on doors for signatures. I also tried to organize young people for the YPA, and wrote and distributed leaflets at textile plant gates—densely worded single-spaced documents that I was told violated every approved standard of leaflet construction, but which seemed to be carefully read by many of those receiving them. Enlivened by the occasional camaraderie of lobster feasts and the electrifying guitars of a Cape Verdean nightclub, it was a vibrantly heady time—a period of emotional identification rather than critical evaluation.

My activist commitment, transferred from the Progressive Party to the Communist Party, survived the shock of Wallace's performance in the November election, in which he ran fourth, behind the splinter candidate of the Dixiecrats. By that time, I had discovered a master narrative that gave a radical meaning to life, and despite this major setback, I was not about to abandon it. Shortly after the election, I was active in the founding of the John Reed Club—a union of the Harvard branch of the American Youth for Democracy and the long-established John Reed Society, in which party people were active—and of which I became chairman after the merger. However, I was much more an activist than a philosophical Marxist. I read *Political Affairs*, the "theoretical" organ of the CPUSA, and various volumes in the Little Lenin Library, but not much Marx beyond the *Communist Manifesto*, nor any seriously philosophical work save Plekhanov's *Essays in Historical Materialism*. At one meeting I shocked more "theoretical" comrades by arguing that there could be no tragedy in a truly socialist society (else what's a heaven for?). Indeed, I was such a "vulgar Marxist" that one comrade (later a very distinguished academic), seated next to me at a branch meeting, held up a book so that he need not risk visual pollution.

During my last semester at Harvard I was busy with political work in the John Reed Club and the party's "peace crusade," and I paid hardly any attention to my academic studies. Among the courses I had signed up for was one in social psychology, given by Richard Solomon, then attached to the Laboratory of Social Relations. Although I had to pass it to have enough credits to graduate that June, I attended few lectures and scarcely cracked a book, hoping that an-end-of-term all-nighter would get me a passing grade, as it had on several previous occasions. This time, however, trying to do a whole course in one night did not suffice, and after staring sleepy-eyed at the final exam questions for an hour, I turned in an empty blue book. Having already decided to answer the party's call for "industrial colonizers," I was ready to accept this as the end of my academic career. However, two more academically inclined comrades encouraged me to throw myself on Solomon's mercy, actually escorting me to the foot of the stairwell in Emerson Hall. Once in his office, I shamefacedly pleaded that to graduate I needed a passing grade in every course, that his was not in my major, and that I would not be able to make it up during the summer or fall—although not going into detail about the life plans that would prevent this. Without committing himself, Solomon said he would "give the matter some thought."

On the morning after the Harvard commencement, I bought a copy of the *Boston Globe*, which published the names of the Harvard graduating class, and could not find my own. Disappointed, but bolstered by my working-class commitment, I was memorably surprised later that morning to receive a congratulatory call from my two comrades, who told me that I had looked under the wrong category. My name was not in the general list, but among those who graduated with honors in "general studies." Mathematically, the D Solomon had granted me still left my cumulative average below the qualifying B—but by that time it was presumably too late to change the diplomas. In 1949, that honors degree seemed a happy if unmerited marker of a major turning point in my life; seven years later, it made possible a dramatic re-turning.[6]

Divergent Family Histories within a WASP Tradition

The summer of 1949 witnessed a second major life-turning event: my marriage to Wilhelmina (Mina) Davis, who had entered Radcliffe in the fall of 1948 and soon became involved in radical groups in which I played a leadership role. Our involvement was not, however, a coincidence, but an outcome of two complex and interwoven family histories, which are in some respects remarkably parallel. Our paternal ancestors were both seventeenth-century English Puritans, our maternal ancestors were German "Forty-Eighters" who fought for the North in the U.S. Civil War, our fathers both went from practical industrial experience to the academic study of economics in the same seminar at Columbia University, both of them were married in unorthodox ceremonies to women with serious academic aspirations, both of them went on to do economic research in Weimar Germany.

Although their careers radically diverged in the 1930s, there was enough in common to mark my marriage to Mina as a major turning point in the story of my life—which bears a rough resemblance to the biblical parable of the prodigal son. After leaving the home of my youth, I took a journey into a far country, where I was embraced as a returning son and married into the family. But after more than a decade away, I returned to the family of my birth, where I was greeted as once dead,

6. In the fall of 1976, when I was a visiting professor in the Harvard Department of Anthropology, I wrote a letter to Solomon (on William James Hall stationery), thanking him for a gratuitous kindness without which my later academic career might not have been possible; he graciously expressed happiness that his "uncharacteristic moment of charity" had such a fortunate outcome.

and now alive again—and in the process stretched almost to the breaking point my ties to the country of my second home. It's a bit of an interpretive stretch, but it does offer a somewhat rickety frame not only to
the story of my life, but also to that of my historiography.[7]

My mother's grandparents on both sides were German-born. Her
paternal grandfather George Reichhardt lost the "t" when his promotion to captain in the Civil War came through without it, and he went
on with his new surname to become a soap manufacturer in New York
City. Her maternal grandfather Louis Schneider was an interior deco-
rator in New York, whose brother died at the Battle of Antietam, and
farther back was a descendant of Huguenot Protestant refugees from
Catholic France, one of whom became Mayor of Stuttgart. Her parents,
Amelia Schneider and George Reichhard, were married in 1892, and
when she was born in 1899, she was named after her mother—and at
some later point became Dorothea Amelia, and by 1920 had dubbed
herself Dorothé. Her father made a comfortable living as realtor and
insurance agent, and the family lived on Central Park West, and later in
Queens, with summers at rented vacation cottages in New York and
New Jersey, from which her father commuted to the city. At the dinner
table there were always lively discussions, but never about politics, because her father was a Democrat and her mother a Republican. Along
with the ardent Schneider temperament, my grandmother inherited
their artistic proclivities, and the family often spent evenings listening
to music on a new-fangled Victrola. By the account of my mother's
sister Edith, who was two years behind her in Hunter College High

7. This section and the next were written in the winter of 2007–8 in response to a very
careful reading by my ex-student Ira Bashkow of what I had hoped was the final draft
of an already overlong "essay." Unlike the rest of the text, which depends heavily on
memory, the present section has involved research of a more traditional scholarly sort—
specifically, reading substantial portions of books by my father and my one time father-
in-law. In the case of material relating to my father and mother, I have relied also on correspondence in my possession and on obituaries and reminiscences, including especially
those of my Aunt Edith and my Uncle Hobart. In the case of those portions dealing with
Horace Bancroft Davis (Hockey) and Marian Rubins Davis (Nanie) I have depended
heavily on their jointly authored book *Liberalism Is Not Enough* (Davis and Davis n.d.).
Part I (1–63), entitled "Direction," was written by Nanie prior to her death in 1960; Part II
(65–261), "Liberalism is not enough," existed in draft form in 1983 (212) and was apparently complete in 1990 (261). The printed version was edited by my daughter Rachel
Stocking, from the "many versions" then in existence ("Acknowledgments" by HBD).

School, she was greeted in every class with "you must be Dorothea's sister. We shall expect great things of you." From Hunter, my mother went on to Barnard, where she majored in English and, like most of her classmates, "bobbed" her hair. She was known for her athletic abilities, scoring second place in the high jump, playing intramural baseball, and serving as organizer of the annual "field day." The verse caption of her yearbook picture in the 1921 *Mortar Board* read "She tackles little things like track and field day last November, for Dorothé of old A.A. is quite the staunchest member."[8] That fall, my mother went on to graduate school in English at Columbia.

Mina's mother, Marian Rubins ("Nanie") Davis, also had German antecedents. Her maternal great-grandfather, an officer in the *Landswehr*, had refused to fire on his fellow countrymen during the revolution of 1848 and fled with his family to the United States. In contrast to my mother, whose later life was actively influenced by her German connections, both personal and cultural, Nanie attributed her own "sense of being German" to her grandmother's "romantic" stories of a childhood in Baden. Her political sympathies, however, can be better traced to paternal relatives from Scotland, and more particularly to her father, who dropped out of high school in Minneapolis and scrounged "for small wages" to help support his widowed mother. He was a Henry George "single taxer," and in the 1920s he encouraged the unionizing of the interior decorating business he owned, against the urging of business associates to join them in "breaking the union." In 1919 Nanie went off to Smith College, where a favorite teacher in a course on classical economic theory piqued her interest in Marx in the process of pointing out his flaws. After graduating summa cum laude in 1923, she went on to do graduate work in economics at Columbia, where she met and married Horace Bancroft (Hockey) Davis (Davis and Davis n.d.:1–63).

Whereas Nanie later recalled Communism attracting her "as Catholicism must beckon to one buffeted by the winds of doctrine," Hockey

---

8. Franz Boas' daughter, Maria Franziska, who as "Frances" was a member of the Barnard class of 1923 and a competitor in field day exercises organized by my mother, must have been known to her. But Margaret Mead, of the same year, had other interests: "Economics, social science, Peggy has advanced ideas. Discourseful quite, with forceful might, she ponders immortality" ("Mortar Board," vol. 21, 1921). As far as I can recall, my mother never mentioned either of these links to my history of anthropology.

My mother, Dorothea Amelia Reichard, on the occasion of her Lutheran confirmation in New York City in 1914. Coincidentally, the lacy organdy shirtwaist dress and the very large bow in her hair are very similar to the ensemble that Karen Anna Baun, the mother of my second wife, Carol, wore at her confirmation that same year in St. Mary's Danish Lutheran Church in Kenosha, Wisconsin.

had to overcome his own resistance and was then initially refused membership—despite the fact that Nanie had already joined—due to suspicion of his upper-class New England background. His paternal ancestors had landed in Massachusetts in the 1630s; his grandfather Andrew, after joining an elder brother's very successful flour mill business in California in the 1850s, came back east in 1882 and invested in the Angier Chemical Company, makers of a patent medicine "emulsion" that treated an amazing variety of bodily ailments—and which provided "a comfortable living to him and his family for many years" (67–68). Hockey's father, Horace Andrew Davis, studied law at Harvard, published two books and several articles on legal matters, and made money on investments, as well as from the Angier Company. But when his son described him on a questionnaire as "a gentleman of leisure," he turned on Hockey "in a rage" (74).

Hockey's maternal ancestors were abolitionist Quakers named Hallowell, whose Philadelphia home was a station on the Underground Railroad. At the outbreak of the Civil War, his maternal grandfather, a member of the Harvard class of 1861, set aside his Quaker pacifism to join the Union Army, was wounded at the Battle of Antietam, and after the war went into banking in Boston. All of his six children attended Harvard or the Harvard Annex (Radcliffe), from which the eldest ("the beautiful Annie Hallowell") graduated summa cum laude in 1894—and after a year in Europe was wooed and won by the brilliant young law student Horace Andrew Davis. After moving to New York upon their return, they had a son named Hallowell, followed in 1898 by Hockey—who in later years was well aware that he had been born into a network of kinship privilege: "having a wealthy extended family does add to one's resources" (123).

Although most of that family on both sides were politically conservative, Hockey included his mother (and "probably my father too") among those with "a social conscience." Two others were Hallowell cousins who supported the Calhoun School, a trade school for Negroes in Alabama, where Hockey spent several weeks during the winter of his senior year in high school, joining in the road work and giving a rousing speech on the virtues of education. A further moment in his political evolution came when his mother, having set out to "reexamine the bases of Quaker pacifism," decided to oppose United States participation in World War I. Between 1917 and 1919, Hockey left Harvard to join a Quaker Mission to France, during which he came in contact with socialists, and his original religious opposition to the war became a political one, as did that of his mother. In 1912, the family had returned to the Boston area, and she used an inheritance to buy a house in Brookline, which at the time of the Lawrence textile strike in 1919 she sold to her husband, so that she could use the money "for worthy causes" (87).

Hockey, who was by then "an eager reformer," spent the summer of 1919 in Minnesota, organizing farmers for the National Non-Partisan League. Early in September he hurried back to support the Boston policemen's strike and to complete his Harvard degree. Entering the competition for the Harvard *Crimson* editorial board, Hockey published a "slashing editorial" calling on President Wilson to withdraw American troops from Russia, "which caused quite a stir," including his "purging" from the board competition. In the spring of 1920 he became one of the leaders in the Harvard student Liberal Club and spent that summer in England, where he volunteered in the Labour Party research department and attended two meetings of the Trades Union Congress. But the "high point" of his English summer was a conference on the future of socialism organized by the Guild Socialists, after which he started "calling myself a Guild Socialist." Having previously changed his major from English literature to economics, with a special interest in labor, he took several graduate level economics courses, with the hope of a career as a researcher in the labor movement.

With this goal in mind he set off in the summer of 1921 for Pittsburgh, to gain hands-on experience in the steel industry. But the mills there were not hiring, and he headed south by rail as "blind baggage" on the platform just behind the locomotive tender, only to be discovered and arrested in Piedmont, West Virginia. After a night in jail, he was set free the next afternoon by a guard who took ten dollars from his wallet as "bail bond" and told Hockey to get out of town. Hitching a ride to Baltimore, where he was able to cash a traveler's check, he took the train to New York City and in the morning registered for graduate work in economics at Columbia.

Although Hockey later recalled that of the graduate students there, the one he "liked best" was George Stocking (108–9), I don't recall any such feeling being expressed by my father. Despite their common Puritan descent, by the late nineteenth century their socioeconomic, religious, and cultural backgrounds were quite divergent. Throughout his life Hockey remained *au fond* an upper-class New Englander, whose radical commitment, although it cost him dearly, was sustained by a sense of his own entitlement. My father, by contrast, was born and bred on the Texas frontier, and his populist impulses were in the long term subordinated to his protestant academic striving.

There were no bankers, no Quakers, no multiple Harvard connections in the turn-of-the-century Stocking family. Considering the role of "race" in my own scholarship, however, it is worth noting that there were some African American links. Thirty years ago, when my Uncle Hobart was updating a Stocking ancestry published in 1903 (C. H. Stocking and H. E. Stocking 1981), I suggested that he might follow up several leads—including two telephone calls from African Americans who thought we might be related and an illustrated article in the *Chicago Tribune* about an African American ostrich rancher in southern Illinois whose name was Stocking. My uncle did not acknowledge my letter, and although I did not attend the family reunion he was instrumental in organizing in 1983, I strongly suspect that no black Stockings were present. However, in reminiscences published after I sent my letter (but without reference to it), my uncle did recall a series of Negro servants who lived for a "meager wage" in the "Little House" in their backyard in Clarendon, Texas—one of whom (the longest in tenure), upon hearing of my grandfather's death in 1918, wrote back from Oregon requesting train fare to attend the funeral—which was forthwith supplied. Another, "Poor-Boy" Williams, accompanied the younger Stocking children "everywhere and so constantly" that their playmates assumed "Poor-Boy" was their father (H. Stocking 1980).[9] My grandfather, Jerome Daniel Stocking, was the first doctor in the Texas Panhandle. Born in Lisbon, New York, in 1849 he came to Texas in 1873, after his graduation from Potsdam State College, when he accepted the offer of a job in the Waco public schools, with the hope that a warmer climate would be palliative for his recently diagnosed tuberculosis. At the end of a year, however, he returned north, with the goal of becoming a doctor. After graduation with honors from the University of Michigan medical school he returned to Texas in 1878 and attempted to set up practice in the town of Lawrence, a few miles east of Dallas. Upon his arrival the physician already established there, convinced that my grandfather was another Yankee carpet bagger, demanded a payment of $500 in cash, to be placed under the newly built railroad bridge,

9. More than two decades after my uncle's death in 1986, Deborah Hanna, who was doing extensive genealogical research on her own complex family history, got in touch with me about her Stocking connections. Following up my suggestion that there might also be African American Stockings, she subsequently discovered information about eighteenth-century slave-holding Stockings, as well as later U.S. census information about Stockings listed as black or mulatto.

Dr. Jerome Daniel Stocking, the bearded man with documents in his hand leaning against a stanchion on the courthouse porch in "Old Clarendon," Texas, shortly after his arrival in March 1885, seven years after the town's founding as a Methodist colony by Rev. J. L. Carhart (who is standing in the lower right corner). Others present included two stage coach drivers, two ranchers, several cowboys, the sheriff and his deputy, the postmaster, the land agent, and Morris Rosenfeld, merchant and school trustee, who was instrumental in bringing my grandfather to the Panhandle. The door on the right side of the building led to the jail; the upper floors of the building on the left were the first home of my grandfather and his family, above the drugstore and the doctor's office.

as the price of being allowed to practice in peace. Apprised of the threat, the sheriff, an upright man, lay in wait and arrested the culprit, who was subsequently sentenced to three years in prison. In the meantime, my grandfather had married Emma Hubble. In 1884 the leading citizens of a recently founded Methodist Episcopal agricultural colony in the Texas Panhandle (named Clarendon after the wife Clara of its chief founder, Rev. L. H. Carhart), invited my grandfather to relocate there, then far away from the nearest railroad. Guaranteed $1,800 a year for the first five years, he accepted, and in March of 1885 arrived with his wife and children after a stage coach trip of more than two hundred miles.

For a number of years my grandfather made his house calls on horseback, frequently being paid in kind rather than in cash—on one occasion the payment was three burros for his children to ride. A

The last gathering (in 1912) of the children of my grandfather, who shaved his beard for the occasion, much to the surprise of his second wife, "Tiny" (b. 1868, neé Sarah Mariah Ward), who was the sister-in-law of his first wife, Emma Hubble, who had died in 1887 after giving birth to two sons: Fred (b. 1879) seated on the right, who became a doctor, and Roy (b. 1881) standing in the center, who became a pharmacist. Also in the back row are the then surviving members of the first set of Tiny's nine children by my grandfather, who were born in close sequence after their marriage in 1889: Homer (b. 1893); Jerome Jr. (b. 1890), who inherited the drugstore; my father (b. 1892); my Aunt Ruth (b. 1891), who had a rich career as teacher, advertising executive, medical doctor, psychiatrist, and director of a children's home. Absent was Myron Ralph (1895–98). Tiny is surrounded by the other four of her children: Frank (b. 1902), a statistician and economist; Collis (b. 1900), also an economist, who held jobs in the U.S. government; Mary (b. 1904); and Hobart (b. 1906), who was a professor of geology and a late-life amateur genealogist.

staunch prohibitionist in a town the cowboys called "Saint's Roost," he was once lured out of town on a fake medical call and held up at gunpoint by a group of masked men who demanded that he end his opposition to the sale of liquor. Taking his money, his gold watch, and his horse, they left him to walk some miles back to Clarendon. Since there was no Congregational group in Clarendon, my grandfather became a pillar of the Methodist Episcopal Church and a founder and trustee of its local college. A staunch believer that "the devil makes work for idle hands," he arranged with patients that his children (as early as the age of seven) would work long hours on Saturdays and

Obviously staged (perhaps by my father—who lurks in the opening on the right), this is the most striking of a small packet of pictures of his year in the Philippine Islands (1915–16), much of it in this isolated village in the shadow of Mount Arayat, a 3,300-foot inactive volcano in the province of Ilocos Norte in northern Luzon. When my parents entered a retirement community in Portola Valley, California, in the late 1960s, I inherited two long spears still in use at the time of his research, along with an arrow-scarred five-pronged shield, as well as a number of metal-tipped arrows—all of them now on display in our apartment.

during the summer vacation for fifty cents a day. On Sundays they went to church in the morning and had home prayer services in the evening—and were paid a penny for each Bible verse they memorized. My father read the Bible through by the time he was thirteen, when he aspired to be a minister.

Like all of the other younger Stockings, my father enrolled in Clarendon College, from which he graduated in 1910. The years immediately after his graduation are not well documented. During this period he apparently sold life insurance and Bibles, taught at several schools in the Texas Panhandle, and during the summer worked as a roustabout in the oil fields. But there were several more notable formative experiences. In 1915 he traveled to the Philippine Islands, where he served in the Bureau of Education, teaching the virtues of "civilization" and hard work to "natives" in the province of Ilocos Norte in Northern Luzon. He had intended to stay for three years, but a severe case of malaria forced his return at the end of the first year, and for the next eighteen months he studied economics at the University of Texas. Although my grandfather had spoken out in a town meeting against American involvement in the war, four of his sons served in the military, including my father, who enlisted in January 1918. Stationed in New Jersey as a cadet in the air force and discharged a few days after the armistice, he returned to the University of Texas, where he completed his undergraduate degree early in 1919.

After serving for some months as superintendent of schools in Clarendon, in November 1919 he returned to the oil fields as an "instrument man" in the geological department of the Empire Gas and Fuel Company, in pursuit of a research project on waste in the oil industry suggested to him by Max Handman, one of his undergraduate professors, who was my godfather when I was later baptized. Handman was an "institutional economist," emphasizing the functioning of the economic order rather than formal value theory—and by one account was the inventor of the label itself in a conversation with Thorstein Veblen in 1916. Encouraged by Handman, in the fall of 1920 my father was admitted to graduate study in the economics department at Columbia, then on the verge of becoming a major center of the "institutional" school (Rutherford 1994). Shortly thereafter, he met my mother on a tennis court and they were married in the spring of 1923.

When Hockey entered the Columbia economics department in 1921, my father had just been granted his MA, along with a Garth Fellowship for further work toward a dissertation on competition and waste in the oil industry. Given Hockey's aborted experience in the steel industry, it is not surprising that despite differences in their backgrounds, he was attracted to someone six years older who had come back from the oil fields to make such a successful entry into graduate study. By Hockey's reminiscent account, however, underlying political differences between them soon began to surface. When my father reported some of his research findings in the graduate seminar, he failed to mention a belief he had indicated to Hockey in private conversation, "that socialism was the only cure for the ills" he had seen in the oil fields. When Hockey remarked on this omission after the seminar, my father ("like an honorable man") asked for the floor at the beginning of the next session and "stated his conclusion." In the very next paragraph, however, Hockey went on to argue that in my father's later anti-trust writings, he had adopted the "atavistic" remedy of "busting the trusts" to reestablish "free competition." Quoting another writer who spoke of my father as "a dangerous reactionary masquerading as a liberal," Hockey went on to suggest "one might have thought he would be leery of unrestricted

My father and my mother, now calling herself Dorothé, were married on June 23, 1923, at the New Jersey home of his cousin Rev. Jay Thomas Stocking (author of an early and somewhat outlandishly embellished version of "The Little Engine That Could") in a ceremony from which she deleted the promise "to obey." Her sisters, Ruth, third from the right, and Edith, partially obscured on the left, came from New York City for the ceremony, but her parents did not, and it was left to the newlyweds to send out the announcement of their own marriage.

competition after his experience in the Panhandle" (Davis and Davis n.d.:108–9).

There was a time when I might have agreed with Hockey. I recall joking with my brother that our father had the finest nineteenth-century mind still around. But he was remembered by others as a Texas Populist and once told me that he had voted for Norman Thomas in 1932. More recently, as I read his first two books, it seemed to me that Hockey must either not have read or since forgotten them. Entitled, respectively, *The Oil Industry and the Competitive System: A Study in Waste* and *The Potash Industry: A Study in State Control*, they form a matched pair, in which the virtues and defects of unrestricted competition, monopoly, and state intervention in particular historical circumstances were discussed in what today might be called "ecological" and "cultural" terms. In neither book did my father advocate socialism directly: in the former, he went no further than to suggest that a solution to the problem "would obviously necessitate a modification of property rights in the public interest" (1925:112). In the latter, he devoted two chapters to the German postwar experience and future possibilities of a socialist government in sympathetic if not optimistic terms—although without reference to the Soviet Union, and in a manner Hockey might retrospectively have regarded as vitiating by compromising the achievement of true socialist ideals.

My father's willingness to discuss socialism in a book published in 1931 (but not in one published in 1925) may have reflected his academic situation. In 1924 his oil industry dissertation was selected by a committee of five nationally known economists (two of them his professors at Columbia) as winner of the $1,000 first prize in the Hart, Schaffner and Marx contest to "direct the attention of American youth to the study of economic and commercial subjects." After three previous one-year appointments, one at the University of Vermont, another with the National Industrial Conference Board in New York, the third at Dartmouth College, he was brought back to the University of Texas in 1925 as associate professor and promoted to full professor a year later. He was on the faculty there for the next twenty years, although more than eight of them were spent either on research leave or in U.S. government service. Over that time there is no doubt that his earlier sympathy for socialism had shriveled into memory.

While there were some parallels between Hockey's career and my father's in the 1920s, by the end of the decade they had radically diverged. During his first year at Columbia, Hockey did not take his graduate work "very seriously" and was more interested in a labor seminar at the New School for Social Research, in which he was encouraged to write a book on the New York building trades (Davis and Davis n.d.:107). But in the spring of 1922, at the suggestion of one of his Columbia professors, he applied for a job in the International Labor Office (ILO) in Geneva, seeking a comparative perspective on the labor movement. Unfortunately, his time in Geneva was "a year of disaster." On the boat over he reactivated an old knee injury, and after emerging from the hospital, he permanently damaged his eyesight working in a dimly lit ILO office. After several months recuperating on the Balearic Islands with wealthy cousins, he returned with them to New York, still on crutches, and then moved to Boston to live with his parents until his knee was completely healed (122–23). During that time he had contact with the Communist Party, but declined to join due to "reservations, pacifist and otherwise" (129).

When Hockey subsequently returned to a dissertation project on the building trades, he was unable to find his notes—only later to recall that he must have left them in a private research library, and then to discover that in his absence the librarian had shot himself and the library had closed (141). In the fall of 1924, Hockey set out again for Pittsburgh, where he got a job in the Braddock plant of the Carnegie Steel Company, a subsidiary of United States Steel. In the aftermath of the unsuccessful strike in 1919 led by William Z. Foster, later the general secretary of the Communist Party, there had been a worsening of conditions by a speeding up of work, a lengthening of hours, and an effective reduction in pay. Although Hockey worked on several jobs in the Braddock plant, the bulk of his time was spent at the "furnace front" with a gang of six whose task was to "tap" blast furnaces in which the molten metal reached temperatures of 2,500 degrees Fahrenheit. In between, however, he had time to observe other processes in the mill, with a particular interest in the issue of worker safety. When he himself had to quit work after straining his back in March 1925, and the company doctor said they did not pay for back strain, he took the "almost unprecedented step of appealing to the State Workman's Compensation Board." The company responded by turning loose a "staff of investigators" to uncover his political background, and the case was still unsettled when Hockey decided to return to Columbia, where upon his arrival he was offered a one-year appointment in the economics department (130–39).

Another motive for his return may have been his marriage to Marian Rubins, to whom he had been introduced in 1924 by the secretary of the economics department. Within seventeen days they had become engaged. On June 25, 1925, they were married in Minneapolis, in an informal "pseudo-Quaker ceremony" they designed themselves, and were duly registered under Minnesota law (143).[10] In the year that followed, when Nanie was teaching at Smith, they saw each other only on weekends. At the end of that year, Hockey had a plethora of possibilities: reappointment at Columbia, a one-year fill-in position at Cornell, an offer from the University of California with the expectation of tenure, and an Amherst Fellowship for study abroad. He accepted the latter, and shortly after the birth of their son, Horace Chandler Davis, the family left for Europe with the idea of pursuing Hockey's interest in job safety comparatively in Britain and Germany. The only significant scholarly publication to emerge from this fellowship, however, was an article on labor courts in Germany, which highlighted the efforts of the socialists and referred to the Communists in rather negative terms. Retrospectively, however, Hockey felt that it was the experience of poverty in Europe that "started us on the way to joining the Communist Party" (146).

When the Amherst Fellowship was extended for a third year, Hockey and Nanie decided to return to Pittsburgh to renew his study of the steel industry. Hockey's later account, however, focused on his role in support of the National Miners Union, a Communist splinter group from the United Mine Workers. Along with liberals on the faculty of the University of Pittsburgh in the American Civil Liberties Union, he protested against the beatings and arrests of the dissidents—with whom on one occasion Hockey spent a night in jail. In the meantime, Nanie, who had a research job at the university, organized protest meetings against the banning of a radical speaker, with the result that a possible research position for Hockey was rejected by the dean, along with the remark that a job for "Mrs. Davis would be even worse" (147–53).

For a year, the Davises lived in Memphis, where Hockey had managed to get a job at Southwestern College and taught a course in anthropology, in which he offered "a dose of Franz Boas with his heretical

10. I have done my best here to resolve several discrepancies between her account and his regarding the dates of several events in this period.

ideas on racial equality" to a class that voted 26 to 3 in favor of lynching. Nanie, who had previously joined the Communist Party in Pittsburgh, devoted her energies to politics, including the organization of a meeting (in which Hockey also participated) protesting the arrest of Communist union organizers at a textile factory in Atlanta. To prevent the meeting from taking place, the police arrested them both and held them overnight in jail, until they were freed by the intervention of a radical lawyer and left Memphis to visit Nanie's parents in Minneapolis. From there they moved to Sunnyside Gardens, Long Island, an early "planned community" close to lower Manhattan, where they were supported by Hockey's mother "Munga," who also used her own connections with the Federated Press to arrange a half-time job for Hockey, with the understanding that he would use the rest of his time to finish his doctoral dissertation (154–60).

When after a year and a half his dissertation on the building trades was rejected by the Columbia department, Hockey turned instead to labor conditions in the steel industry, but once again lost the manuscript—this time leaving it on the seat of a taxicab. The driver looked at it closely enough to decide it was Communist propaganda, which he showed off to his buddies at a local bar. Fortunately, the display was witnessed by a Communist sympathizer, who managed somehow to abscond with the manuscript and deliver it to the left-wing Labor Research Association, which returned it to Hockey. Although he had not at first thought of it as a dissertation, he decided to show the manuscript to a member of the Columbia department, who told him it would be acceptable if he deleted the last part as "tendentious." As a result, the published version appeared in two editions, both published by the International Publishers, one of them his seven-chapter doctoral dissertation on the living and working conditions of steel workers, the other with four additional chapters on the steel trust, profits, the history of unionism, and the steel strike of 1919 (Davis and Davis n.d.:16off.; Davis 1933a, 1933b).

With his doctorate in hand, and his reservations about party membership finally resolved, Hockey planned to continue living in New York for a while; but on September 1, 1933, he received a call from the Brazilian consul asking if he would be interested in coming to teach at the newly founded Escola Livre de Sociologia e Politica de São Paulo. Required to lecture (in French, until he learned Portuguese) on the New Deal, Fascism, and Communism, his opinions on the latter topic upset the local Communist Party until reassurance came from the New York party "that we were O.K." However, the academic authorities were not so easily reassured, and Hockey, by a 4 to 3 vote of the school's directors, was told that his appointment would not be renewed at the end of the year (Davis and Davis n.d.:168–70).

By the time the family arrived back in the United States, Hockey had received an offer to teach at Bradford Junior College in Haverhill, a one-time shoe manufacturing town north of Boston. Impressed by his Columbia record, and unable to reach Hockey in Brazil, the principal had telephoned his father to determine if Hockey was "a gentleman"—and was reassured by the patrician quality of the answering voice that he must be (177). While at Bradford, Hockey worked on a book on the shoe industry commissioned by the Labor Research Association, whose members also assisted in the research. He seems to have spent most of his free time and energy, however, in radical political activity. Retrospectively, he emphasized his disagreements with the Communist Party line on such issues as "self-determination for the Black Belt," support for Boston's Mayor James Michael Curley in the congressional elections of 1938, and the failure "to have a more open discussion of the purges" in the Soviet Union (188). But he followed the party line in signing a loyalty oath that Harvard liberals were resisting. Even so, he got into trouble when he was picked up by the police in a nearby town for selling pamphlets against Father Charles Coughlin, and lost his job when he testified in public against the refusal of the city council to rent the municipal auditorium to the Communist Party for a birthday celebration for Ella Reeve "Mother" Bloor, one of the founding members of the CPUSA. He had barely started to look for another position when he and Nanie were offered jobs at Simmons College in Boston, where the head of the economics department was a liberal who knew and "approved" of Hockey's earlier activities in the Harvard Student Liberal Club (181).

Although his appointment at Simmons was as assistant professor without tenure, it lasted for five years before things fell apart. The college provided funds to pay students who collected research material for professors writing articles, and after publishing several of these Hockey thought he might write a text in economics or on labor problems. In the end, however, all he managed before the war broke out was to see through publication his book *Shoes: The Workers and the Industry* (1940). He was a popular lecturer, drawing on material he had previously used at Bradford, but Nanie was "miles ahead" in popularity and managed, improbably, to convey so much of her own enthusiasm for statistics that "the girls" asked for a second semester of the course. Hockey seems not to have been politically active, in part because he was critical of the party's "united front" policy. But he was quite active in the American Federation of Teachers, which over time irritated the president of Simmons, who, although ostensibly a liberal, told Hockey that he wanted to get rid of him and would refuse to recommend him for other academic jobs. At first Hockey was going to fight the issue, but the local Communist Party was reluctant to do so, unless he and Nanie agreed to stay permanently at Simmons, and when the teacher's union refused to support them, an agreement was negotiated by which they each got substantial dismissal pay (Davis and Davis n.d.:193–200).

Over the next several years, Hockey was employed in a sequence of positions in the labor and left-wing movements. With the idea of being "an intellectual in the labor movement," and on the basis of his recently published book, he was research director and editor for the United Shoe Workers union for a year, while living in Silver Spring, Maryland. Quitting that job early in 1943, he worked for three weeks in the Office of Strategic Services in Washington, D.C., until his radical past again caught up to him, and he was barred from government work. From there he moved to Cumberland, Maryland, where he was editor of the Western Maryland edition of the CIO News, and then he took a job as local representative of the United Furniture Workers. But when he was offered a promotion to the job of business agent for the whole district, headquartered in Baltimore, he turned it down because he did not want to "make unionism a way of life." In Cumberland he was publicly active for the Communist Party, and at the 1944 state convention he opposed the proposal of Earl Browder that communism and capitalism could coexist, and that the CPUSA be abolished and replaced by a Communist Political Association. Momentarily disillusioned, Hockey was receptive to an offer from the Farm Equipment Workers Union to work in their national publicity department in Chicago, and the family moved to Winnetka, Illinois, where they bought a house with a $25,000 legacy Hockey had received from his recently deceased mother. However, the CIO unions generally were moving to the right in this period, and within nine months Hockey was again out of work and was forced to patch together jobs with left-oriented organizations in the Chicago area. After first working with the Chicago Committee for Spanish Freedom, he and Nanie taught at the Abraham Lincoln School and then worked with the Chicago Civil Liberties Committee—until it became evident that "making a living in the left-wing organizations [was a] vanishing proposition." Fortunately, by this time higher education was booming with the return of war veterans and the GI bill, and in 1947 Hockey was able to reactivate a job offer he had received several years previously from the University of Kansas City. Although it was the longest lasting of his academic appointments, and he was in fact voted tenure in 1953, he was fired that same year, after he was called before the Jenner Committee in Chicago and refused to answer questions about his membership in the Communist Party (211–31).

If Nanie's life with Hockey was integrated by mutual participation in a struggle to change the world, the division of domestic labor in their marriage was in many respects quite traditional. She never completed her doctorate, and she bore five children, losing a sixth sometime during her years at Simmons, after a "long bumpy ride" from a speaking engagement. When I knew Hockey at their summer house on Shawme Hill in Sandwich, Massachusetts, he took evident pleasure in doling out food at the dinner table (sometimes arbitrarily), and in the years after Nanie's death from cancer in 1960, he settled into the role of patriarch, catered to and later cared for by his extensive progeny. But in the years before her death Nanie was the matriarch at the center of life on Shawme Hill. With its outdoor Shakespearian stage in the wooded hollow behind the house and its nearby lakes and beaches, it was the setting of almost mythical memories for the children who came there each summer—even when its maintenance became a sometimes disputatious burden for the second-generation offspring, who became its effective inheritors.

My father and mother had a very different life together and apart. His books regularly contained acknowledgment of her "valuable assistance," but she did not participate meaningfully in his preoccupying professional life—as he in effect acknowledged in 1969 in a letter informing me that she had "retired after years of service" as the typist of his almost illegible first drafts. During her early years in Texas she was preoccupied by pregnancy, including two lost babies, before my birth in 1928, followed in 1930 by that of my brother Myron. Less than a year later, she received "permanent high school" certification entitling her to teach in "all grades of the public schools of Texas"—only to have the Texas legislature pass an anti-nepotism law that applied to her as the wife of a professor at the state university. By this time the initial exotic aura of Texas had dimmed, and with her career plans frustrated, my mother was glad to enjoy whatever travel opportunities presented themselves.

The Stocking family at home in Clarendon, Virginia, during 1934 when my father was chairman of the National Recovery Act Petroleum Labor Policy Board. The two boys (Myron on the left, me on the right) were already showing signs of coming down with the mumps.

In 1932 she spent six months in Mexico City when my father won a Guggenheim Fellowship to study the Mexican oil industry. The following year when he was invited to Washington along with troops of academics who filled the lower ranks of the Roosevelt "brain trust," she sailed with her two small sons on a coastal steamer to New York, with a brief stop in Florida, before joining him in Clarendon, Virginia. For the next two years my father commuted daily to Washington to work long hours in the effort to save the free enterprise system from the disastrous consequences of its own excesses, as member and then chair of the National Recovery Act Petroleum Labor Policy Board. When this was augmented by the chairmanship of the National Longshoreman's Mediation Board in 1935, my mother sailed with her sons on the S.S. *Koenigstein* to Antwerp, Belgium, from which we traveled south through France and then to Catalonia before settling for the summer in Madrid.

It was during the year following our return that my parents built the "first modern house in Austin" as what I have since assumed was a kind of peace offering from my father. With a mural of *Afternoon of a Faun* over the living room fireplace, and a two-story entrance hall color-keyed to a reproduction of a large Van Gogh print to the left of the glass front door, it clearly reflected my mother's modernist cultural inclinations. Appropriately, given her own family history, it was designed by a young German-born architect/artist, "Bubi" Jessen (1908–79), who after receiving a prize-winning degree from the University of Texas in 1928, a master's at M.I.T. in 1931, and five years of working in the WPA, won a state prize in a competition sponsored by the Portland Cement Association for a concrete house to be built at the Texas Centennial Exposition in Dallas. Although there is no specific mention in available biographical sources that Jessen designed our house, the fact that it was built of the same material at approximately the same time suggests that it, too, was his work (N. Sparrow, Architecture Library, University of Texas, personal communication). We moved into it in January 1937, two weeks after the adoption of my sister Sybil, and for the next three years the home my mother named "West-Away" was our primary residence.[11]

11. That it was the first modern house in Austin was a matter of debate some years ago between me and a local architectural historian who had in print given that accolade to a house built in 1937. That ours was actually built in 1936 and occupied by January 1937 is evident from both external and interior photographs, including one of me seated next to a window with Sybil in my arms.

The north face of West-Away, the "first modern house" in Austin, shortly after its completion early in January 1937 (at a cost of $25,000). I am standing on the front walk waving to my mother. Although remodeled in 1970, my sister Cindi recently discovered that it is currently on the market for an asking price of $3.25 million.

During the summers, however, my father continued to have extra-academic commitments, several of which involved moving the family away from Austin for extended periods. In the summer of 1938, we lived in Baltimore, where he was a consultant for the Amoco Oil Company in its suit against Standard Oil. In the summer of 1939, we lived in Palos Verdes, California, from which he commuted to Los Angeles for a consulting job that does not appear in his bio-bibliography. After returning briefly to Austin, we were off in 1940 for Washington, D.C., where he worked first for an advisory committee to the Council of National Defense, then as head of the consent decree section of the antitrust division of the Department of Justice, and finally as director of the fuels division of the Office of Price Administration, before returning to Austin in the fall of 1942. The following summer my mother took her three kids to Saltillo, Mexico, where by virtue of my considerable height advantage I starred on the basketball team of the Protestant Centro Social. And in the summer of 1944, we were off to New York City, where for the next three years my father and his friend Myron Watkins did research on international cartels and national monopolies for the Twentieth Century Fund.

Events at the University of Texas during his absence convinced my father that he should look for another job. In 1941, the university's liberal president Homer Price Rainey resisted an attempt by the Board of Regents, sparked by the hillbilly band leader and state governor W. Lee "Pappy" O'Daniel, to fire four members of the economics department alleged to be dangerous radicals, including Clarence Ayres, an institutional economist and close friend of my father's. Unfortunately, Rainey's continued resistance to political intervention—which included an attack on the classroom use of John Dos Passos's novel *U.S.A.*—led to his own firing in November 1944. His subsequent failed attempt to run for governor in the Democratic primary must have been on my father's mind in the summer of 1946, when he entered negotiations to become director of a new institute in social sciences and head of the Department of Economics at Vanderbilt University, where he remained until his retirement in 1963.

Exiled for years in what she regarded as a virtual cultural desert, my mother did her best to enrich the cultural lives of her offspring and in the process vicariously to satisfy some of her own frustrated cultural aspirations. For her, there was the American Association of University Women, as well as literary groups of faculty wives; for me, a bookcase full of inexpensively bound literary classics. For both of us, there was the local "community concert" series, including performances by such international stars as Jascha Heifitz. She even drove my brother and me a hundred miles to San Antonio to hear Paderewski play the *Moonlight Sonata*, and more than twice that far to Dallas to attend two performances of the Metropolitan Opera in one day—*Faust* in the matinee and *Die Walküre* in the evening. Although it was decades before I could appreciate Wagner, I did subscribe to a record club that gave me a life-long devotion to Mozart and Beethoven. There were, of course, also art lessons for me and piano lessons for Myron and me from Mrs. Hollander—an elderly woman who taught us nothing about harmony, but rather to play "pieces," including shorter works of Beethoven, to perform at a "concert" in our living room. Later, after we had moved to New York City, my mother became a "stage mom" for Sybil (who played to favorable reviews during a short run on Broadway) and managed also to find modeling jobs for Sybil and her sister Cynthia, who had been adopted in 1941.

I remember my mother's Kulturkampf of the 1930s in positive terms as a lasting enrichment of my own life—although in some respects a superficial and somewhat uneven one. In contrast, my brother's early

The completed Stocking family, posing for a Christmas card in front of our home in Arlington, Virginia, in November 1941 when my father commuted to work in Washington, D.C., as economic consultant to the U.S. Department of Justice and I enrolled in a Georgetown junior high school, while Myron went to grade school locally and our mother cared for our sisters, four-year-old Sybil and recently arrived Cynthia.

memories of her, focused perhaps by an understandable sibling rivalry, tend to emphasize several quite painful experiences: lessons of hell-fire and damnation in a Lutheran kindergarten, and the time he was spanked three times and put in a closet when he persisted in saying "I can't" while practicing one of Mrs. Hollander's concert pieces. We agreed, however, that our mother's life with our father was in many respects an extended depressive experience, lightened perhaps by cultural sublimation and occasional episodes of travel, which in some cases seem more like escape attempts. Many years later, when we were discussing the extent of her unhappiness in the 1930s, Myron, by then a psychoanalyst, had a vague memory that she was hospitalized for a "nervous breakdown" and agreed with me when I suggested that she may have had an affair with a German bandmaster who wrote for her a march called "The Texas Belle" and later drove down from Baltimore once a week to give us after-school music lessons (Myron on the guitar and me on the violin). When we were living in New York in the 1940s, I distinctly remember overhearing bitter late-night arguments between my parents, in which her angry voice was by far the dominant one. One of my sisters recalls a failed suicide attempt in the 1950s, and my wife Carol remembers that when my parents came to visit us after our marriage, my mother at one point commented on "how things will be different with my next husband."

In contrast to my father, who escaped a right-wing political attack by migrating to a better job, Hockey's encounter with the Jenner Committee effectively banned him from employment at mainstream academic institutions. Returning to an earlier family tradition, he wrote offering his services to African American colleges in the South, many of them religious foundations from the post–Civil War period. For several years he taught at Benedict College in Columbia, South Carolina, where Nanie also taught in the last years before her death. By that time, Hockey's past had once again caught up with him, and when the president of Benedict was threatened with loss of its tax exemption, Hockey's offer to resign was "immediately accepted"—although the president did write letters of recommendation to other African American colleges, one of which led to Hockey's appointment for two years at Shaw University in Raleigh, North Carolina.

Hockey's last teaching position was at the newly founded University of Guyana, to which he was invited in 1963 by Cheddi Jagan, who was for a brief period chief minister of what was then still British Guiana. Among the early faculty were several victims of McCarthyism recommended by Jagan's wife Janet Rosenberg, a Chicago radical to whom he was married in December 1943, when he was a dental student at Northwestern, and who must have known Hockey in the period after he lost his job with the Farm Equipment Workers. Although the Guyana episode was unmentioned in Hockey's memoirs, my colleague Raymond Smith, who was briefly acquainted with him at the time, recalls that "Horace Davis" was quickly disillusioned by the academic conditions there and left at the end of the year, when labor and racial strife led to a British military intervention provoked by the United States. Working as an independent scholar, Hockey went on to publish several books on the history and theory of Marxism and nationalism (1967, 1976, 1978). In the years before his death at 101 he divided his time among three of his children, enjoyed extended family reunions at Sandwich, and was a skilled and enthusiastic Scrabble player.

In contrast, my father continued as chair of the Vanderbilt Department of Economics until he had a stroke in 1958. By that time he had been chairman of the Social Science Research Council and president of both the Southern Economic Association and the American Economic Association. In 1950, he was asked by the Committee of the South to do a study of pricing in the steel industry in its relation to the postwar economic development in that region, which was expanded into a more general work, *Basing Point Pricing and Regional Development* (1954). At the end of the decade, he published a collection of his recent essays, *Workable Competition and Antitrust Policy* (1961), with an opening essay entitled "Saving Free Enterprise from Its Friends." His last published work was *Middle East Oil: A Study in Political and Economic Controversy* (1970), based on a year's research while teaching at the American University in Beirut three years after his retirement from Vanderbilt in 1963. At his death in April 1976 in a retirement community in Portola Valley, California, he left an unfinished manuscript, "The Evolution of Federal Anti-trust Policy." Three years before, my mother had died of kidney cancer—six months after she shot a hole-in-one on the Stanford University golf course. When I last saw her on her death bed, she could barely speak, and when I leaned close to her face, I thought I heard her say that she wanted to end the suffering, but when she heard me suggest this, she responded in a perfectly clear voice: "Are you crazy?"—which I took as an affirmation of life, rather than of deathbed conversion.

Imagining a Future with Wilhelmina Davis

In choosing to marry Wilhelmina (Mina) Davis, the second of Hockey and Nanie's four daughters, I was aware that I was choosing a very different life and future expectations from those to which I had been born and bred—and at the time I thought the choice was a permanent one. Writing now after fifty-five years, with a fading memory and across the chasm of a painful divorce, it has not been easy to recapture the passionate urgency of that moment of choice. It is clear, however, that in the beginning Mina and I shared a vision of the political future and of our role in achieving it. And for the next fifteen years we were together for better and for worse, sharing (albeit unequally) in the early life of our four daughters and a son. The months of our courtship and marriage were, in short, a critical (and still determinative) turning point in my life, and I have here tried my best briefly to reconstruct them, drawing heavily on a packet of letters we exchanged in the early weeks of the summer of 1949.

To begin with, we were both very young: she was still eighteen and I was only twenty, and both of us sexually inexperienced. Myself, especially: I cannot recall today any attachment in the three years between those "girl friends" at Lincoln High School and Mina, who was (at the time and in memory), my "first love." She was a vibrantly attractive young woman, full of the bloom of youth. We were very much alike physically: blond, brown eyed, fairly tall but neither of us skinny. She was very intelligent (later tests, taken when our first two children were young, indicated a higher IQ than mine). And despite the differences in our family backgrounds, there were similarities in our recent family and collegiate experience. Even before Mina came to Radcliffe, she had already in effect left home, staying with relatives in Winnetka to finish her senior year at high school when her family moved to Kansas City. We were both alienated from Cambridge academic life—she from the premarital training school she experienced at Radcliffe, I from the apolitical academic striving at Harvard. I was a senior and a leading campus radical; she was a freshman aspiring to be a radical and knew all the left-wing folksongs. I had been a wilting male wallflower at Radcliffe "jolly-ups," but with Mina, who was an ardent square dancer, I found a dance form I could really enjoy. Small wonder, then, that we were drawn to each other.

Initially, however, there was a problem: Mina was involved with another guy, the grandson of a major German sociologist and a senior in the math department, who was known to her mathematician brother Chan—and at one point mistakenly assumed by him to be the man she might marry. For some weeks she was seeing both of us, much to my chagrin, until I insisted that if we were to continue to be involved with one another, she must choose between us—which she did.

During the spring of 1949, Mina hosted a number of weekend gatherings of young radicals at the Davis place in Sandwich, which was still in a state of some disarray (and a cause for mild irritation) when her family arrived in early June for their annual summer stay. But when I showed up several days before my graduation, they welcomed me with warm embrace, as a kind of surrogate prodigal son who, unlike my father, had decided that "liberalism was not enough" and was about to set forth on a life of dedication to the working class. And I responded with enthusiasm, winning over Mina's two much younger sisters with improvised bedtime stories about a whale named Wumpus and a cowboy named "Wild Bill." After I left Sandwich on June 27 to hitchhike down to Silver Spring, Maryland, where my parents were living for the summer while my father was working in Washington, Mina reported to me that "The Cindy Kid" and "Two-Gun Terry" were quarreling over whose "boyfriend" I was.

Over the next twenty-one days Mina and I exchanged sixteen letters in which we discussed future plans. In the first of Mina's, she queried me as to whether I was going "to break the bad news to your parents this week. . . . I hope they take it as well as my parents think they will." Since we had not yet been discussing marriage, I assume the reference was to my decision to leave academic life for a job in industry. However, I decided not to spoil my parents' pleasure with my degree cum laude, because "I might not see them for several years" and did not want their last memories to be bitter ones.[12] I did, however, have a political conversation with my mother, in which she confided her dissatisfaction with the banality of life as a faculty wife in Nashville, and I gave her a somewhat presumptuous lecture on the status of women under capitalism, remarking later to Mina that *she* was "lucky" to have "a life with a purpose."

The precise nature of that purpose was under discussion in several venues after I took the train back to Boston on July 3 and moved into 185 Warren Avenue in the South End, where a small group of our Harvard

---

12. Although I have vivid memories of the mise-en-scène and cast of characters present when I announced my membership in the Communist Party, and at first assumed that it must have happened on this visit, the lack of reference to the specifics of the "bad news" in correspondence with Mina tends to confirm my brother's recollection that it occurred on a different occasion. Be that as it may have been, I know that whenever it was, it caused great pain when I told them.

party friends had established a cooperative. We spent a lot of time in intense conversation on the criteria of house membership and the rules of procedure—notably in the case of a seriously disturbed young African American working-class woman, who was not invited to join. There was also much discussion of party policy and political activity—including whether it was out of touch with the working class and about our role in Club Emancipation, a local community branch of the nonparty Young Progressives of America. And there was a lot of talk about personal problems and postgraduation plans, including whether Mina and I should get married and whether she should leave academic life to enter industrial concentration. Mina herself was still at Shawme Hill, where the communards had all spent time, and they were aware of her parents' mild but palpable resistance to her not returning to Radcliffe in the fall. It was also just at this time that the Communist Party revived its youth group, which had been dissolved during the Browder years, in the form of the Labor Youth League, in which leaders of the Boston Communist Party expected that I might play a central role, along with my industrial concentration.

All of this, and much more, filled those letters of late June and early July: my comments about my father "living in the wrong century" as "a slave to a "hypocritical impartiality"; Nanie's worries about the Warren Avenue situation, and whether we would have to sleep together; Hockey and Nanie's wanting to talk over Mina's plans with me, because I was "a very sensible person." Most of all, however, the letters were filled with our professions of loneliness and pledges of undying love, which by July 8 we were discussing in terms of marriage. It was not easy for Mina to "walk out of the life [she] had been calling home for eighteen years," but by July 17, in the last letter of the sequence, the issue had been decided. Commenting on the strength, enthusiasm, and "wonderful optimism" of several leaders of the party who had been visiting at Shawme Hill, Mina proclaimed the coming millennium: "we have to be optimistic, because we know what a fine world is coming . . . promise me you'll never leave me." A month later, we were married.

By that time, Mina had convinced her parents that she, too, should enter "industrial concentration," delaying to the indefinite future any further college education, and they were more than willing to accept me into the family. Unfortunately, my parents were not ready to reciprocate. In Massachusetts, a woman could marry at eighteen without parental consent, but a man had to be twenty-one—which I was still four months short of. So on August 17, Mina left work at the garment

Wilhelmina Davis Stocking and me with members of the Davis family in 1952 at their summer home on Shawme Hill in Sandwich, Massachusetts. Mina's parents, Nanie and Hockey, are in the center of the top row. To the right of Mina's grandmother are the Crowleys—Robin and Barbara Davis Crowley, who is holding their daughter Regan. On the left, Mina is holding our daughter Susan. The youngest Davis, Cindy (Cynthia Quentin), is on the right; her elder sister Terry (Esther Fisher) is on the left with their much-loved dog, Timmy Bulge. Absent were Horace Chandler Davis and Natalie Zemon Davis.

shop at which she had been hired the week before, and two of our Warren Avenue comrades drove us to our wedding in the town clerk's office in Nashua, New Hampshire—where the minimum age for males without parental permission was only twenty. That next weekend the Davis place on Shawme Hill was the site of one in a long series of Davis family wedding celebrations, which my own belatedly relenting parents attended with reasonably good grace—though they never really approved of my new family-in-law, and certainly not of my career choice. Years before, my mother had once told me that she didn't care what I did in life, so long as I tried to be the very best—even if it was only as a garbage man. But I knew that was not for her a serious option, and after my marriage she blamed the Davises (and especially Nanie) for having somehow bewitched me—and was probably a bit jealous of Nanie's status as matriarch of the annual gathering place of an extended progeny.

Even before Mina and I were married, there had in fact been forebodings of future marital difficulty. Before the Nashua service could take place, I had to have my blood drawn, and my life-long problem with floppy veins caused me to faint from the prolonged probing. While that omen should not be taken too seriously, there were others during our courtship that in retrospect perhaps should have been. For one brief moment early in our premarital correspondence Mina seemed to include me among the "everyone" who felt that she had not thought about what she was doing, and she proceeded to document her case by a systematic presentation of reasons for not going back to Radcliffe (1a, 1b, on through 4: "if I did decide to get married it would not substantially change any of these plans")—to which I responded with my own "a, b, c, d" of reassuring but slightly cautionary comments—along with a joking complaint that she had said "I" and not "we." In retrospect, it is clear that there were other subtle signs of future troubles. Despite our mutual affirmations of undying romantic love, there were occasions when our love was in fact significantly asymmetrical: not only did I seem to mediate her relation to her family, but I sometimes assumed or was cast in the role of mentor on the issues of her future. When I wrote to her about my mother's alienation from faculty life, Mina replied, "your comments on women under capitalism started me thinking . . . about the disgusting attitude toward life" that was "just about universal among the girls in the dorm": "At best, they were at college to get training for a short 'career' before marriage, and at worst they were there to pass the time pleasantly on their parents' money while they fished for a rich husband." Our love was to be different, and for a time it was. But in the longer run she felt forced to sacrifice her career to mine and began to wonder if life might not offer something or someone better.

Life in the Working Class during the McCarthy Era

In the first several years of our marriage we lived in a series of cheap apartments (one next to the railroad tracks, another above a bakery) in the then heavily black or Negro (not yet "African American") South End and Roxbury neighborhoods of Boston, from which on summer weekends we often hitchhiked down to Sandwich. We both had jobs in industry: Mina's primarily as occasional garment worker, mine in a wider range of "industrial" activities. My first job in the working class was as laborer on a water tunnel project in Brookline, which might have given me greater upper body strength had I not been laid off after ten days. After some weeks of unemployment, I went to work in a small furniture factory in Chelsea, where for six months I sanded the legs of television tables preparatory to their final finishing—though it was more than a decade before we ourselves owned a TV. With no prospect there of significant trade union or political activity, I quit that job in March 1950 and in May was able to find one in a shop more important to the working-class struggle: the Colonial Provision Company, in the North End meatpacking district. Colonial was one of the two biggest plants in the amalgamated Local 11, the largest (and most militant) in the New England district of the United Packinghouse Workers Union—which only that year had reluctantly decided to comply with the provisions of the Taft-Hartley Act.

In applying for a job at Colonial, I did not indicate I was a Harvard graduate, nor did this ever become known to my fellow workers. Nor was I marked as a Communist, though after a time it was evident that I associated with members of the small cadre of party people and the penumbra of sympathizers (mostly Italian immigrants) who helped make Local 11 a stronghold of the Left. After I had worked for a few weeks on a gang that prepared loaves and pork butts for smoking, my foreman decided I would do better across the elevator shaft in the "washroom"—where, along with two of the small minority of African Americans, we were left unsupervised to clean the meat residue from equipment sent up from the various departments. For many months, I was only slightly active in union affairs—attending union meetings, playing on the local union's basketball team, bowling in a union league, staying occasionally after work for a few drinks in a North End bar—becoming accepted, more or less, as one of the guys.

Sometime in the spring of 1952, when I was well enough established at Colonial Provision to take a more active role in union affairs, I helped to edit and produce a mimeographed local union newspaper. When the contract of the local's sausage division came up for renegotiation, and one of the issues was the elimination of the male-female wage differential, I spoke out in a Colonial shop meeting urging the election of a woman to the negotiating committee; instead, the women united to nominate and elect me. Although a split between the Colonial representatives and more conservative ones from Boston Sausage forced us to accept less than we asked for, my role in the shop was now assured—first by election to the shop grievance committee and later as chief shop steward.

I was very conscientious—aggressive, even—in pursuing griev-
ances, but the company, long a family-run venture, at about this time
brought in a professional personnel manager, who was also conscientious and aggressive, resisting grievance settlements and introducing
arbitrary new shop rules. Early in February 1953, matters came to a
head when the company announced that the crew of the "pump room"
on the first floor (where pork shoulders and hams were trimmed and
injected with pickling fluid preparatory to smoking) would no longer
be allowed to go to the rest room before their morning coffee break—it
having long been common practice, in answering "nature's call," to escape occasionally from the wet and cold for a smoke. When members of
the crew responded by going to the rest room in groups during the pro-
hibited period, two of them, after being warned, were suspended for a
week, and the department steward rushed up to the fourth floor to tell
me that the pump room crew planned to walk off the job. I asked them
to delay until noon, while we tried to work out the matter with the company; but the management stonewalled, having perhaps planned this
"union-busting" provocation. We took the bait, and at noon the grievance committee went through the plant from the top floor smokehouse
to the first floor receiving dock, leading four hundred or so workers off
the job in support of the pump room crew. The following Monday there
was a mass rally in historic Faneuil Hall—the "cradle of liberty" in the
American Revolution—at which I made a rousing speech to a packed
audience of white-coated packinghouse workers from Colonial and
other market shops. Although it was greeted with militant applause,
the denouement was a great letdown: after a ten-day strike in violation
of the Taft-Hartley Act, a national union representative brokered a
settlement in which four shop leaders, myself included, were removed
from union positions and barred for two years from union activity in
the shop.

By 1957, when I received my last copies of the local's newspaper—
and Colonial in the interim had been through a strike of many
months—others of the February four were back in union leadership.
But in 1953, when I was working in that wet and steamy washroom,
barred from union activity, remaining at Colonial seemed politically
and personally futile, and after four months, with the party's permission I left to go to work in a nonunion Roxbury machine shop. Meeting
the piece-work rate drilling gun-sight fittings seemed at first hopeless,
but like many workers faced with the challenge of beating Frederick
Taylor at his own game, I was able to borrow from others or invent for

myself shortcuts enabling me to meet the rate, after which I could slack off, lest the rate be changed. That fall I took trade school classes to further my career as machinist, with a plan to move west to Springfield, an area of party concentration to which our closest party friends had moved some months previously. On a quick trip to Springfield just before Christmas I was hired as a lathe operator at the American Bosch plant, where several thousand workers were under contract with the International Union of Electrical Workers, formed four years before when the "Communist-dominated" United Electrical Workers had been expelled from the CIO. On January 1, 1954, our family (including our daughters Susan and Rebecca) set up housekeeping in the first-floor apartment of a two-flat house on Greene Street, separated by a grape arbor from the home of our Italian immigrant landlord.

Four months later I was laid off at Bosch and then found a series of unskilled jobs. For three weeks I worked in a one-room nonunion shop on a small drill press. Unable to endure the boredom of pulling down the handle all day at an hourly rate, under the constant surveillance of the foreman, I found a job at the Monsanto chemical company, throwing heavy bags onto skids for shipment—though not enough of them to pass the trial period. I then settled back for some months into the unsurveillable nonskill I had learned at Colonial: cleaning the equipment and the restrooms in an A&P butter-packaging plant after all the daytime employees left—tasks that my co-worker and I got done with several hours still left before midnight to listen to the radio in the shop lounge. In February 1955, I was called back to the swing shift at Bosch, while Mina worked days as a stitcher, and our two daughters stayed at a babysitter's during the late afternoon when neither of us was at home—until Mina left her job prior to the birth of our third daughter, Rachel.

Although my copies of the IUE local news indicate a fair amount of union turmoil at the Bosch plant (including complaints about latrine permission and a one-day strike that September), I don't recall any personal union activity before I was laid off again in January 1956. Nor do I remember much party political activity, in a period when the party had to all intents and purposes been driven underground—though I still have clippings from the *Springfield Union* of letters on various civil rights and peace issues (the latter written over the pen name "Geneva Spirit"). I do, of course, recall the intraparty turmoil provoked by Khrushchev's "Secret Speech" to the twentieth Soviet Communist Party Congress on February 25, 1956. But despite the dimming of "the

Stockings together in 1955 at the Greene Street house in Springfield, Massachusetts. In the front row are Susan, Dorothy, Rebecca, and Wilhelmina; in the back row are the two Georges and Cynthia (who is standing in front of a hi-fi cabinet I built.).

light at the end of the tunnel," I did not immediately abandon life as a member of the working class. After three weeks putting leather handles on the shafts of golf clubs at the Spaulding plant in Chicopee, and evenings trying to sell Babee Tenda Safety Tables to new parents, I managed to get a job with a more likely working-class future, as apprentice machinist in a specialty shop in Agawam that built large machines of various sorts—including a printing press fifty feet long and fifteen feet high, of which our five-year-old daughter Susan, there for a "family night," afterward drew from memory a remarkably accurate picture. Although I still looked forward to becoming someday a toolmaker, my job was at the less-skilled end of the process, and in August 1956, when I stupidly failed to tie down adequately a piece I was drilling, it swung around into my left wrist. Rushed to a local hospital emergency room for a half-dozen stitches, I left behind a trail of blood to mark the end of my career in the working class.

American Civilization and Positivist Historiography at the University of Pennsylvania

By this time, I had been forced to question and then to abandon the master narrative that for seven years had sustained that career—in a period when external repression and internal deterioration had reduced party life to furtive if not clandestine meetings plotting, not revolution, but simple survival. Although it took a while for the full impact of the Khrushchev revelations to sink in, by the summer of 1956 I realized that they had effectively undercut the moral bargain that made possible my joining the Communist Party in the first place: rather than justifiable responses to conspiracies by anti-Communist powers intent on undermining the world's first socialist state, the "Moscow Trials" were show trials, initiated by Stalin to purge those he regarded as political enemies, their scenarios closely following the pattern described in Koestler's *Darkness at Noon*—on the basis of which thousands of party members were executed or sent to Siberia for alleged anti-Soviet activities. In the course of long discussions with our closest party friends, Mina and I gradually came to the conclusion that there was no hope of any substantial change in the American party. By the time of my accident, there was little to sustain me in a life to which I was not born—in which my wandering mind might someday again put my careless limbs at risk. Fortunately, however, I had a readily available life alternative: to re-embrace my liberal academic patrimony.

In retrospect, I came to view my Communist Party days as the continuation of a powerfully oedipal adolescent rebellion.[13] My father and I had argued bitterly about trivial matters since my high school days, and my joining the party greatly raised the stakes, since the issues involved were fundamental to his liberal identity: to delegate one's intellectual freedom to some external authority (whether it be the Communist Party or the Catholic Church) seemed to him a fundamental violation of individual freedom of thought. For me to persist in violating the major dogma of his otherwise anti-dogmatic liberalism gave me, if not the moral high ground, then at the least the upper hand in our struggle of wills—and in the months after I revealed my membership brought him several times to tears. Rather than rejecting me completely, however, my parents on several occasions offered to loan me the money for graduate school, presumably on the assumption that a serious commitment to the life of the mind would necessarily involve my leaving the Communist Party. Having done that, the painful wounds of oedipal rebellion were almost instantly healed and my parents followed through on their offer to loan me the money. Fortunately they lived long enough to share with my children the dedication of the book that eventually emerged from my dissertation (1968a:v).

Like other disillusioned radicals trying to place their personal experience of the "failure of socialism in the United States" in a larger interpretive context, I returned to graduate school seeking to understand why American culture was so resistant to radical social change. In 1956, a likely place to do this was in one of the programs in American civilization that flowered in the Cold War period, when the uniqueness of American values seemed an issue with international political significance. Although it was very late to apply for admission, in the days after my accident I explored three options: Harvard, where the earliest possibility was not for another year; Yale, where there was a chance in February 1957; and the University of Pennsylvania, where I was told

13. As evidence of the oedipal nature of my Communist commitment, I offer a glimpse into a darker corner of my black box. Drinking with comrades around a kitchen table one evening, we discussed whether revolutionary violence might be justified if the future of socialism lay in the balance. If my vague memory is correct, I imagined a situation in which unarmed workers approached a locked capitalist armory guarded by my father, who refused to give us the keys, and the only way to gain entry was to kill him. I have repressed my choice—or perhaps only dreamed.

that I could start when the semester opened in two weeks—and which, fortuitously, differed from other programs in its social scientific rather than literary/historical emphasis.

Somehow, we managed in those two weeks to pack up and ship our worldly goods (including the large console that I had built to hold our hi-fi components), load our three daughters (the oldest, five years old; the youngest, not yet two) into our second-hand Hudson, and drive to our new home on the second floor of a three-flat at the end of the Baltimore Avenue street car route in southwest Philadelphia. There were two small bedrooms in the back for the three girls, who (we learned several weeks after our arrival) were to be joined the following June by yet another child, whom we named Melissa. In the center of the apartment there was a dining/kitchen area and a bathroom, and at the front a large room that became a combination bedroom/study and occasional living room. I took the street car every day to campus, treating my graduate education as another job: even if some lectures were dull, I took careful notes in every class and somehow managed to finish assignments on time, working much harder than I ever did at Harvard. Nor did I spend time on political work—any lingering activist impulses being quickly smothered by the Soviet suppression of the Hungarian Revolution three weeks after the term opened. Putting aside for the time being her own reawakened academic aspirations, Mina shouldered the bulk of the responsibilities of 1950s domesticity—including keeping daughters quiet and amused when I was not on campus, while I read and wrote in the doorless room at the front, behind an improvised curtain and the sound barrier of a small batch of classical favorites played over and over on our hi-fi. And she did this with only occasional help from me, and with a "good spirit" that for some years survived our mutual reading of Simone de Beauvoir's *Second Sex* (1952).

In contrast, I was experiencing a challenging intellectual awakening, largely under the guidance of Murray Murphey, who (unbeknownst to me then) had been a classmate at Harvard before undertaking graduate work in American pragmatic philosophy. By the time I took the required one year proseminar in methods, Murphey had moved on to an anthropologically oriented study of American civilization, in the positivist spirit of the recent Bulletin 64 of the Social Science Research Council, *The Social Sciences in Historical Study* (Cochran et al. 1954). After a run-through of major figures and issues in American historiography, posed against Morris Cohen and Ernst Nagel on scientific method (1934), as well as sessions contrasting Francis Parkman with Irving ("Pete")

Hallowell on the cultural personality of the Ojibwa Indians, the pro-seminar turned more seriously to the application of social science to American civilization. Emile Durkheim, as "the Newton of the social sciences," provided a model of method in his study of suicide. There was a dose of functionalism in anthropology (Bronislaw Malinowski, somewhat critically) and in sociology (Robert Merton, more sympathet-ically). The "new criticism," exemplified in Wallace Stevens's "Anec-dote of the Jar," demonstrated the possibility of greater methodological rigor in literary studies. The course culminated in a presentation of "content analysis" as compromise between qualitative and quantitative methods. Although I also enrolled in more conventional courses in American literature and history, in the second and third years I focused on the social sciences, taking courses on sociological method, race rela-tions, and social psychology, as well as two semesters with Hallowell (including one on culture and personality) and summer courses at Brandeis with Vann Woodward on southern history. But it was Mur-phey (and behind him Thomas Cochran, the business historian who had chaired the SSRC Bulletin 64 committee) who defined my initial historiographic orientation. For my first major research paper, I chose a project tangential to my special interest in race relations and the Ameri-can South: a study of "The Negro in the Philadelphia Press," based on a content analysis of relevant articles in the *Philadelphia Enquirer* every fifth year between 1890 and 1915.

If Murphey was the major influence on my methodology, when it came to subject matter the mentoring role was played by Hallowell, a scholar of wide-ranging but conceptually integrated interests. Trained in the Boasian historical tradition, he had developed a distinctive neo-Freudian approach to the culture and personality and worldview of the Berens River Ojibwa Indians, among whom he did fieldwork in the 1930s—including an interest in the relative acculturation of different groups along the river and the changes revealed in the historical record of contact. In the postwar period, however, he recast his personality interests in a much longer temporal framework, speculating about the evolutionary emergence of the psychological prerequisites of a cultural level of adaptation. There was an analogous "great transformation" in Hallowell's course on the history of anthropology: starting with an interpretation of the spatial and temporal orientation implicit in the medieval worldview, he traced the emergence of "scientific" anthropol-ogy out of "proto-anthropology." If his cultural relativism had thus a limit in regard to his own profession, Hallowell was nevertheless intent on treating the history of anthropology "as an anthropological problem." His sources were restricted to published materials, which he employed in rather conventional historical terms, but he was a serious and conscientious historian of anthropology—who over the longer haul not only influenced my approach but greatly facilitated my career (GS 2004).

By the time I chose a dissertation topic early in the third year, my interest had shifted from race relations per se to social scientific thought about race. Having visited Mina's parents in South Carolina, I was aware of the stirrings of the civil rights movement in the context of "massive resistance" to the Supreme Court desegregation decision of 1954, with its appeal to the findings of social science. Although the question "What Happened to Race?" had recently been treated in an essay by Oscar Handlin (1957), it was a topic that I felt deserved a more rigorous treatment, based not on the thought of a few "representative men," but on a content analysis of a representative sample of the work of a broad range of scholars in all social science disciplines—both as an application of Murphey's methods and as a test of their applicability. Seeking a present reference point for the analysis, I used the 1950 UNESCO "Statement on Race" (qualified the next year by a second somewhat more biologically oriented statement) to break down the "modern" social scientific position on race into six major analytic categories: the definition of race; misuses of the term "race"; issues of race classification; the origin of race differences; the significance of race differences; and the effects of race mixture. On this basis, I worked my way through 551 articles by 228 authors in 21 social science journals published between 1890 and 1915, recording relevant passages on McBee Keysort cards. Applying my categories (which grew by subdivision to 96), I clipped the corresponding holes around the card-edges, so that I could (in that pre-computer age) use a kitchen skewer to shake out all the cards with information in any particular category.

Gradually, however, I became aware of many problematic aspects of this positivist historiographic method—among them, that of defining who in a period of incipient academic professionalism would qualify as a social scientist, as well as what to do about articles that did not contain the word "race" but nonetheless seemed relevant to the problem of human differences. During the summer of 1959, while my family was in Sandwich, I suffered a week-long and profoundly depressing epistemological crisis—reminiscent, perhaps, of my agonizing over Pascal's wager. Content analysis had facilitated important insights: notably, the revelation that the neo-Lamarckian assumption of the inheritance of acquired characteristics was not a regressive quirk in the thinking of particular figures, but the linchpin of what I would later think of as a "paradigm" of thought about the nature of human difference, in which there was a circular causal relationship between habit and instinct, and thereby between culture and race. Neo-Lamarckism as such, however, was manifest in less than half of my 228 authors, even when I classified as implicitly Lamarckian passages that someone less sensitive to its presence might have interpreted in purely cultural terms. And the fact that of my 228 authors only Alfred Kroeber (1915) seemed aware of the critical paradigmatic role of Lamarckian assumption provoked further historiographic angst: had he not been aware, would it have been any less "true"? And what did this imply about an actor-oriented historical approach? How was I to weigh the influence of Franz Boas's 1888 essay on "Alternating Sounds"—the very first of those 551 articles that I read, in which the word "race" did not appear, and which was not widely cited, although upon later rereading, it seemed clearly to imply an alternative paradigm. But if these issues shook my faith in social scientific history, and my later historiography was in a more conventional intellectual historical mode, I was not about to abandon a project on which the future of my family depended. After a week of worry, I put aside my methodological angst and soldiered on to the rapid completion of a 600-page dissertation (1960a)—which Hallowell told me he liked so much that he read it "almost word for word."

While I never again attempted a systematically quantitative content analysis, my dissertation research left a permanent mark on my scholarship. Unpublished as such, it nevertheless marked a major episode of intellectual capital accumulation, serving both as germinal reference point and as permanent empirical resource for much of my later work. When I think about the history of anthropology, I tend to think forward and backward from that turn-of-the-century period, and particularly from Franz Boas, in whose work were reflected or refracted many of the tendencies in that history—including a never-resolved epistemological tension that made him intellectually very congenial to me. And if my subsequent work has tended to focus on major canonical figures in the history of the discipline, there was one byproduct of the dissertation that mediated a more broadly focused approach: an account of the founding of the American Anthropological Association in 1902. Based on my baptismal archival research, first in the Boas papers and then in the archives of the Bureau of American Ethnology, this paper (my first published effort) foreshadowed a frequent opening gambit of my later work: the analysis of a "revelatory" microcosm (1960b). This might be an event, or a text, sometimes fortuitously discovered—even one of those short passages I later began to call "juicy bits"—in which larger processes seemed to be embedded, and from which one could extract a range of larger meanings. A closely focused analytic description of such microcosms enabled me to move outward, through specific interactional or institutional contexts, from individual intellectual biography to larger "external" historical contexts. Although epistemologically, methodologically, and ideologically problematic, this approach has been more congenial to me than an interpretation moving in the opposite direction, in which the "stuff" of history seems all too easily subject to manipulation in terms of some a priori master narrative.

Political Disillusion and
Historiographical Assumption

That I should have adopted this bottom-up approach no doubt reflects my seven years in the Communist Party. There were a number of experiences in those years that in retrospect articulate with its then commonly prevailing image—but that I managed at the time to see as "necessary" means to a utopian end. On one occasion I served as temporary depository for a small package of gold coins left with me by a regional leader who knocked at our door in Springfield late one night—although it was not Moscow gold, but American, not yet renegotiated as the currency to sustain his harried "underground" existence. Other moments seem in retrospect more disturbingly revelatory—including the time at Harvard when we mobilized party people and sympathizers for a meeting of a "Trotskyite"-led peace group, in order to vote it out of existence. And there were some experiences that came to seem like microcosmic reenactments of the Moscow trials, nonetheless retrospectively troubling for having been played on a smaller historical stage, and without guns. On one occasion I agreed to stage-manage the expulsion from the John Reed Club of a comrade for unspecified "crimes" the nature of which could not be revealed to me (I later surmised that he had got an African American woman pregnant and refused to marry her, though he volunteered to pay for an abortion).

As the "struggle against white chauvinism" intensified, I was myself implicated, when I took "criticism and self-criticism" so seriously that I voluntarily wrote a long document (since lost) recounting all the "revelatory moments" of my relations with "Negroes," going back to the time in Austin when I went along with my mother into a nearby enclave of segregated premodern poverty to leave our laundry for a poor black woman to wash and iron—or when I gave up my seat on the bus to an elderly Negro woman. Not all of the early interracial experiences I recalled for my comrades were so innocently liberal, however. There was also the time when I made an offensive remark (now long repressed) to the Cherokee-Negro "yardman" who accompanied our family to Washington, D.C., in 1941 to serve for several years as man-of-all-work— and he picked me up and angrily told me that I was never ever to talk like that to him again. Delving into my unconscious, I suggested that despite my active participation in the struggle against Jim Crow, it might be that I would have trouble taking leadership from the African American woman with whom I served on the New England district executive committee of the Labor Youth League. All of this, only to discover later that my scrupulously and painfully reflexive "self-criticism" was being circulated in the party as an unrepentant and recalcitrant admission, demonstrating how the cancer of "white chauvinism" had spread even among people in responsible positions.

Reflections on my Communist Party experience preoccupied me during those years of intellectual awakening at Penn, often in moments of historiographic or moral musing. Surviving journal notes suggest that "my disillusionment and my sense of history" grew in tandem. Still very close to my party experience, I decided that "any historically meaningful characterization of Marxism must be based not on an 'ideal' conception of an 'unspoiled philosophical approach,'" but "on the theory as expressed in the practice of that group which has for better or worse appropriated to itself the heritage of Marxism: the world Communist movement." While my philosophical predisposition remained in a general sense materialist, I rejected "the 'superstructure' formulation": my party experience suggested that the "grossest errors of Communist dogmatism" were "the oversimplification and too facile categorization of complex phenomena, and the modification, distortion, or selection of reality in order to fit or justify theoretical preconceptions." Reading Kroeber's "Eighteen Professions" (1915) for my dissertation research, I reformulated the sixteenth as "history deals with conditions without which a relatively unique event would not have occurred—or better, the peculiar concatenation of events which led to its occurrence"—a foreshadowing of my later tendency to think in terms of context rather than cause.

Reading more Koestler—this time *The God That Failed* (1950)—I came to the conclusion that my own experience in the party had been "in the deepest sense religious." But unlike many other Communist Party apostates, I never embraced an extreme anti-Communism. Rather than demonizing my erstwhile comrades, I have continued to think of most of them as good and intelligent people who sacrificed self-interest for what they felt to be a higher goal—however dogmatically mistaken and misguided they may have been. Repelled by the means, hopeless of the end, I became instead a relativist—albeit with a reawakened personal conscience. Although I was by habitual inclination judgmental, yearning for moral absolutes, I now questioned my own moral standards and strove to understand how others might act in ways that seemed to violate them—as I had myself done. Despite having abandoned my faith, I tended for a long time to think of myself as an apostate. I felt guilty for having given up "self-sacrifice" for "self-realization" and worried that a "thoroughgoing relativism" was depriving me of "the capacity for righteous indignation." While seven years in a political wilderness may have denied me scholarly resources I might otherwise have accumulated, I still regard my party membership as an understandable choice and an enriching educational experience in many ways determinative of my later career as an historian of anthropology.

Social History and Historiography at Berkeley during the Free Speech Movement Years

In late November 1958, after I had begun work on my doctoral dissertation, I sent out fifty-five letters to history departments in the Northeast, the Midwest, and California inquiring about job possibilities. It was just before the great Sputnik expansion of American higher education, and the letters produced only one serious response. It came, however, from the department at the University of California, Berkeley—which "had already heard about me" from my professors at Pennsylvania. I assume that this "old boy" connection was mediated by Thomas Cochran, whose Bulletin 64 was produced the same year my father served as chairman of the Social Science Research Council. Be that as it may have been, I met with several Berkeley historians at the annual meeting of the American Historical Association and received a letter in March 1959 saying that "after surveying an extensive field" they had decided I was "the man we wanted to invite here," once their budgetary situation was clearer.

In response to my follow-up inquiry later that year there was a further talk with Berkeley department members at the Chicago meetings of the American Historical Association that December. A month or so afterward, the appointment had proceeded far enough that I was requested to submit "a biography" and to sign the loyalty oath that had been a matter of great controversy at Berkeley in the more extreme anti-Communist environment of the early 1950s. The oath required a denial of membership, during the preceding five years, in any organization advocating the overthrow of the United States or California governments "by force or violence or other unlawful means except as follows." After consulting a lawyer friend from Progressive Party days, I decided to follow his suggestion that I might sign, but should attach a qualifying statement. So I signed, indicating the exception of my membership in the Communist Party until 1956—but with a footnote saying that while it was widely thought of in those terms, it had not in my experience advocated violent overthrow (Gardner 1967).

Kenneth Stampp, then acting chair of the Berkeley history department, responded by saying that although my "past political activities [were] quite irrelevant and not even a proper subject for discussion," he nevertheless felt that the matter should be presented to President Clark Kerr—though he "would be surprised and disappointed if it made any difference to him." It was, however, a matter that Kerr wanted to discuss with me personally, and I was invited to come to Berkeley at the university's expense for a meeting early in March 1960. Leap-frogging directly into the jet age for my first-ever airplane trip, I was cordially hosted in Berkeley by the very small circle who had been made aware of the problem and met for an hour with Kerr—who unbeknownst to me was a professional acquaintance of my father. Focusing first on the nature of the Communist Party, we discussed whether the CPUSA, whatever its recent position on force and violence, was not in some objective world historical sense effectively the agent of Soviet international policy. Turning to a more practical point, Kerr wanted to know what I would do if called before an investigating committee. I replied that I would testify as to my own membership, but would not discuss the activities or affiliations of any other person—in my mind thereby risking a jail sentence, which several close friends had in fact endured near the height of the McCarthy period. At the end of the inquiry, Kerr said that he would present the matter to the Board of Regents at their next meeting and, as I left, surprised me by offering his "best wishes" to my father. Several weeks later, I was informed that "after consulting the

Board of Regents," Kerr had approved my appointment as lecturer. I have occasionally since then imagined scenarios for that regents' meeting—whether it was specifically discussed, or somehow slipped in without a vote under "miscellaneous new business." I suspect, however, that Kerr's role in defending my personal academic freedom made it difficult for me to accept the rather dark image of him as evil genius of the "multiversity" during the subsequent Free Speech Movement (cf. Kerr 2001:27–74).

I was hired at Berkeley as a social historian and did in fact twice give a large lecture course on early American social history, drawing on what I had learned at Penn, augmented by a range of further reading in secondary and primary sources—notably, Walt Rostow's *Stages of Economic Growth: A Non-Communist Manifesto* (1960), and the psychologically complex diary of the Puritan divine, Thomas Shepard. I also gave seminars on topics in race and culture. But from the point of view of the development of my historiography, the more important Berkeley experience was my assignment, as the "new boy" in the Berkeley department, to take charge of History 101, the required historiography course for history majors.

In this capacity, I was responsible for overseeing a dozen or so teaching assistants, each of whom supervised the "original" research projects of the dozen or so students in their section—and I attended each section at least once. It was a demanding but on the whole rewarding experience for all concerned. The TAs (one of whom later married Henry Kissinger) were among the best graduate students in the department, and several of them were unusually adept at involving and drawing out even the least forthcoming students in class discussions— a skill that I greatly admired but have never successfully emulated. My own primary responsibility was to lecture on the history of historical writing and historical method from Herodotus to Bulletin 64. I spent a month after our arrival in Berkeley writing the first lecture, two weeks writing the second, a week writing the third, and after the term began managed somehow in the intervals between twice weekly lectures.

Like my years at Penn, History 101 was a formative episode of intellectual capital accumulation. It was my first extended experience of European intellectual history, going back to the Greeks and the Romans, and, more importantly, to French and German historians—all of them in translation, since while I could make my way in Spanish and French sources, I remained for most purposes monolingual (cf. Stern 1960). The book that most engaged me—agonistically, given my abiding materialist predisposition—was Collingwood's *Idea of History* (1946), which more than any other made me realize that idealists might have something to say that, however difficult to follow, I must take seriously—and which in fact illuminated my own historical practice.

But it was Berkeley historians, partly through reading, but also by a kind of conversational osmosis, who perhaps had the most influence on me. While I was not close to Tom Kuhn personally, his *Structure of Scientific Revolutions* (1962) had a considerable impact—not so much as a systematic theory of scientific development, but because his idea of "paradigms" suggested fruitful ways of thinking about certain phases in the past history of anthropology. I also found food for historiographic thought in Joseph Levenson's *Confucian China and Its Modern Fate* (1958, 1965), with its emphasis on intellectual history as the history of men thinking rather than the history of thought. Conversationally, however, I was a bit closer to Carl Schorske, with whom, in memory, I associate a strengthening of the version of "bottom-up" historiography with which I was left after my disillusion with master narratives: as an historian, one's primary commitment is to the "stuff" of history, and while one might draw on various general concepts or theories (not to mention predispositions ingrained by personal experience) in order to make it meaningful, it was the "stuff" of history (problematic as that concept may be) that was both the beginning and the end of historical understanding. And there were other conversational influences as well—for the Berkeley department was an exciting place in the 1960s.

Already in the 1950s, there had been several key appointments that laid the basis for its transformation from a gentlemanly group of California scholars into a leading world center of historical research and training. I recall one of those earlier appointees telling me of a critical moment in the process, when then Chancellor Kerr encouraged the submission of a strong minority report to provide a basis for overriding the refusal of the department's then-conservative majority to approve Joseph Levenson's appointment. My own hiring was one of the first of an explosive expansion, in which the younger members of the department—all of them touched by the fire of 1960s Berkeley—developed a sense of group identity unusual in the academic world—including, for me, intimate and enduring friendships.

Despite my prior disillusion and growing depoliticization, it was impossible in this milieu not to be affected by both world and campus political issues. In 1961 I signed petitions protesting the ill-fated Kennedy/CIA invasion of Cuba as likely to "trigger World War III." Three

Free Speech Movement marchers coming through the Sather Gate on their way to the meeting of the University of California Regents in University Hall on November 20, 1964. On the right in the background is the student union building; on the left is Sproul Hall. Mario Savio is on the right turning backward. (Steven Marcus Photograph, courtesy of the Bancroft Library, University of California, Berkeley)

years later, I was involved with other Berkeley American historians in a study of the treatment of "The Negro in American History Textbooks" in use in California public schools (1964b). In 1965, I took advantage of an expense-paid job interview at Emory University to join a national contingent of American historians who traveled by bus from Atlanta to Montgomery, where we walked on the last leg of Martin Luther King's march from Selma, joining a rally of thousands in front of the state capitol. Later that year, I marched with some fellow members of the history department from Berkeley to Oakland in a demonstration against the Vietnam War. But the local focus of political activity—through which many national issues were mediated—was, of course, the Free Speech Movement (FSM).

I still recall, with a welling resonance of activist adrenaline, Mario Savio exhorting the crowd in front of Sproul Hall in November 1964, to "put their bodies on the gears and upon the wheels" of the university's bureaucratic machine, and later that evening joining a group of faculty observers who tried unsuccessfully to negotiate with the campus police the basis for a peaceful withdrawal of the more than eight hundred students who were sitting in the hallways of Sproul Hall. In the preceding two months I had been one of a group of young historians who were in and out of each other's offices in Dwinelle Hall discussing faculty participation in the FSM, writing letters to the press, and drafting motions for meetings of the faculty—including a brief motion ("the Stocking preamble") that was "kept in hand" (although not actually offered) to counter anticipated opposition at the December 8 meeting, where the faculty voted 824 to 115 in favor of the major student demands. Two years later, at the time of "The Little Free Speech Movement," I was one of four who signed an appeal to the Academic Senate in favor of Mario Savio's readmission to the university as "symbolic of the positive achievements" of that previous vote. Three weeks later, I was one of three faculty observers at a sit-in against recruitment into the U.S. Navy in the lower lobby of the student union, watching the police drag the participants away, and on January 19, 1967, testifying as a defense witness at the trial in which they were found not guilty.[14] But if the activism of the students sometimes evoked in me a retrospective empathy, it also provoked in the present an anxious ambivalence. As a member of the last cohort of the "Old Left," I had "been there, done that"—or something like it—and having already suffered a painful disillusion, I could not fully identify with a "New Left" formed half a generation later. I was disturbed by what sometimes seemed the absolutism of student radical demands and the extremism of their tactics (which occasionally recalled those of my own Communist Party days). Concerned about means and ends, I worried also about the unanticipated consequences of actions, however well intentioned. And I was constrained by an inclination to see the "other side"—the rationality, in their own terms, of positions that were not my own. Although tending to incapacitate me for action in the present, that relativism (personal, anthropological, and historical) has been essential to my historicist understanding.

14. Although I have no memory of a "Stocking preamble," it is referred to in my close friend Reggie Zelnik's account of the role of the Berkeley faculty in the FSM events (2002: 311, 336). Following up that account, I recovered files on top of a bookcase in my office, in which there were contemporary documents, including a letter to Henry May on January 1, 1965, analyzing the FSM appeal to various categories of students (cf. J. Freeman 2004).

The Berkeley Experience:
Divorce, Family Breakup, and Consciousness Raising

Although my appointment at the University of California marked the successful beginning of my academic career, it also led to the dissolution of my marriage and my family. Leaving aside its most intimate aspects, which were traumatically transformative for all concerned, the breakup was both culturally constructed and historiographically consequential. Like many divorces in this period, it was a microcosm of the cultural process of women's liberation. Mina and I had been too poor to share fully in the consumption revolution of the 1950s; our domestic lifestyle was closer to the Cramdens' than the Cleavers'—although not owning a TV, we watched neither of them at the time. But we did experience our own baby boom; and though I helped to put our daughters to bed with improvised stories and sometimes went with them to museums on weekends, it was Mina who cooked and cleaned and took care of them on a daily basis. So long as my scholarly self-realization was a prelude to her own, she carried the domestic burden willingly. But when we moved to Berkeley, and I became increasingly preoccupied by the tenure process, her future life seemed to offer simply seven more years of subjection of self. Supplementing our family income by taking home typing jobs, she did her best for a time to play the role of "faculty wife," even to the extent of managing a "dinner party" for faculty colleagues. But it was not a role she found congenial—the less so, perhaps, as our political trajectories, roughly parallel in the early 1950s, began to diverge. After a phase of rebellion and alienation, I had moved back toward my family's academic liberalism; she, after a briefer distancing, moved back toward her family's academic radicalism. And while I, too, read Betty Friedan's *Feminine Mystique* (1963), and encouraged Mina's return to school to complete her BA, that was not easy for her to manage after the birth of our son Thomas in December 1962. Over the next two years, things fell apart, and after a trial separation, we were divorced in 1965—I, unwillingly, with well-intentioned promises that things might be different; she, the initiator, soon to be remarried to an old friend from our radical past, with whom she later sailed to the Caribbean to carry on fieldwork for a PhD in anthropology (see Caulfield 1969).

It was in this context of domestic breakup and self-redefinition that I experienced the cultural ferment of Berkeley in the early and middle 1960s—some of it personally, some of it indirectly or vicariously through colleagues, friends, and others close to me. One had only to

The Stocking children—Melissa, Susan, Thomas, Rebecca, and Rachel—on a holiday in the High Sierras near Mount Lassen early in the summer of 1967, when they may not have been aware that their father was soon to be leaving Berkeley (as it turned out, permanently).

venture south of campus to enter one of the classic venues of 1960s countercultural and New Left radicalism—or, if you will, of "flower" and "people" power. A walk on Telegraph Avenue would take one past student and faculty radicals reenacting a long tradition of coffee house discourse, as well as long-haired tie-dyed sidewalk entrepreneurs, barefoot teenage runaways of both sexes seeking handouts, even Hell's Angels who had come to sample the action. It was in some ways an ominous world—in a sharply personal way, to a reluctantly divorcing father of teen and pre-teen children. My children had friends who were permanently scarred; several others close to them literally did not survive: their step-brother was murdered, one of their closest friends committed suicide, and another died in a tragic automobile accident.[15]

15. For richly moving personal accounts of the dilemmas and the tragedies of adolescence in this Berkeley milieu, see Melanie Bellah, *Tammy: A Biography of a Young Girl* (1999) and *Abby and Her Sisters: A Memoir* (2002).

My own children, however, were among the luckier ones. Despite the major traumas of divorce and remarriage (including my departure from Berkeley in the summer of 1967), they emerged from their experience there in the 1960s and 1970s relatively unscathed. In the 1980s, they all returned, along different paths, to Davis/Stocking academic roots. That they were able to do so was facilitated by an event that occurred in the year we arrived in Berkeley: the passage in 1960 of the "Master Plan for Higher Education in California" establishing a three-stage sequence from local junior colleges to regional state colleges to the multicampus University of California—a path that each of them followed. My eldest, Susan, after classes at a junior college, graduated summa cum laude from UCLA in psychology and carried on her career as teacher and sculptor. Rebecca, after courses at a junior college and a semester at the San Francisco Art Institute, attended San Francisco State for two years, and after a quarter at the University of California at Berkeley transferred to Harvard, graduating summa cum laude in 1982, and later went on to medical school and a career in clinical and computer medicine. Rachel went from junior college to a summa cum laude at San Francisco State, then to a PhD in medieval history at Stanford, and after that to a tenure position at Southern Illinois University (see R. L. Stocking 2000). Melissa, after courses in a junior college, graduated summa cum laude in sociology followed by an MS in clinical psychology from Cal Poly Pomona—where she continues to play a leading role in their Learning Resource Center. Thomas got a BS in applied mathematics at Berkeley in 1987 and went on to become a computer programmer and entrepreneur in computer software. Between the five of them, they and their spouses have produced ten gifted grandchildren and, so far, three great-grandchildren.

Although I have avoided direct discussion of some of the experiences of my children in the Berkeley years, I should say something about my own in the years between my separation from Mina and my departure from Berkeley in 1967. Although they were for me painfully traumatic and worrisome years, they were also an exciting time for a long-monogamous man in his late thirties, suddenly free to decorate his own bachelor pad, adorn his chin with a beard, and, in a hesitant, experimental way, explore the possibilities of a new persona in the emerging world of "sex, drugs, and rock 'n' roll." I traveled more than once across the Bay to the Haight-Ashbury district during the "summer of love" and went to several of Bill Graham's rock concerts—and two decades

Pondering the possibilities of a new persona as bearded bachelor in 1960s Berkeley, California.

later still had a psychedelic poster of Big Brother and the Holding Company hanging in our weekend place in Beverly Shores. I danced (without "steps," but with a liberating total body movement) at both student and faculty parties—for this was a period when some faculty members, too, moved their shoulders, and even their hips, to the beat of "White Rabbit" and "(I Can't Get No) Satisfaction." I never took an acid trip, but I had close friends who did, and I did briefly experiment with marijuana. I can still recall my embarrassment when the hostess at a faculty dinner asked me if I had smoked it, and after a moment's hesitation I described the experience to colleagues. And I did, during the break between more than fifty years of two strict monogamies, have relationships of varying seriousness with other women.

Looking back, it seems clear to me that my personal as well as academic and political experience during the Berkeley years contributed significantly to my emerging historicist orientation. In a way analogous to the impact of my years as Communist in the working-class, the experience of family breakup and divorce strengthened my appreciation of the over-determination and multiple consequences of historical events, as well as the transvaluation often implicit in their later reconstruction. Life changes experienced and evaluated in one way as they occur can be very differently perceived in the retrospect of memory, and also in the context of changes in life experience and personal relationships.

In the case of my four daughters, I recall the psychological impact of the breakup as a mixture of the mutual sadness of loss (perceived by at least one of them as abandonment) and a sense of my own guilt (as having contributed to the events that led me to "abandon" them). By that time, however, our relationship already encompassed between eight and thirteen years of a potent, if complex, closeness in which was embedded a powerful achievement motivation. Shielded by distance from the traumas of adolescent rebellion, my relation with them was largely empathic and supportive financially. Mina also offered a model of achievement motivation, but its impact was more problematic, due to her direct involvement in their adolescent rebellions—which in each case led to her daughter leaving a home she no longer found welcoming. The case with my son Thomas (aka Tomas) was quite different. He was only two years old at the time of the separation, and his subsequent experience of me as father was limited—this, in contrast to his experience of Mina's second husband. Tomas and I did have some memorable brief visits, including an afternoon in Santa Monica when I taught him to swim in the hotel pool, and a flight from California to

Chicago when the plane made a forced landing in Denver, surrounded by fire engines and ambulances. But there was nothing to compare with month-long sail boat voyages to Mina's fieldwork site in the Caribbean, skippered by her second husband, sometimes braving near-hurricane winds, and on one occasion running aground on a reef near Cuba, where they were interned for three weeks before being allowed to sail on to Florida. Over time, travel as adventure became a major theme of his life, in which his adolescent and early manhood experiences were less traumatic than liberating. While we have long experienced a kind of closeness, it is perhaps better described as avuncular than as paternal.

Over the years, my daughters' experiences in self-realization made me much more sensitive to the problems of aspiring women, and I have been able to see Mina's experience of our marriage and its breakup more empathically. However, it has long been my sense that her view of these events changed dramatically in the early 1960s, in a process she may recall as "consciousness raising"—and that she would remember its impact on our children very differently than I do. But in the black box of my own retrospective understanding, I tend to privilege my own perspective—as even relativist historians are sometimes wont to do.

Tenure without a Book:
Essays toward a New History of Anthropology

When I arrived at Berkeley in the summer of 1960, it was as an un-tenured instructor in American social history; when I left, in the summer of 1967, it was as a recently tenured associate professor without a book, but already identified with a new tendency in the history of anthropology. It was against this background that the tumultuously transformative experiences of life in 1960s Berkeley took place, although what is background and what is foreground is a moot point. I knew at the time that I was demon-driven, and at one point thought of writing an essay on "The Psychological Atrocities of the Tenure System"; but I do not now recall seriously considering opting out, except perhaps in the most devastating moments of family breakup.

Within that tenure system I had in fact a relatively privileged position, and although I did not produce the book normally demanded, I was able to sustain the impression that in due course I would produce a major work. At the end of my first year I was promoted to assistant professor and given a summer research fellowship; at the end of the second year, I was given a second summer fellowship, had in press an important essay on Lamarckianism in American social science (GS 1962), and was already applying to the American Council of Learned Societies for support during a half-sabbatical year (which became a full year off) to finish a book-length reworking and expansion of my dissertation. As then envisioned, the book was to consist of four major parts (Context, Continuity, Change, Causation), composed of sixteen chapters (3/5/5/3). In the application, six of these were marked as "complete," seven as "incomplete," and the other three (including a conclusion looking forward to the present and an essay on method) as in the "research and planning stage." I got the money ($6,400), which with six months' sabbatical pay ($2,600) and what Mina made by typing, was to sustain a family of six for a year. Not, however, without cost to my marriage and family. When I was reminded in November 1964 that I had not sent in the required report on my fellowship activities, all I could do was plead unnamed "personal difficulties which greatly hampered my work." In reply, I received a sympathetic note accepting this as my final report, and hoping that my problems would soon be "satisfactorily resolved."

I had in fact published two essays that year: one of them an occasional piece in the institutional microcosm mode entitled "French Anthropology in 1800" (1964a); the other, one half of a long paper on the culture concept in the work of Tylor and Boas (1963), which was written for the Social Science Research Council conference on the history of anthropology in April 1962. Planning for the conference had begun two years prior to that, in a committee chaired by my mentor Hallowell. Although at that time my dissertation was not yet complete, it was taken for granted (as I later discovered in researching a biographical essay on Hallowell) that I was to contribute a paper on race and culture in American anthropology. The conference participants included historians and sociologists of science (among them Bernard Barber, John Greene, and Harry Woolf) and leading representatives of the "four fields" of anthropology (among them, Joseph Casagrande, Frederica de Laguna, Melville Herskovits, Dell Hymes, Harry Shapiro, Carl Voegelin, and Leslie White—as well as two leading figures of the Chicago department, Fred Eggan and Sol Tax). In the spirit of Hallowell's seminar, the conference was intended to establish the basis for a new history of anthropology—one that, in contrast to the "brief, sketchy or semischolarly" and generally "out-of-date" historical treatments of the field, would be both anthropologically informed and seriously historical. In the account prepared by Dell Hymes for the Council's publication *Items* (1962), I was given exemplary billing and soon after was invited to give a version of my paper to a plenary session of the annual meeting of the American Anthropological Association. In short, I was there at the launching of the "modern" history of anthropology and embarked on it with the imprimatur of some of the discipline's leading figures.

Dell Hymes and I had arrived at Berkeley at the same time, and over the next several years I had through him some contact with the anthropology department (including an oral examination at which a rock was thrown on the table, and the student was asked to say whether it was an artifact or had simply been kicked by a cow). In moving away from American social history, I moved not only toward anthropology but toward an emerging subfield of the history of science. When the psychologist Robert Watson sought to represent anthropology on the editorial board of his proposed *Journal of the History of the Behavioral Sciences*, he asked me to serve, and I suggested also Dell, with whom I was already involved in discussions of the historiography of anthropology. When I subsequently responded critically to Watson's somewhat ahistorical opening editorial, he asked me if I would like to write one, and I suggested that Dell and I might cooperate. Writing, however, has always been for me a solitary process, and after several months had passed without a draft, I decided to write the essay myself. Drawing on Berkeley influences (notably Kuhn and Levenson), the position I argued was strongly "historicist," in a sense influenced by Herbert Butterfield's *Whig Interpretation of History* (1963). In a phrase I have come to regret, I suggested that the historian approached history "in the spirit of the mountain climber attacking Everest—'because it is there'"—holding to one side "presentist" preconceptions about the progress of disciplinary knowledge. However, I immediately qualified the position by incorporating a passage from Hymes that made the case for an "enlightened presentism," and over the years I have retreated further from the "strong" position (GS 1965c, 1999).[16]

16. Since the words "historicism" and "historicist" appear frequently in this essay, the particularity of my usage merits comment. Although historians of anthropology associate the opposition to "presentism" with my name, I have no proprietary interest in either term. That "presentism" may have been my coinage is suggested by the phrase in which I first used it: "Whiggish history is a variety of what I would call generally 'presentism' in historical study" (1965c:4). Needless to say, however, I had not in 1965 done an Internet search, and it is possible that I missed it in sources I did consult. However, when I went on to offer my own frankly "loose" and "polemically convenient" definition of "historicism,"

In addition to the historicism essay, I published four others in the middle 1960s: an application of the presentism argument to a controversy between anthropologists over the interpretation of E. B. Tylor (1965a), two essays on Franz Boas (1965b, 1966a), and a survey of current work in the history of anthropology (1966b). However, although I had signed a contract with one of the several publishers who had read about my project in the *ACLS Newsletter*, and had actually managed to write 120 pages during the summer of 1966, the book I had been led to believe was a precondition of tenure was still far from completion.

Thus it was that the tenure decision in the fall of 1966 was based on nine published essays and a book manuscript less than three quarters complete. I was not optimistic; indeed, I was very anxious. But to my surprise and great relief, I was informed in December that the department had recommended my promotion to permanent tenure as associate professor—unanimously, but with cautionary thoughts about the future direction of my work. Some, including Kenneth Stampp, felt that I was in striking distance of having a major work in American intellectual history and should plow through to the end. The Germanist on the committee offered a double-edged compliment: "George, you really must learn German—you think like a German." Carl Schorske felt that while I had "a fine instinctive grasp of the main currents of German intellectual history," my substantive background was weak, and that this was especially a problem, "since the most important groups in my audience (American historians and anthropologists)" would have no appreciation of my weaknesses in this area. Implying also that the project was so tied up with my personal psychological problems that it might be difficult to finish, he urged me to put it aside for the time being.

In reporting all this shortly after Christmas to Dell Hymes, with whom I had previously been discussing various options, I was still in doubt as what to do. I did, however, include in the letter an outline almost identical to the published table of contents of *Race, Culture, and*

---

in terms of a series of oppositional attributes to "presentism," I specifically indicated that "historicism" already had a long, complicated and sometimes contradictory history (Lee and Beck 1954). In the years since, "historicism" has undergone further transformation, most strikingly in the movement referred to as the "new historicism" (Gallagher and Greenblatt 2000:1–19). When I refer to myself as an "old historicist" (below, p. 163) I have in mind an opposition to the "new historicism"—and not to the varied uses antedating my own appropriation of the term.

Evolution (GS 1968a). I also discussed plans for coming to Penn for the fall semester of 1967 under a National Science Foundation Fellowship I had just received for postdoctoral training in anthropology—this, with further work in the Boas papers and the possibility of a Boas biography in mind. At Penn, I audited courses in linguistics, French social theory, Oceanic ethnography, and cultural theory and wrote the methodological reflections that preface each essay in *Race, Culture, and Evolution*. But with my later work on British social anthropology already in mind, I had planned to spend the second half of the fellowship year at Chicago, long the center of British influence in American anthropology, where the anthropologists were already interested in my work—and had in fact broached the possibility of my accepting an appointment.

From History to Anthropology
at the University of Chicago

In 1968 the University of Chicago Department of Anthropology was in the later stages of a transformation that had begun a decade previously, in the aftermath of the death of Robert Redfield and the departures of Lloyd Warner and Sherwood Washburn. In 1960, it had hired three brilliant young social anthropologists from the Berkeley department: Tom Fallers (a Weberian previously trained at Chicago), along with Clifford Geertz and David Schneider (two products of the Harvard Department of Social Relations, both strongly influenced by Clyde Kluckhohn and Talcott Parsons, albeit in differing ways). All three had ties to British social anthropology, with which the Chicago department had been linked since Radcliffe-Brown's six-year stay in the 1930s, and more recently through Fred Eggan, who in 1963 was influential in arranging a conference of the British Association of Social Anthropologists in which several younger Chicago anthropologists participated (Gluckman and Eggan 1963).

By the time I arrived, the personnel of the anthropology department had more than doubled since its low point in the early 1950s. The new appointments included several who had trained at the University of Chicago and who retained a commitment to the distinctive interdisciplinary character of its undergraduate education and the embracive "four [or five] field" training of its graduate anthropology program. However, what some have called "the sacred bundle" of anthropology was already coming unraveled, and younger anthropologists were more inclined to see themselves as specialists in a particular "subdiscipline." In an expansive period of readily available funding and high academic mobility, the more distinguished or promising subdisciplinarians could realistically expect to pursue their research interests at other institutions. However, their situation in Chicago, which their appointments had helped to reestablish as "number one" in the country, was a very privileged one, with light and flexible teaching loads defined by their own research interests, taught mostly at the graduate level, and with freedom, in effect, to accept any research leave for which they could manage funding. Within the Social Science Division the department had not only a large measure of autonomy but also a sympathetic ear at higher administrative levels for any appointment it felt necessary to maintain its status and to strengthen any particular line of research that seemed relevant to this goal. In 1968, that included the history of anthropology (see GS 1979b).

Shortly after my arrival in Chicago, I became aware that the department had previously voted in favor of my permanent joint appointment in anthropology and history, but had run up against the historians' expectation that tenure demanded at least one published book. By then, however, *Race, Culture, and Evolution* was in press, and over the next several months, negotiations between the two departments continued, in which Barney Cohn, a member of both, played an important role. His voice carried considerable weight especially among the history department's younger members, and early in April the matter was resolved when the historians finally voted favorably, albeit with several abstentions. The anthropologists immediately pushed the appointment forward to the higher levels—which, fortuitously, included an economist divisional dean, as well as a university president with whom my father had worked several decades previously in Washington—and by the end of April I received a formal offer to join the University of Chicago faculty.

Although I had arrived in Chicago knowing that this offer was a possibility, it was not an easy decision to accept, given my strong sense of belonging in the Berkeley history department, and the fact that I would be moving two thousand miles from my five children. But like most of the turning points in my life, it was overdetermined. Back in Berkeley, the particular circumstances of my divorce allowed me to see the children only once a week, in often hectic group situations not conducive to easy enjoyment, and even less to effective parenting. And there was no other academic position in the country so uniquely favorable to pursuing the history of anthropology as Chicago—which Raymond Firth, at a later departmental anniversary, hyperbolized as "not a cluster, but a galaxy of stars." Given virtually complete freedom to pursue my research in the anthropology of the past, I could at the same time absorb through conversational osmosis and participation in department activity a great deal of the anthropology of the present. So I decided to accept the offer—with the understanding that my children's college tuition anywhere would be matched up to the amount of tuition at Chicago.

During the spring of 1968, I was preoccupied completing papers on Boas for two conferences to which I had previously been invited. For the first, on the history of linguistics organized by Dell Hymes, I wrote an essay entitled "The Boas Plan for the Study of American Indian Languages" (1974a) and a shorter methodological essay on "transcending textbook chronicles and apologetics" (1974b)—both of which I circulated with some trepidation, fearful that specialists attending (who included the world-renowned Roman Jakobson) might question my critique of a previous "presentist" account of Boas by a linguistic anthropologist who was also at the conference. For the second conference, on "National Traditions in Anthropology," I wrote a paper on "the Boas tradition" (1974c) for an audience that included Marshall Sahlins (fresh from the barricaded streets of Paris) and Margaret Mead (one of three women among a group of distinguished or soon to be distinguished male anthropologists, whom she seemed able to dominate every time she rose to speak). Embodying so much of anthropology before and after, Boas remained for me a permanent reference point in all my work. But lacking German, and daunted by the demands of biography—in perfectionist principle, to read all that a person wrote and read, and to understand all the contexts of their writing and acting in the world, down to the present—I soon abandoned any idea of attempting a full-scale study.

In the meantime, I had also taken advantage of the intellectual resources and opportunities available to me in the anthropology department, including the new curriculum instituted by the social anthropological group in the early 1960s. The evolutionary concerns that had been a major focus of Chicago anthropology in the 1950s were now relegated to a sequence on the "Human Career," which sociocultural students were no longer likely to take. In contrast, archeology students— whom I recall as worrying whether archeology had a "paradigm" (and if not, how to get one)—were still required to take a new sequence that had been organized in Parsonian terms around "the concepts of personality, society, and culture as systems." Increasingly, however, "systematic analysis" at Chicago focused on the study of culture, as symbolic systems rather than patterns of behavior. Although I attended the course on personality, it was David Schneider's variant of "systems" (reviewing the literature of kinship and relativizing it to the point of its disappearance as a universal category) that was especially relevant to my developing research interests (cf. Bashkow 1991).

By the time I accepted the Chicago offer, these interests were shifting decisively to British anthropology, which was at once closely related to and distant enough from American anthropology that it might illuminate and be illuminated by comparison. I had already published essays on E. B. Tylor (1965a, 1966a, 1968d) and Bronislaw Malinowski (1968b) and had been approached by Robert Young, an expatriate Texan historian of psychology with a broader interest in the behavioral sciences, about the possibility of my spending time at King's College, Cambridge. By April 1968, this had eventuated in an invitation to participate in a seminar he was organizing at King's on "Science and Society." To make this possible, it was agreed, as part of the Chicago offer, that I would be given paid leave to go to England after teaching two courses in the fall quarter. In ways that went well beyond the discussions in the seminar itself, those months in Cambridge were to have a foundational influence on my further work in the history of British anthropology, which by then was envisioned as a multivolume enterprise.

Multicultural Travels with Carol Bowman:
From Srpski Itebej to King's High Table
across Boundaries in Time and Class

During the months before my departure for England, however, my personal life situation was transformed when I met Carol Bowman. After accepting the appointment at Chicago, I had moved to an apartment building in walking distance of the campus and shortly thereafter was introduced by my colleague Ray Fogelson to Carol, who lived in the same building. Daughter of a Serbian father (Steve Bowman, born Bolyacz) and a Danish mother (born Karen Baun), Carol spent the first eight years of her life in Kenosha, Wisconsin—where her mixed parentage was viewed as exotic, if not verging on miscegenation. In the late 1930s, however, her parents moved to Oak Park, a suburb on the west border of Chicago, where Carol, although self-professedly an indifferent student, so impressed one of her high school teachers that she was urged to apply for early admission to the University of Chicago. However,

Carol, who thinks of herself as "adventuresome" but only anxiously so, was intimidated by the prospect of college at the age of fifteen—and was already dreaming of living in New York City. When her parents subsequently insisted that she go to college within a one-day driving radius of Chicago, so that they could visit her (although they never did), the farthest she could get was Oberlin College in Ohio. But upon her graduation in 1953, she was able to convince them that she should undertake graduate work for a master's degree in English literature at Columbia.

For the next ten years she lived in New York City, for part of the time in Greenwich Village. Working "as little as necessary" to support her "New York habit," she relied on a series of temporary jobs to get her through periods of unemployment. There was, however, one extended stretch in the late 1950s when she worked at one of the most important sociological institutions in the country: the Bureau of Applied Social Research at Columbia University. Although she began as a temp typist and later worked as a secretary, this somewhat tenuous sociological connection foreshadowed her career after returning to Chicago in 1963, where she was working when Ray Fogelson introduced me to her in 1968. Shortly thereafter, she agreed to water my plants when I went to visit my children in California. In the weeks after my return, we got to know each other better, she introduced me to her parents, and on September 29, 1968, we were married in Libertyville, Illinois. For the next twenty years, during which she obtained a doctoral degree in sociology at the University of Chicago, she worked at the National Opinion Research Center, starting as coding supervisor, and by the time we met was a senior survey director.[17]

Although Carol discourages glimpses into her black box, she would probably grant that one of her attributes is a self-effacing modesty. She "cringes" when I recall the later comment of our eldest grandson: "Carol is just like everyone else—except she dazzles." Among the many

17. In that role in 1984, Carol went to the Soviet Union under the auspices of the National Academy of Sciences for a one month visit to continue work on an international comparison of secondary schools with large data sets collected in the United States, several Soviet republics, and Japan. During her stay in Moscow, she consulted with members of the Soviet Academy of Scientists. The following year, she left NORC and became director of research at the Center for Clinical Medical Ethics at the University of Chicago. Since 2000, she has also served as senior research project professional in the Section of Geriatrics. She has published widely in numerous medical journals.

On September 29, 1968, Carol Bowman and I were married in an abbreviated Serbian Orthodox service at the St. Sava monastery in Libertyville, Illinois, where Carol's Serbian grandparents are buried. Among the wedding guests were her own parents, Steve and Karen Bowman, two of her childhood friends from Kenosha, Wisconsin, several of her colleagues from the National Opinion Research Center, and her very close friend Valetta Press. My guests included University of Chicago colleagues David and Addie Schneider, and Raymond Fogelson, who still takes quite seriously his responsibilities as my "kum" (ritual relative).

ways in which she dazzled me was the quality of her mind. In contrast to my memory sieve, Carol remembered in detail things that happened when she was three; her imagination leapt, mine labored; when we worked crossword puzzles together, she got the themes and puns, I filled in the crossings (sometimes, when she was not around, with help from the Internet—which she regarded as cheating). However, it was not only her quicksilver wit, but also her inborn generosity and deeply engrained sense of familial responsibility that quickly won over my parents, my children (who think of her as a very special friend, not a step-mother), and later their progeny, for whom she has been a world-class "Grandma Carol." Most importantly, she stuck with me, through

Carol Stocking with her very proud father, Steve Bowman, just after she received her PhD in sociology from the University of Chicago on September 1, 1978.

bad times as well as good. Over the years she even succeeded in loosening up a bit what she thought of as my "Clarendon" values and "Cotton Mather" personality.

Among Carol's many other influences on my life there is one that stands out historiographically: the experience through her Danish and Serbian relatives of complexities of cultural otherness in historical time and social space. Before our marriage she had been to Yugoslavia, without meeting any of her relatives, and to Denmark, where she met several family members, including one who had "the gift" and was able to locate dead bodies for the police, as well as amber by the bucketful on North Sea beaches.[18] During the 1970s and early 1980s we took four trips together to Yugoslavia, twice with her father Steve—and on two occasions stopping off in Denmark.

---

18. For skeptical readers (part of myself included): her distant cousin Anders could also "cure" both mental and physical problems (by talk therapy and by massage)— including those of a patient who flew in from Montana when he had an episode of "insanity."

Everywhere we went, we were stuffed with food. In Denmark, the scattered offspring of a single farming family returned for a festive dinner at the ancestral farm near Hurup in Jutland, close to the site of the Thisted witchcraft obsession of 1698—family tradition being unclear as to whether their ancestor was a witch or a witch hunter. The contents of the home, accumulated over generations, ranged from a large seventeenth-century Bible (annotated in pen) to the latest Danish modern furniture. In contrast, the barns around the central courtyard were very up-to-date, with six tractors of varying sizes, as well as tiled floors for the Holstein cows and the spotless pink pigs.

An even more striking contrast between tradition and modernity was evident in Srpski Itebej, remembered by Steve as the place to which he had been carried on his uncle's shoulders the seven miles from Zitiste to visit maternal relatives named "Rajic." When we first arrived in Itebej, we went to the town office to see if we could find a Rajic. After a failed search of large volumes of late-nineteenth-century records gathering dust high up on the office shelves, one of the local officials recalled that there was a "baba" (old lady) on the far side of town whose maiden name was Rajic. Contacted by telephone, her grandson Pera Marenkov, a talented mechanic who augmented the family income with a modified corn-husking machine more efficient and less expensive than the one run by the state, soon arrived in his Yugoslav Fiat to drive us over deeply rutted streets to the family domicile. There we were greeted by four generations of relatives, whose ebullient baba Dusanka informed us that a Gypsy who "read" coffee grounds had recently predicted visitors from "far away."

The numerous Proustian memories of our visits in Itebej (where Carol, after taking a course in Serbian, later visited for a month by herself), in Bavaniste (where we met another branch of Steve's peasant relatives), and in Belgrade (to which their daughter Bozana had moved when she was married) invariably involved food and drink. In a dirt-floored peasant cottage near Itebej where we arrived unannounced, a distant cousin offered us a fabulous sour cherry strudel. Before we sat down for dinner in Bavaniste, Steve and his Lazarov cousin Dragomir had a knee-to-knee *starac* (old man) face-down, won, of course, by Steve, elder by seven years and a guest to boot. At Vinograd, near Belgrade, Bozana and her Montenegrin husband Vukota Roncevic entertained us at a restaurant high above the south shore of the Danube.

In the spring of 1984, when Carol went to the Soviet Union to continue her research, I came along for the first leg of her trip (see footnote 17). On the way, we stopped in Yugoslavia, where we visited her Rajic/Marenkov relatives in Srpski Itebej. Posing here in front of Pera Marenkov's workshop are (from the left) Pera's wife Verica, their younger daughter Radoslava, Carol, Pera's parents Milena and Radovan Marenkov, their older daughter Milena, and Pera's grandmother Dusanka (who was, in Serbian terms, Steve Bowman's "sister"). Several years later, Pera and Verica came to visit us in Chicago and at our summer place in Beverly Shores, Indiana, where Verica (a wonderful cook) complained that our food lacked "fat"—but herself took an immediate liking for Oreos. In 2010 Pera died after a brief illness, during which there were many calls to and from Serbia about therapeutic possibilities that Carol, as a relative and a medical researcher, might be able to recommend.

But the most memorable aspect of these visits was to experience the changes in Steve, as he reentered a world of legend, language, and social structure that he had previously revisited briefly on a trip he and his wife Karen made to Yugoslavia and Denmark in 1969. On our first visit to Yugoslavia in 1973, as we traveled by train from Budapest to Belgrade, he began to tell us stories that Carol had never heard before. And when we took him to the Kosovo field on which the great battle between Serbs and Turks had been fought in 1389, he suddenly realized that the stories his uncles had told him of the combatants being so closely entangled that the rain could not reach the ground were probably not literally true. Most striking, however, was a transformation in the cultural personality of Steve himself. After decades in which he had made a point of not speaking Serbian and assumed the social role of a crotchety and opinionated front-porch commentator on the passing Oak Park scene, he now conversed easily in his slightly archaic native tongue with relatives he had never met, but among whom he quickly assumed the exalted status of *starac*. In the process, Steve (now "Deda Stoyan") gained access to memories stored in another part of his brain—and apparently repressed again when he returned to his lower-middle-class home in Oak Park.

In 1976, however, his *starac* personality was resurrected when Vukota and Bozana, who spoke no English, visited us for two weeks during our year at the Palo Alto Center for Advanced Study. Although I was shut out from the conversation, I managed to get myself rebuked several times for "not knowing how to behave"—that is, for not showing the proper respect for Steve's reassumed *starac* status. When Steve vigorously discouraged my attempt to invite Vukota to see Sylvester Stallone in *Rocky*, I persisted—on the grounds that the film was effectively a silent one—and I was perhaps a bit smug when Vukota later bubbled over, in Serbian, about how much he enjoyed it. And when I managed to involve both of them in the translation of Serbian kinship terms, using Lewis Henry Morgan's kinship categories, and in the process confirmed the problematic character of ethnographic elicitation through intermediaries, it was Steve, after some debate with Vukota, who imposed his own authority as *starac*.

All of this was in the future, however, when Carol and I arrived at Cambridge in January 1969 in response to Bob Young's invitation to participate in his seminar. Fortunately, Carol was able on the basis of her prior experience in survey research to attach herself to an ongoing project in industrial sociology. Braving workers' whistles on shop floors, she collected data on why young men in the full employment labor market of Peterborough might choose to enter a lower-paying entry-level job when higher-paying options were available. She also had a taste of life at King's College, and on one occasion was one of the first nonfaculty women to dine at high table, where she was seated next to E. M. Forster—although (as she remembers it) the only words that passed between them were her request that he please pass the salt. Meanwhile, I tried to think of something intelligent or humorous (or better, both) to say to other dons, it being understood that at high table one did not talk about one's work.

During the months at King's there were a number of revelatory incidents of class and culture, some with overtly political overtones. On one occasion, when I stepped aside in a narrow passageway in favor of a butler carrying a heavily loaded tray, there was an extended moment of silent impasse until I realized that I was expected to go through first. There was another time when a North Country working-class student lamented at a radical gathering that he would never achieve the accent that fellow students acquired by birth. I recall also two occasions when the college was decorated with radical slogans: once, when "Women, Communism, and Freedom" was emblazoned in large red letters on the boundary wall behind King's College Chapel (the issue of admitting women to the college being then a matter of public debate); another, when a large abstract painting on loan in the student common was over-printed in black, "Art sells out for 30 pieces of silver." Although during our stay we became friends with several refugees from the Berkeley Free Speech Movement, there was nothing comparable to Mario Savio on the Sproul steps. The only surviving memory analogue was the time I witnessed a small "demonstration" at which a dozen or so King's students took tentative footsteps onto a lawn that had been nurtured for centuries, on which only "ducks and dons" (myself included) were privileged to walk.

By the end of July, when we watched the moon landing on a borrowed telly in our flat in Mulberry Close (along with my visiting daughter Rebecca), I had taken advantage of the time between seminar sessions to work in various manuscript archives—most importantly, the papers of Alfred Cort Haddon in Cambridge and those of Malinowski at the London School of Economics. While I had previously done some archival work on Boas, it was in England, during this trip and a second one in 1973 (when I was academic visitor at the London School of Economics), that I had the Rankean experience of total immersion in another historical country. On several occasions I savored the historical explorer's anticipation of discovery, when I was the first to open a dusty box of still uncataloged papers, as well as the eureka feeling when I chanced upon a particularly revelatory document. But there was also a kind of oceanic epistemological malaise, when I went through file after file in larger collections with only a vaguely emerging sense of context— as if the pieces of several jigsaw puzzles were passing in a jumble on a conveyor belt, rather than sorted into boxes, each with a picture on the cover.

In addition to manuscript archives, there were the antiquarian bookstores, which at that time still included relatively inexpensive nineteenth- and early twentieth-century materials relevant to my research. By the time I returned to Chicago I had accumulated a small library of books that I have relied on ever since, including most of the works of James Frazer, William Rivers, and Herbert Spencer. Some of these were real "finds," including the five volumes of James Cowles Prichard's *Researches into the Physical History of Mankind*, which, like the work of Boas, Tylor, and a few other major figures, became for me one of a series of observation towers from which I could roughly map, forward and backward, the intervening historical territory, as well as the immediately surrounding contextual countryside.

In addition to the physical materials, there were also the oral. Although they scarcely qualified as fieldwork, I had many conversations or interviews with important actors in the more recent history of British anthropology, or others close to them—including John Layard, who had accompanied William Rivers to Melanesia in 1914, Alfred Haddon's son, the daughters of Malinowski and Radcliffe-Brown, and a number of the surviving generation of their students. When one of the forty or so places at the Association of Social Anthropologists (ASA) conference in Sussex was opened up by illness, I was driven there by Edmund Leach, with a breakdown on a hedge-lined road and a stop at his daughter's London home for lunch, and he filled the hours of our trip with anecdotes about Malinowski's seminar. At a larger ASA conference in 1973, I recall a garden party at an Oxford college, where Evans-Pritchard, lying on the lawn propped upon his elbow, held forth to a surrounding circle of standing anthropologists. Later, he invited me to lunch in All Souls College, where he confided that Radcliffe-Brown was a lower-middle-class midcountry poseur who could not read Durkheim in the original French, and that Malinowski, by contrast, was "a cad, a shit, and a genius."[19] There were also meals at the London clubs of several anthropologists—most memorably, when

19. My last direct personal contact with Evans-Pritchard occurred after lunch at All Souls College when we walked toward central Oxford with an attractive female student on his left and me on his right. Keeping up as best I could with their conversation, I banged my forehead rather badly on a low street sign at Banbury Cross; after directing me to the nearby Radcliffe Infirmary, where my wound required several stitches, he and his friend proceeded to central Oxford.

Raymond Firth invited me to lunch at the Athenaeum, and we stopped on the stairs while he talked to a retired colonial official (who had been, it suddenly struck me, in a related line of work). Although only a few such incidents made it into my books, they were an essential part of their referential present context—and would have been unavailable to me if I had not come from Chicago, which gave me an outsider's limited entree into the still rather small and close-knit tribe of British social anthropologists.

From Huey Newton's Poster
to the Harvard Twenty-fifth Anniversary Report:
Settling in to a Cautious and Ambivalent Historicism

Nor would these anthropologists have been so readily available had it not been for Bob Young's invitation to come to King's, where for a short time our intellectual trajectories crossed—his to carry him leftward along a path of radical enthusiasms vigorously pursued from institutional margins (http://human-nature.com/rmyoung); mine moving further away from radicalism along a path of cautious and ambivalent liberal historicism, pursued from a major disciplinary center. When I first arrived in Chicago, I had decorated my office in the Social Science Research Building with a poster of Huey Newton as Black Panther chieftain, seated in a raffia throne chair holding a spear. But during the climactic year of 1968, I was very much involved with professional and personal matters and had little time or inclination for political activity. While Carol and I were courting, we did once go down to Grant Park during the Democratic National Convention—withdrawing, however, before any confrontation with club-wielding cops. Mostly, I watched the events of 1968 from a safer distance, including a view, from Ray Fogelson's downtown penthouse apartment, of the west side of Chicago aglow with flames in the aftermath of Martin Luther King's assassination. Over the next several years, I was observer rather than participant in the upsurgent radicalism of the younger anthropologists at the annual AAA conventions, where discussions centering on Vietnam and the responsibilities of anthropologists ran on into the wee hours—in dramatic contrast to the meeting I had attended in San Francisco in 1963, when, as I recall, politics intervened rather as buzzing waves of disbelief and shock at the news of Kennedy's assassination. When I returned from England in 1969, I had only limited sympathy for the campus radicals, and even less when some of them participated in the

Weathermen's "Days of Rage" in downtown Chicago that October. When I returned from my second trip to England in 1973, there was little of the radical spirit left in me[20]—other than ambivalent and apolitical empathy, and the stirrings of a concern that the universalist meritocratic standards of the anthropology department (we hired the "best" in the world, without regard to the specifics of identity) were serving in effect to maintain it as a male preserve.

By 1974, however, the anthropology department had become my permanent academic home. More than once since I became a member my anthropological colleagues had voted to promote me to full professor, only to be blocked by the historians—who may have been put off by my evident identification with a group higher in the pecking order of university and national academic prestige. According to gossip that trickled through the sometimes leaky wall of confidentiality, the historians were primarily concerned that while I had written some excellent "vignettes," I had not shown that I could paint the "big picture"—a charge I could not dismiss out of hand, since at that point my one book (rather than the two then normally required) was, in a formal sense, simply a collection of essays. Taking heart from the rumor that the "good guys" had all been in the minority that voted for me, I proposed to the dean—then a member of the anthropology department—that I might be professor of anthropology and associate professor of history. However, that boundary-transgressive hybrid was not one he felt the university could allow, and instead I resigned from the history department. Thus did I become, after a fashion, an anthropologist—despite a growing sense that my characteristic mode of thought was more historical than anthropological.

Just as I worried in the late 1950s that I had lost the capacity for righteous indignation, I worried in the early 1970s that my world was

20. In 1984, I accompanied Carol on her research study to the Soviet Union. During our first week in Moscow, we stayed in a hotel for visiting scientists that we all assumed was bugged. I had a long interview with the leading Soviet historian of anthropology (through a translator whom he several times corrected) (GS 1984b), and we did a lot of sightseeing, including Red Square and Lenin's tomb. At the end of our stay, we watched the May Day parade before Carol left for her research in the Baltic countries and I flew back to Chicago. Although the Moscow visit only confirmed in many more details than this footnote can include my prior disillusion of 1956, it was in an odd way moving to have visited what had once been for me a sacred site.

egocentrically contracting, with outward extending circles of commitment embracing first Carol and my five children, and then my
students and colleagues, and then the profession and the history of
anthropology—beyond which lay a void of pessimism, into which I
sent, without much hope, occasional conscience-salving donations to
favored liberal causes. As I look back now, I see a certain analogy to my
favored mode of historiography, which extends in concentric circles
outward from individual anthropologists, through their institutional
interactions, into a darkening realm of "context," which I do the best I
can to illuminate. But despite my cosmic pessimism, I was still able to
report, in the Harvard Class of 1949 twenty-fifth anniversary volume,
that I got up every morning "looking for the sunrise," and bicycled
"madly along the lake shore for an hour every day, head down, ass up,
as if I was really going somewhere."

Blocked Projects, False Starts, and Miscast Roles: The Travails of an Interdisciplinary Hybrid

It was close to two decades after my arrival at Chicago, however,
before I published the first volume of my imagined history of British
anthropology, and the better part of another before I felt more or less
comfortable with my hybrid interdisciplinary identity. In addition to
the conference essays on Boas's linguistics and on the Boasian tradition, I managed in the early 1970s to prepare two important edited volumes with substantial introductory material, one on Boas's early work
(1974c) and a second on American anthropology in the interwar period
(1976). Taken together, along with an essay entitled "Anthropology
as Kulturkampf" (1979a), these mark in effect the completion of the
Boasian phase of my work. In the meantime, there were several "occasional" pieces that fed into the British project: a publication, with commentary, of a diary Tylor kept of his experiences among spiritualists in
the 1860s (1971a); an account of the prehistory of the Royal Anthropological Institute published in the centenary of its founding in 1871
(1971b); and a reprinting with extended commentary of the original
one-volume 1813 edition of Prichard's *Researches* (1973)—as well as
an essay on the life and work of the Scottish moral philosopher Lord
Kames, originally intended as introduction to an aborted reprint of
Sketches of the History of Man (1975). I also drafted as course lectures a
half-dozen chapters for what had metastasized into an ambitious
three-volume project then called "Scholars and Savages." But when I

tried to put all this together in book form during my year at the Center for Advanced Study in the Behavior Sciences at Palo Alto (1976–77), I spent a lot of time spinning wheels. By the end of my stay, I still had not finished the last two chapters of what was to have been the first volume—a failure I was then inclined to explain in oedipal terms (one chapter, on sexuality, having to do with my mother; the other, on authority, with my father). Be that as it may have been, it is clear that what started as a writer's block had blossomed into a full-fledged "midlife career crisis."

With the hope that a temporary change of focus would enable me later to resume productive work on British anthropology, I decided to undertake what I mistakenly assumed would be a more manageable project: a history of the Chicago department, for which my prior work on the American and British traditions might be relevant background, given the department's relation to them both—this with the somewhat grandiose hope of establishing by example a new model for the institutional history of anthropology. Rather than treating the department's history as a celebration of its growth or the achievements of its personnel, I would treat it as a mediating contextual site between the thinking and research of a group of individual anthropologists, established and aspiring, and the larger world to which their thinking and research was in part a response.

Even before I had begun serious work, however, the department history project became entangled in planning for the celebration in 1979 of the fiftieth anniversary of the department's existence as a separate Department of Anthropology. Initially, it had seemed logical that as resident historian I should play a leading role in the planning of the celebration, into which my history might somehow be integrated. I did not anticipate, however, how challenging it would be to write the history of a group in which I was an active and dedicated member in a manner that would compromise neither my commitment to an historicist understanding nor my commitment to the present welfare of the group. In the event, it was a challenge I was unable to meet.

While I was still at the Palo Alto Center, I received an invitation to come for a quarter to Harvard as visiting professor. It was an offer that as prodigal alumnus son I could not refuse, although it meant spending most of my time preparing lectures on the history of anthropology in Britain and the United States from the Enlightenment to 1950. Prior to going to Cambridge, however, I did manage to prepare a questionnaire that was sent to all holders of advanced degrees from the Chicago department. After my return from Cambridge in December I resumed intensive work on the departmental history and was able to draft two chapters by the end of February. During the next several months, however, the pace slowed; by the end of that academic year the third chapter was still incomplete, and further progress ground slowly to a halt. By the end of 1979 the materials relating to the department history were confined to a file drawer, where they remained untouched for the next two decades. Since this was not the only unfinished project in my career, one may assume that there were deeply rooted psychological reasons for its abandonment. But the more accessible ones have to do with the technical difficulties of the project as I had conceived it, with the tensions between my roles as departmental historian and as a primary planner of its fiftieth-anniversary celebration, and between my own feelings of disciplinary marginality and my aspirations for disciplinary recognition—as well as my political history as a one-time member of the Communist Party.

The technical problems may be marked by the increasing length of the three chapters: thirty-one, forty-one, and forty-five pages, the last still in an unfinished state. With each, the cast of characters grew larger, along with the bodies of source material and the range of interpretive issues. By the time I abandoned the third chapter, it had become obvious that the three additional chapters I originally projected to carry the history down to the early 1960s would take much more time researching and writing than anticipated. And since the department history had been undertaken as a manageable alternative to my stalled but not yet abandoned history of British anthropology, time spent on the former had eventually to be weighed against the effort to break through the blockage on what was intended to be my magnum opus.

With the department history stalled and the anniversary drawing closer, my historical energies over the academic year 1978–79 were devoted largely to the preparation of the anniversary celebration scheduled for the autumn of 1979, including the selection of speakers in a lecture series and the mounting of an exhibit on the history of the department in the Special Collections Research Center of the Regenstein Library. In order to place that exhibit history within a broader anthropological tradition, we (two research assistants and I) filled each of twenty-two display cases with documentary and other material illustrating a particular phase or topic from the Enlightenment to the

The 1979 University of Chicago Anthropology Department. Front row: (left to right) K. Barnes, R. Tuttle, D. Schneider, S. Tax, M. Sahlins, B. Cohn. Back row: N. McQuown, G. Stocking, P. Friedrich, V. Valeri, T. Turner, R. Klein, R. Smith, R. McCormick Adams, M. Nash, Jean Comaroff, K. Butzer, M. Singer, L. Bisek, R. Braidwood, A. Dahlberg, F. Eggan, R. Nichols, L. Freeman. Absent: John Comaroff, R. Fogelson, M. Marriott, N. Munn, D. Rice, R. Singer, M. Silverstein.

present.[21] Thus the illustrated exhibit catalog, *Anthropology at Chicago: Tradition, Discipline, Department,* began with facing pages describing the first display case ("The Savage and the Civilized"), illustrated with the frontispiece of Rousseau's "Discourse on Human Inequality," and ended with the twenty-second display case ("Toward the 1990s"), illustrated by a group picture of the departmental faculty (GS 1979b).

As the catalog subtitle indicated, the exhibit's purpose was not simply to display documents from the department's past, but to suggest their usefulness as "the stuff" of a departmental history "of a somewhat unusual type, with special historiographical problems," including the "obvious limitation" that relevant source materials were "still lodged in the active files of participants." The introduction went on to suggest

21. One of the perquisites of teaching at the University of Chicago is the generally high quality of graduate students, among whom over the years I have been able to find outstandingly capable, energetic, hard-working research assistants who are able to perform not only the day-to-day functions of the position, but also to participate creatively in the research process itself, even to the extent of entering into extended discussions of specific interpretive problems (cf. pp. 116 and 191).

that the attempt to write recent history "by a member of the community being described" was a "difficult undertaking"—although the handling of "presently problematic" themes had been left "entirely to my discretion." Exercising that discretion, there were some themes in the exhibit materials that I only "touched upon"—leaving it to viewers/readers to make their own interpretations (GS 1979b:3). In general, the result was an historical account that, despite a certain documentary richness, was not only sketchy but also a bit more *gemeinschaftlich* than a more serious historical treatment might suggest. And as the project proceeded, there were several moments at which the "difficulties" of writing such a history about a group of which I was a marginal but dedicated member in the present were brought sharply home to me. In the spring of 1979, when I was called upon to give a presentation on the department's history to a visiting committee of the university's Board of Trustees, I was congratulated by the then department chair for "not having hurt us" by "demystifying" our reputation within the Social Science Division as an internationally esteemed elite department. Six months later, after the talk I gave at a celebratory dinner opening the exhibit, I was privately criticized by the new chair for discussing problems facing the department in the present "in too frank and homiletic a manner." Another colleague expressed similar doubts about the whole department history project on the grounds that the "objectification" of our previously informal history gave to it a "constitutive role," providing to current differences within the department "concrete reference" that they had previously lacked.

Aside from the concerns of the faculty, there were issues with its degree-holding students, whom I had intended to include, not simply as recipients of doctorates who might sustain the department's elite status, but also in terms of their experience in the department as aspiring anthropologists. Among the two hundred or more responses to the questionnaire I had sent out in the fall of 1977 were a small number who had received terminal master's degrees, or left Chicago for other institutions, or could not get jobs in anthropology, or simply had mixed or even bitter memories of their Chicago years—in short, all those whose experience of the department was more Darwinian than *gemeinschaftlich*, but who were also part of the department's history as I conceived it.

The most personally poignant response was that of Robert Gelston Armstrong, who had come to Chicago in the fall of 1939 and at the same time joined the Communist Party. After four years of military service in

World War II, he resumed graduate school in 1946, taught at Atlanta University in 1947–48, and then for a year at the University of Puerto Rico. In the fall of 1949 Armstrong returned to the department to work on his dissertation and drafted more than a hundred pages of an overly ambitious Marxist theoretical "preface." After negative feedback from both faculty members and comrades, he put the preface aside and went on to complete a dissertation on "State Formation in Negro Africa" based on a comparative analysis, still cast in Marxist terms, of recent British social anthropological monographs. For the next two years, he did fieldwork among the Idoma in Nigeria, returning to Chicago in June of 1953 with the hope of finding academic employment. As it happened, his mentor Robert Redfield was going on leave that fall and invited Armstrong to take over his course. This was the very moment that the McCarthyist campaign against "Communists" in the universities was reaching its climax, and before Armstrong could assume his appointment, the FBI informed the dean of the Social Sciences Division that Armstrong had until 1948 been a member of the Communist Party. Although Redfield, Eggan, and Tax continued to support the appointment, it was forestalled by the opposition of the department chair, Sherwood Washburn, whose dissenting voice was effectively a veto, given a university policy that politically problematic hirings required unanimous faculty support within the appointing department. In the event, Armstrong could not find an academic job until the fall of 1956, when he returned to Atlanta University, where he remained until he won a fellowship from the Social Science Research Council for linguistic research in Nigeria in 1959. Save for occasional visits back to the United States, he lived in Nigeria until his death in 1987, serving for a decade as director of the Institute of African Studies at Ibadan and carrying on research among the Idoma, who gave him full chiefly honors at his burial in Otukpu (see GS 2006).

Save for its last decade, Armstrong's saga was recounted to me in his response to my questionnaire, including what he called the "unfinished business" that had destroyed his sense of the Chicago department as an anthropological *gemeinschaft*. Given my broadly contextual approach, which in principle included the experience and subsequent fate of its students, his story should have become a part of the departmental history. But as an historian concerned with the verification of evidence, I felt obligated to pursue the issue with members of the department who had been involved in his exclusion, and the two elders I was then able to contact (Tax and Washburn) both denied memory of the events.

When it came to filling those exhibition cases and writing the text of the catalog, I made no mention of the "the Armstrong case."

In retrospective moments of moral angst, I have been inclined to attribute the abandonment of the departmental history to my inability in the 1970s to come to terms with Armstrong's "unfinished business." However, I have found no evidence in my diaries to indicate its priority. Rather, there is a sense of generalized "intellectual crisis" continuous with that I had felt at the Center for Advanced Study in 1977. If Armstrong's case became its retrospective icon, it was, I suspect, rather as a manifestation of a more general problem of the "anxiety of influence" (see Bloom 1973) that I was not then able to resolve: a reluctance, in the face of real technical difficulties and from a position of disciplinary marginality, to confront the authority of members of a group in which I sought to establish a hybrid disciplinary identity. Be that as it may have been, both memory and surviving evidence suggest that the abandonment of the department history was not a conscious decision, but a gradual letting go.

There was, however, one "revelatory moment" (in the event, a turning point) in which all the undercurrents of my disciplinary marginality bubbled to the surface: the week in July 1982 when I was chosen as chair of the Department of Anthropology. It was a moment when the department faced a number of short- and long-term problems, including adjustment to the anticipated absence of six members during the next year and, more generally, to the more restricted academic economy of the post-expansion period. Two more likely candidates for chair having just undertaken long-term commitments, I was apparently thought of as "available." In considering the possibility, I wrote for myself four single-spaced pages of "reasons for" and "reasons against." The former included, first and "ultimately the strongest," my "ego/ sense of identity": although I remained "really an historian," I was gratified "to have been accepted" as an anthropologist, and "this puts a kind of seal on that." Beyond this there was my "sense of responsibility" as a member of the department, and then, as an afterthought, a desire to experience the "dispersion of power in bureaucracies . . . in the modern world." Not least, there was my feeling that it would provide "an ironclad excuse" for not finishing my history of British social anthropology. Among the fifteen "reasons against," the most prominent were several limitations of my intellect and personality: the fact that I read, thought, and wrote slowly; my "perfectionism" and "inability to compartmentalize"; my tendency on the one hand to "agonize" over decisions and on the other to "react precipitously"—as well as my "mood swings." Still others had to do with the immediate "no win" situation in the department in terms of the impact of faculty absences on graduate and undergraduate teaching—as well as a longer-run concern that it might perhaps be a "sinking battleship." There was also my inability to "represent" the department both in the profession (since I was not really an anthropologist) and to the university administration (since I was neither "old Chicago" nor "effectively pan-professional"). And ultimately, there was the concern that further delay might forestall completely the finishing of the book on which I had been working "for the last ten years" and perhaps mean "the end of my productive scholarly life."

All of these "reasons against," enhanced by others of a more personal nature, should have led me to reject out of hand the offer of becoming chair. But as I noted in my diary, "part of me lusted after it even so"—perhaps for oedipal reasons, my father having been for many years the chair at Vanderbilt. So I wrote a memo to the selection committee specifying a number of "understandings" that would enable me to "preserve the strong positive impulse I now feel in my scholarly work," as well as posing several issues regarding personnel and course staffing—which might have "the beneficial effect of indicating to the department something of how I would approach the chairmanship, and to me perhaps also something of what I might expect in that role."

To make an issue of staffing problems was, in effect, to go against the then prevailing culture of the department, which viewed itself as a collection of individual stars of the first magnitude (in practice, almost exclusively male) who were given great freedom to choose what and when they were going to teach, as well as to take leave whenever they found external support—a freedom I had also enjoyed. But in a memo to the department in December 1980 (entitled "For a Full and Various Fruit Basket in a Time of Famine") I had expressed concern that the "universalistic norm which has ostensibly governed all our appointments in the last twenty years," and had "worked well enough in a period of expansion," might be less appropriate "in a period of declining resources." And in my private ruminations prior to the deciding meeting, I noted a personal bias "in favor of appointing women"—or, posed more generally, "in favor of non-universalistic scholarly criteria," in order to get "someone who will contribute to a range of activities of the department." To pose the staffing matter in such counter-cultural terms was likely to arouse disagreement, and in the ensuing meeting I found myself alone against the department (one of whom at one point said "let's throw him a bone, and invite a visitor"), and at a certain point I retreated to my office to allow my colleagues to consider the whole matter. When, after an hour, a delegation urged me to reconsider my concerns, I persisted in them, even to the point of emphasizing undergraduate education in a department devoted to the production of academic major leaguers. In the end, it was mutually agreed that it would be better for the department, and for me, if they looked for someone else.

At the time, I wondered if I had been "standing up for some (misguided) principle or shooting myself in the foot to avoid the draft." Surprisingly, there were no permanent scars, although for a while there were some joking references to my having been "queen for a day."[22] Whatever the unconscious decision-making processes involved, and however embarrassing the event, it seems in retrospect clear that the outcome was best for all concerned. As chair, I would have been at best ineffective and at worst disastrous for the department, and in the process I might have lost all positive momentum as an historian of anthropology.

Disciplinary Marginality as a Condition of Productive Scholarship

There had already been positive momentum, along somewhat different lines than the failed department history. A year prior to the chairmanship fiasco, I had been invited to give a guest lecture at the annual spring meeting of Cheiron: The International Society for the Behavioral and Social Sciences. Projecting my own writer's block on a larger historical screen, I called it "Books Unfinished, Turning Points Unmarked: Notes toward an Anti-history of Anthropology." On the basis of unpublished manuscripts in various archives, I suggested that a sequence of "paradigm" changes in the history of British anthropology could be traced in the failed attempts of major figures (Tylor, Rivers, Malinowski, and Radcliffe-Brown) to complete large-scale synthesizing projects to which

22. It would not surprise me if colleagues who were "there" had different memories of this "event." Indeed, my own memory of it was more schematic than the reconstruction offered here—which, however, is based on contemporary personal documents, from which quoted passages are taken. *Queen for a Day* was a radio and then television show for twenty years after 1945 in which women told sad stories of their lives, and the one with most applause received a shower of gifts.

their careers seemed to be pointing. Although my attempts to generalize were a bit improvisational, the lecture went well, perhaps because it resonated with the personal experience of many in the audience. As a warm-up for the Cheiron presentation, I had given the lecture locally to the members of the Fishbein Center for the History of Science and Medicine. Both topic and sponsorship were consistent with the redirection of my institutional and research energies away from the department of anthropology and its history, and back toward the history of British anthropology and of anthropology in general as one of the human sciences (GS 2001a:330–51).

In December 1978, I had taken the lead in establishing an interdisciplinary seminar of scholars in the Chicago area who had "serious research interests in the history or sociology of the modern social and behavioral sciences and in the intellectual and institutional context from which they have emerged." Calling ourselves the Chicago Group in the History of the Social Sciences, we met three times a quarter over the next four years to discuss work in progress. Early in January 1980, drawing on several of the papers presented to the Chicago Group, I came up with an idea for a conference on "The Division of Labor in the Human Sciences." Unfortunately, however, an attempt with two colleagues to get Social Science Research Council funding, although greeted favorably, was not in the end successful. Three years later, having in mind a paper that had been presented to the Chicago Group on Freud's use of himself as a paradigm for psychoanalysis, as well as Clifford Geertz's proposal for an "ethnography of disciplines" and my own work on Malinowski, I suggested to a colleague the possibility of a collectively taught course attempting to compare disciplines in terms of their founding myths, their paradigms, their social structure, their mode of initiation, and what I called their implicit "methodological values." Instead of a course, this became in 1984 the topic of the first year of the "Workshop in the History of the Human Sciences" organized as part of a new program implementing the Baker Commission Report on Graduate Education at Chicago. Core members of the Chicago Group became the most active faculty participants in that workshop, and its first year was devoted to the theme "Paradigms, Networks, Myths and Values: Aspects of Discipline Formation in the Human Sciences." And in 1986, I joined with my former student David Leary in organizing a summer institute at the Center for Advanced Study in the Behavioral Sciences on "Disciplinary and Interdisciplinary Perspectives" in the history of social science inquiry.

Despite the fact that the human sciences, and anthropology among them, long had a somewhat marginal relation to the history of the "harder" sciences, there was a rapprochement in the late 1970s. During that period I attended several meetings of the History of Science Society, was for two years nominally on its council, and was for five years on the editorial board of *Isis*. Since then my participation has been as reviewer of books and evaluator of manuscripts, and several times as member of committees advising on the future of the history of science at particular universities. Locally, I was a member of the Morris Fishbein Center for the History of Science and Medicine from the time of its founding in 1970 in the context of contention between historians and philosophers of science. Continuing dissatisfaction with its early leadership led to the appointment of a temporary director in 1976, and after his illness and death, I was selected as his replacement in 1981 and served until my resignation in 1992, since which time I have been only a marginal and occasional participant.

Back in the years around 1980, however, there were a number of symposia and conferences at Chicago in which I played an active role, including "The Hospital in Historical Perspective" (1981), "Persistent Controversies in Evolutionary Theory" (1982), and "The History of Science and the Humanities" (1985). The most dramatic of these, however, was a conference in 1979 on the sociology of science at which a presentation on the "peer review" process seriously disturbed several of the scientists present. One of them suggested in conversation that there were some topics that should not be investigated "because there are big bucks at stake"; another, a member of the National Academy of Scientists, managed to get a rule passed in the Fishbein Center that the topics of symposia had to be approved by vote of the full membership, including scientists who rarely if ever attended meetings.

Many of these activities were already underway at the time of the chairmanship fiasco and figured in my listing of "reasons against." Also noted were institutional and intellectual efforts more closely related to anthropology but cast in a broader framework than the history of the department. In 1973, I had joined with several other scholars in founding a semi-annual *History of Anthropology Newsletter*, which included not only bibliographic sources but also documentary materials illustrating various phases in the history of anthropology from the Enlightenment to the twentieth century. In the fall of 1977, I submitted to the University of Chicago Press a proposal for an annual journal analogous to the recently established *Studies in the History of Biology*. Three years after this proposal failed to be picked up, I sent a revised one to the University of Wisconsin Press, under the title "Anthropology in World History," in terms reflecting my then current involvement in a team-taught course we called "Europeans and Others." Moving beyond the history of modern anthropological ideas in an academic discipline or department, the proposed annual volume would reach "back in time and out in space to encompass a wide range of thinking about human variety in relation to the emergent world historical system of which it is both reflection, and, to some extent, determinant." In addition to the development of the culture concept, or of particular "subdisciplines," or of "museums, government bureaus and universities" as anthropological institutions, the new series would consider missionaries, government anthropologists, and academics as ethnographic reporters, the role of anthropologists in "different colonial situations," the links between anthropology "and the literary and artistic *avant garde*, the contrast between different national anthropological traditions," as well as "anthropology in the third world"—any one of which might provide the focus for a "thematic" volume (as indeed, several of them later did). By the time of the chairmanship fiasco, the first volume of *History of Anthropology* was already in preparation, and the very active editorial role I then and later played was among those "reasons against."

Lurking behind all of them was a "strong positive impulse" in my own research and writing. Absent the threat of the chairmanship, my situation in the anthropology department was close to the best of all possible academic situations, insofar as it allowed me to maintain a limited participant observation in an elite department while also pursuing activities on the other side of my double marginality. I had a light teaching load, with small classes and very good students, including a memorable graduate seminar in 1976 on "Anthropology between the Wars." Graduate students were often interlocutors in my research, and a sequence of them were my research assistants. The few for whom I had primary dissertation responsibility in fact enriched my understanding of the ethnographic process through sometimes extensive correspondence from the field, and I was able to draw on their experiences in a course I gave on "the field experience in anthropology."

That I gave such a course was seen as a bit presumptuous by some of my colleagues. Although several of them had suggested during my early years in the department that I should do some actual fieldwork, I had never done so. Despite those visits with Carol's Serbian and Danish relatives, or tagging along on the trips she took in 1984 to the Soviet

Union and to Japan as part of a comparative sociological study of high school students, I remained in many respects a provincially American monoglot. I was always uncomfortable at international meetings, and when Carol and I traveled in Southeast Asia after I joined her in Japan, it was frankly touristic rather than ethnographic. Even so, my very anxiety and discomfort in such culturally and linguistically contrastive situations, filtered through my strongly self-reflexive tendency and enhanced by vicarious experiences of fieldwork in teaching and research—as well as in thesis proposal hearings, dissertation defenses, and departmental seminars—gave me food for historical thought about the fieldwork process. While the book I once thought of writing on the fieldwork experience never got off the drawing board, by 1982 I had written a long essay entitled "The Ethnographer's Magic: Fieldwork in British Anthropology from Tylor to Malinowski" (1983), which was included in the first volume of the *History of Anthropology* series. That essay was one of several I was able to draft after putting aside the department history, three others of which were featured in the next three volumes of the *History of Anthropology* series (1984a, 1985, 1986).

There were other changes in my life situation that facilitated the breakthrough. In 1979, Carol and I bought a house near the shore of Lake Michigan in Beverly Shores, Indiana, where over the years we hosted many dinners and parties for students and faculty colleagues. Although Carol's job allowed her to enjoy the house only on weekends, it became for a time the primary locus of my writing, on long weekends and for lengthier periods, as academic job flexibility and summer vacations permitted. Free of casual interruption, save by the quirks of my attention, I could seek my own balance of manual and mental activity. I became an avid gardener, an aspiring distance runner, and a designer/stitcher of large needlepoint Christmas stockings—over the years, sixteen of them, one for each of my ten grandchildren, one for each of my children, and one for Carol. I also managed to get quite a bit of scholarly work done, facilitated by a technical innovation: a small-screen Osborne computer, urged upon me as the coming thing by one of my research assistants. Previously, the pencil drafts that were the first stage in my writing process would become so covered with cross-outs, interlineations, and marginal insertions as to be virtually indecipherable for transcription by typewriter. In contrast, a text on computer was easily malleable without becoming illegible and was much more congenial to my characteristic thought and writing process, which tends to be complexly qualified and parenthetic. Although writing continued to be a

Surrounded by ten of the sixteen Christmas stockings I created starting in 1980, several years after I had begun doing needlepoint while watching sports events on TV, in order to justify to my workaholic self that I was not really "wasting time." Although the first of the stockings was made from a needlepoint kit, I soon decided that I could design a better one myself with specific detail about its recipient-to-be. In 1993 I arranged to gather them together for Father's Day at the home of Tomas and Ari in Sausalito, California, from which I was commuting to Berkeley for research in the Bancroft Library. The stockings I later designed for each of my children included one for Tomas as "Commander Casual of the Cool Cat Crusaders" with Santa on percussion, Rudolph playing keyboard, and with tiny reproductions of prior stockings done for Samantha and Dorian on the mantelpiece behind the band. Each of the stockings took over thirty-five thousand stitches, not counting hundreds more removed and replaced because the design or the colors I had planned did not seem quite right, or because I had been distracted by the Bears game on TV. My Christmas stockings are the manifestation of my creativity that I allow myself to be unabashedly proud of (see footnote 5 and page 208). I am a little troubled, however, by the wider implications of praise sometimes received from people close to me: "I can't understand a word of your books, but I love your Christmas stockings." The T-shirt I am wearing in the picture was made for the occasion by my daughter Melissa.

painful, labor-intensive process, it is clear to me in retrospect that the Osborne, first in a series of computers, each with bells and whistles that I cannot play, inaugurated a revolution in my scholarly mode of production.

Finally worth mentioning is a developmental change in mental makeup that I owe largely to the last of six lifetime episodes of various forms of psychotherapy—during my year as Guggenheim fellow (1984–85). There were epiphanal moments, as when my then therapist commented: "You are always talking about your father. Tell me about your mother." But for the most part, he was simply very supportive of what he took to be my better and creative self. As he put it near the termination of therapy: "I chose to work with your good side, rather than digging through the shit." But the change was also due to my own dawning realization that I faced a choice: spend the rest of my life in an impossible search for perfection, or settle for the best that I was able to manage after extended effort and then get on to the next task. The critical moment came in August 1985, when after a session with my therapist the manuscript of my Victorian book rushed to an end. The documentation was still incomplete, and the text might require revision here and there, "but it exists! after fifteen years! . . . I could die tomorrow, and it would be published!" In the event, however, it took another six months of revisions before I was willing to declare it finally finished, and in a moment of expansive optimism I sent it off to the publisher preemptively retitled *Victorian Anthropology* (with no qualifying colon). When it finally appeared in print in December 1986 there were jacket accolades from my friend Dell Hymes and from Claude Lévi-Strauss, whom I had never met, but who apparently knew of my previous work, since he referred to the new book as "another masterpiece."

From Academic Striver to Disciplinary Doyen

That imprimatur, along with very favorable early reviews in publications read beyond the disciplinary boundaries of American anthropology, must surely have had something to do with a letter I received early in February 1988. Coming out of the blue, it was an invitation I could hardly refuse: a full year away from academic responsibilities, all expenses paid, at the Getty Center for the History of Art and the Humanities in Santa Monica. For the next academic year I was to be one of nine "Getty Scholars" (most of them from other disciplines and other countries) "who have investigated the production of culture through its artifacts, ideas and disciplinary practices"—the topic chosen by the Center as its annual "theme." After almost two decades at work on British anthropology, I was already debating whether to continue in that vein into the twentieth century, or instead to tackle a project of even larger scope: "if not a general history of anthropology, then at least a general statement about anthropology as an historical phenomenon"— as I put it in my response to the invitation. For the last few years, I had been devoting my undergraduate teaching to such issues: first, the "Europeans and Others" course, and then a very successful one entitled "The Idea of Culture" (from Herodotus to Sahlins). In what proved yet again a reach beyond my grasp, I suggested to the Getty that I would begin work on a book that would provide a "general presentation of the anthropological viewpoint, as it has evolved in relation to its central concept, over the last several centuries, realized through the lives of its central figures—including their actual ethnographic experience with non-European others."

When it subsequently became evident that the announced "theme" of the Getty year was little more than a hopeful emblem, an informal discussion group of topics "in and around the idea of culture" was organized by George Marcus (one of the three anthropologist "Scholars"), in cooperation with one of the group of younger and less privileged pre- and postdoctoral "Fellows." Meeting fortnightly during the early months of 1989, with the occasional participation of such distinguished outside scholars as Carlo Ginzburg, the group proved particularly stimulating in heightening my awareness of "the nature of disciplinary boundaries" and the "character of disciplinary cultures"—as well as of "postmodern" discourse. For the most part, however, the "Scholars" were left in gilt- (or guilt-) edged isolation to "do their own thing," whatever its relation to the idea and production of "culture." For me, this included the preparation of the sixth volume in the *History of Anthropology* series ("Romantic Motives: Essays on Anthropological Sensibility"), to which I contributed a long essay that did in fact relate to the Getty annual theme: "The Ethnographic Sensibility of the 1920s and the Dualism of the Anthropological Tradition" (1989). I also began work on an essay for the seventh volume (*Colonial Situations: Essays on the Contextualization of Ethnographic Knowledge*), focusing on Malinowski and two of his predecessors in New Guinean ethnography ("Maclay, Kubary, Malinowski: Archetypes from the Dreamtime of Anthropology" [1991]). But by the end of the year, I had abandoned the fantasy of a book on the "idea of culture" and instead noted in my year-end report that a paper comparing Franz Boas and E. B. Tylor ("The Adhesions of Customs and the Alternations of Sounds") had provided the "hook" (or prologue) on which "to hang the chapters of a sequel volume to *Victorian Anthropology*"—four of which I had managed to complete.

Perhaps the most striking manifestation of the "production of culture" during the Getty year was the "culture" of the Getty itself. George Marcus, in fact, published a critical anthropological account, "The Production of European High Culture in Los Angeles" (1990), based on his year as a participant observer—for which he had several times recruited me as ethnographic informant, when I was at some function he was not able to attend. My own much briefer comments were offered in the required year-end evaluation, in which under the heading "Comparison to Other Institutions" I contrasted the cultural atmosphere of the Getty and that of the Center for Advanced Study in the Behavioral Sciences as two styles of "elitism." At the Palo Alto center, there was a more informally egalitarian style that was "the transparent medium in which a school of academic goldfish swam for a year"; in contrast, at the Getty there was a self-consciously European style in which the "Scholars" inhabited a "privileged silken chrysalis within a large, elite, hierarchical and bureaucratic structure, [and] were made conscious of this fact in both large and petty ways." For me the year had been a culturally problematic experience. On the one hand, it had heightened my "self-consciousness" of being in some respects "parochially American" among a group of comfortably polyglot European scholars. On the other, it had given me a glimpse into a world where art and money intermingled—including on one occasion a dinner-table discussion with a member of the Getty family on the problems facing aesthetically gifted women balancing artistic with reproductive creativity—women like my eldest daughter Susan, who hosted a large end-of-year barbecue for Scholars, Fellows, and staff at the homestead she and her husband had created in the Malibu Mountains. In ironic political contrast, there was my interaction (for it was not really a relationship) with the distinguished Russian medievalist Aron Gurevich, whose first exchange with me was to ask where he could buy a good pair of American "blue jinskies"—but whose historical writings included subtle allegorical critiques of the Soviet regime.

Although I had predicted that the sequel to *Victorian Anthropology* would be finished by the fall of 1990, *After Tylor* in fact dragged on until 1995. In the meantime, however, the volume on colonial situations, augmented by the continued availability in paperback editions of all

Seated on the running board of my daughter Susan's trailer workshop at a barbecue she hosted for my colleagues at the Getty Center in the spring of 1988 at the ten-acre mountain homestead on which she and her husband were building (piecemeal, with their own hands) what is now a two-floor, solar-powered house with a wonderful view of the Pacific Ocean. On the days when she is not teaching in the Malibu grade school, a half-hour drive each way on a curving mountain road, or making wine from the vineyards she planted next to their house, Susan works on her multimedia sculptures in a large octagonal workshop they recently built nearby.

the preceding volumes in the *History of Anthropology* series, as well as of my early work on Boas, were enough to sustain my growing reputation as historian of anthropology. Shortly after my year at the Getty, I was invited to a conference on "The Life Sciences, Social Sciences, and Modernity in the Western World" at the Rockefeller Conference Center in the Villa Serbelloni, high on a hill above Bellagio on the shores of Lake Como—another experience that made me feel parochially American, "culturally insecure but with a certain raw intellectual strength." Upon my return to Chicago early in June 1990, I was greeted with the news that I had been elected (as an anthropologist) to the American Academy of Arts and Sciences and at the same time named Distinguished Service Professor at Chicago—which, with a characteristic mixture of pride and self-denigration, I interpreted as not unrelated to the fact that the provost of the university (a neighbor of ours in the Indiana Dunes) had been a member of the AAAS nominating committee and noticed that I was the only one of five Chicago inductees without that local honor.

Self-denigration aside, however, I began to think of my work as an oeuvre, and of scholarly status not as a goal to be achieved, but as an accomplishment to be sustained by continuing productivity during the time left to me. In early March of 1991, I suggested to Betty Steinberg, my editor at the University of Wisconsin Press, the publication of a collection of my "heretofore scattered" essays, under the title *The Ethnographer's Magic and Other Essays in the History of Anthropology* (1992)— this, not only to incorporate them more prominently into the body of my work, but to close the widening gap in publication since *Victorian Anthropology*. Overcoming anxieties that my "auto-deconstructive" introductions to each essay would give ammunition to critical reviewers ("fuck 'em, it's time I stopped worrying about such things"), I managed to send off the manuscript within six months of its conception.

In the meantime, mulling over the problem of what to do once *After Tylor* was finally finished, I still harbored the notion of a history of anthropology through fieldwork. In applying for a fellowship in 1992–93 at the Institute for Advanced Study at Princeton, I entitled my project "On the Ground of Otherness: Toward a History of Anthropology through Ethnographic Fieldwork"—the wording ("toward") carefully chosen to embrace both the "completion of my previous research on the history of British anthropology" and a "move forward toward a more general history of anthropology." Although the proposal was devoted mostly to an explication of the latter, the greater part of my year in Princeton was devoted to the former, as well as several other scholarly projects, including the eighth volume of the *History of Anthropology* series, which endured a long and difficult gestation. Originally conceived as a volume on "national traditions in anthropology," it finally appeared in 1996 as *Volksgeist as Method and Ethic: Essays on Boasian Ethnography and the German Anthropological Tradition.*

Just as at the Getty Center, there was a "theme" for the 1992–93 year in the Institute's School of Social Science: "Science Studies: The Sociology, History, and Philosophy of Science." But this time there was a more systematic attempt to pursue it. The participants were chosen to represent the three disciplines of the theme's subtitle, covering a wide range of epistemological and methodological approaches, and soon after their arrival were encouraged by Clifford Geertz to organize themselves into a fortnightly seminar. It quickly became evident, however, that within the seminar there were two sharply opposing points of view, which may be loosely characterized as "positivist" and "constructivist," and the sessions quickly became "spirited" almost to the point of acrimony. After the second session, at which we discussed an essay of Bruno Latour's, I sent a memo to Geertz suggesting that the opposing viewpoints were "the functional equivalent of lost, drastically attenuated, or sublimated religious belief" and that it was not surprising that the "emotional energy lurking beneath the surface of discourse" should be expressed "in an agonistic way." Despite that tension, the fortnightly seminars continued throughout the year, focusing on the research of individual fellows. But parallel to this a rump group was organized—the membership of which seemed to me "constructed to exclude anyone deemed unable to participate constructively in 'constructivist' discourse." Despite my own professed "epistemological ambivalence," I participated in the rump group's meetings at Geertz's home, profiting especially from sessions at which, prodded by other members of the group, he discussed his own ethnographic orientation, which was in practice more traditional than that of some of the constructivists. As I noted in my diary after one session: "it all has to pass through him, not as 'data' but as experience transmuted by rhetoric—but you have to be there, and there is not here, and it is not navel-gazing, and we (anthropologists) can tell the difference between good and bad ethnography, if not between 'true' and 'false.'"

Lunching with Clifford Geertz and other colleagues at the Institute for Advanced Study in Princeton, New Jersey, in the spring of 1993. (courtesy of Walter Jackson)

If the rump sessions (and the fortnightly seminars) provided food for thought about ethnographic method, the closest thing to a history of fieldwork in anthropology that I wrote during the institute year was a long essay drafted in response to my selection as Huxley Lecturer for the 150th anniversary meeting of the Royal Anthropological Institute. Recalling that 1993 would also be the centenary of Thomas Huxley's Romanes lecture, I began by reading his "Evolution and Ethics," with the thought of writing in general about ethics and anthropology in colonial context. But when I started serious work, that topic seemed more than could be managed in the two months I had allotted for the essay (which, by coincidence, was the period of the rump session meetings). Not for the first time in my career, rather than attempt to paint the "big picture," I chose instead to do a narrowly focused miniature. I would simply read in succession all of the editions of *Notes and Queries in Anthropology*, the field manual of the British Association for the Advancement of Science, from 1841 to 1951 (which was roughly the period of my work on British social anthropology). This, to see what a close reading of a set of related but changing texts might suggest about a range of issues in the history of ethnographic method (some of which did after all relate to problems of "Evolution and Ethics"). The result was a longish essay called "Reading the Palimpsest of Inquiry" (1993a), which had to be cut by more than half for after-dinner oral presentation at Oxford in July 1993 on the occasion of my receiving the Huxley Medal and was not published for another eight years.

As in the case of other scholarly Shangri-las in which I have been fortunate enough to reside, there was a very large gap between the reach of my initial self-presentation to the Institute for Advanced Study and the grasp of the essays I was able to produce. But in many ways the year there was the most productive. Although I did not enjoy the monastic isolation from Carol, with only occasional weekend visits back and forth between Princeton and Chicago, it did make possible very long workdays, beginning often before dawn and broken only by a nap, or a run in the Institute woods, or a Sunday movie, or work on needlepoint Christmas stockings (three of which I created while in Princeton). But despite the generally stimulating intellectual atmosphere, my actually realized scholarship was either in the editorial or vignettish modes; there was still no big-picture history of anthropology, nor was there ever to be one. At the end, I cut short my Princeton stay by several weeks, after a series of severe headaches convinced my doctor in Chicago that I

After I received the Huxley Medal at Oxford in July 1993, Carol and I took a week's vacation in France, where we first visited World War I battlefields (long a special interest of Carol's) and then spent several days in Paris, where our Chicago friend and colleague Bill Sewell took this picture of us in front of a bistro on the Boulevard Saint-Germain. From Paris we traveled west to Brittany, where we stayed at a seaside hotel in Cancale near Chartres, in a room with a spectacular view of the island monastery of Mont Saint-Michel, which Henry Adams might well have appreciated.

should return for diagnostic tests—which revealed nothing more than stress, compounded perhaps by hypochondria.

Conversations across a Widening Generation Gap

A year away from one's normal institutional situation may sharpen one's sense of disciplinary change; at the Getty, it was my awareness of "postmodernism"; at the Institute for Advanced Study, it was my awareness of "generations." At age sixty-five, I was part of a departmental cohort of elite white male anthropologists who had been there twenty years or more, and who were beginning to pass from the scene— preceded by the survivors of their own elder generation, who in 1990 were still a fading departmental presence. While I was in Princeton, the university introduced a scheme of modest retirement incentives with an application deadline of January 1, 1995. Upon my return to Chicago in June 1993, my friend and colleague Raymond Smith, who had already committed himself to retiring, made a point of urging that in the interests of academic renewal I had a responsibility also to do so—an argument seconded by my daughter Rachel, then on the academic job market as a newly minted PhD in history. After vacillating for a year, I chose the half-time option, with reduced benefits and a commitment to full retirement in 2000.

My decision to do so was no doubt affected by a sharpening sense of a "generation gap" as I reengaged in teaching in the months after my return from the Institute. After several decades of worrying experimentation, I had managed to develop a pedagogic style especially suited to the Chicago anthropology department, where small classes focused on one's research interests were the norm, and (if one did not have an appointment in "the College") it was possible to avoid undergraduate teaching entirely. While my own appointment was in fact only in the department, I enjoyed teaching undergraduates, whose minds could be stretched without the responsibility of getting them academic jobs in a contracting market, and I made a point of teaching one upper-division undergraduate course each year. There were no exams or term papers, and the emphasis was on regular attendance and participation. I lectured informally from a detailed outline handed out at the beginning of each class, to which every student was required to bring a report on a previously assigned primary source relating to the day's lecture topic, addressing a standard set of questions designed to force a close textual and comparative engagement: "briefly summarize the argument of the selection"; "why do you think it was assigned?"; "comment on a passage that seemed to you obscure"; "how does this source relate to prior readings in the course?" These reports were graded on a four-point numerical scale (with plusses and minuses), with the total course point accumulation converted into a letter grade, which I guaranteed in advance would be no lower than B for all who attended regularly and took the assignments seriously. The system demanded a great deal of students, but there were few absences, and most of them responded to the challenge. It also demanded a great deal of me, since there was no teaching assistant, and I read and commented on their answers, which among more involved students turned into short essays—and I also very strongly encouraged students to come to my office hours at least once for extended one-on-one conversation. The moments of pedagogical exhilaration substantially outnumbered those of perfectionist depression,

Responding to a student's question in an undergraduate course given in the spring of 1994 on "The Practice of Anthropology: Native American Ethnography since 1850." According to the catalogue of classes, the ethnographies were chosen "with a view to their methodological, theoretical, and contextual resonance so that each episode may stand as a microcosm of an historical phase in the life of its subject people." The photograph was taken by Matthew Gilson for an article in the University of Chicago Chronicle on the winners of the Quantrell Award for Excellence in Undergraduate Teaching.

and there were quite a few unsolicited testimonials then and later from students, reinforced in June 1994 by a Quantrell Award for Undergraduate Teaching—an honor I suspected might have been affected by academic political considerations, since I knew of unrecognized colleagues at least as deserving.

By that time, however, I was becoming more sharply aware of the depth and width of a gap between my own historicist understanding and the taken-for-granted assumptions of many advanced undergraduate students. Although they were anxious to get an overview of the development of fundamental anthropological assumptions about "race" and "culture," they entered the class with a very shallow historical sense and an assortment of postcolonial, anti-canonical, and otherwise "critical" historical assumptions picked up in two years of lower-division courses with instructors more than a generation down from me. The gap was brought sharply home to me by a note appended to one of the class reports: "do ANY of the anthropologists we are reading still have any kind of veracity in modern anthropology? or would ALL of them be considered loonies?" More than a little taken aback, I realized that a similar question might have been asked by others in the class. Whereas in the nineteenth century, it was "savages" who were the "loonies" whose beliefs had to be rationalized, now it was the beliefs of the anthropologists who studied them, and a readily available rationale was that their theories of primitive ir/rationality served ideological and imperial purposes—as no doubt they could, although for me that did not exhaust but only set the problem of historical understanding. Fortunately, there were a number of students whose historical understanding was enriched; but the net effect was nevertheless to make me wonder if I had not better devote myself primarily to graduate teaching during the five remaining half-time years before retirement.

My own role in the actual production of PhD's was limited. I performed a certain service function for a few students, by providing an historical context for their specific anthropological interests, as well as a chance in my fieldwork course for them to pursue the history of ethnographic work in their anticipated fieldwork site. While there were several graduate students who wrote MA theses on historical topics, in general I discouraged doctoral dissertations in the history of anthropology, on the ground that fieldwork was (until the late 1990s) still effectively a prerequisite for employment as an anthropologist. But if my burden of student supervision was light relative to other members of the department, there were a small number of graduate students (and several aspiring undergraduates) with whom I developed the kind of interactive "transference" relations that can make for effective mentorship. And there were a larger number whom we invited to our place in the Dunes for parties, dinners, or barbecues, with croquet on our gopher-burrowed lawn and walks in the woods and along the beach.

More generally, I maintained an interest in graduate education as an issue facing both the department and anthropology as an academic discipline. As chair of the Graduate Affairs Committee during 1991–92, I was involved in reformulating the graduate program and preparing a new brochure on "Graduate Studies in Anthropology." Already then, however, there were signs of a growing "generation gap" at the graduate level. During the winter quarter that year I participated in the "systems" course for the first time in ten years, along with two others of the department's "Boasians." At a class meeting on the second day of "Operation Desert Storm," we were greeted by the question "What is the anthropology department going to do?" and although I had nothing constructive to offer, the reflections of my colleagues on the League of the Iroquois and sanctions as the equivalent of "shunning" among the Amish seemed scarcely to the activist point the students were raising. In addition to the lectures, there were also weekly sessions discussing illustrative ethnographies, and as the term progressed it became clear that the students had serious difficulty engaging such works as Clyde Kluckhohn's *Navaho Witchcraft* (1944). When I suggested that they were "tough minded" when confronted by "scientism" and "tender minded" toward "interpretation," one of them responded that they needed to be both "romantics" and to have "hubris": the former to enter anthropology and the latter to get a job. I found this particularly moving because I had just been doing calculations indicating that historically less than half of our entering cohorts actually achieved the doctorate.

There were further manifestations of discontent as the year progressed, including complaints about the large world map on the second floor of the Haskell Hall stairwell, with markers indicating the locations of student and faculty fieldwork, which some students were inclined to analogize to the maps of agents compiled in the Langley CIA headquarters. There were also complaints about the totem pole recovered from the basement of the Museum of Science and Industry in the late 1980s and erected at the base of the Haskell stairwell. The map is still there today in only slightly modified form, but at the time we did put up an explanatory text near the totem pole indicating that it had been made for commercial purposes after World War II, along with photographs and text from a student-organized dedicatory ceremony/critique at the time of its erection. Even more striking from the point of view of traditional anthropological methodology, however, was the suggestion of one student that he had not entered anthropology to study "strange people in far away places."

During the year after my return from Princeton (when I was a member of the Student-Faculty Liaison Committee), the implications of such issues were brought home to me dramatically at a conference at Stanford and Santa Cruz in February 1994 on "Anthropology and 'The Field': Boundaries, Areas, and Grounds in the Constitution of a Discipline" (Gupta and Ferguson 1997). Rather than going "there" to study "others," a number of the graduate students present were working in American urban situations, often exploring topics related to their own issues of personal identity. They complained at some length and with more than a touch of bitterness that they were effectively excluded from research support within the then still dominant "area-studies" framework of granting agencies (although since then the granting agencies have become much more inclusive). At the time, such incidents (and others like them) seemed to me to call into question the subject matter, the methodology, the politics, and the ethics of traditional anthropology.

With these experiences of the "generation gap" in mind (and with a gnawing sense of the "contradictions" within the academic system in which I was embedded), during the academic year 1994–95 I played a role in organizing a symposium series for the following year entitled "Anthropology Postwar/Premillennial: Intergenerational Conversations." There were ten major papers by elder anthropologists, reflecting on careers begun in the years after World War II. Each of these was preceded by a "contextualizing introduction" offered by a middle-generation member of our faculty, and followed with a commentary by a current graduate student. The individual sessions were very lively, but when it came to publishing the proceedings (which it had been assumed I would edit), I begged off, in part because I had "heard privately from students" that the student reaction had not been "so uniformly favorable" as that of "the sponsoring generation," and in part because it would have required a major effort in the pre-retirement half-time period I had just entered.

By this time generation change had also become an issue within the faculty, as the need for departmental renewal in the context of retirements and of changes in anthropology began to be more sharply felt. Although there had been significant hirings in the 1970s and 1980s, the male appointments were of or near the postwar generation, and of the seven women who during those years entered a traditionally male preserve, only two became permanent members. In the winter and spring of 1992, I had played a minor contributory role in the initial stages of renewal, on one occasion speaking strongly in support of a candidate whose generally "postmodern" interests were somewhat discomfiting to the more traditionally minded; on another occasion volunteering a report documenting the sorry history of women in the department. Over the next few years, the pace of change gradually accelerated, and the newer tendencies within anthropology (globalization, gender, science studies, etc.) began cautiously to be incorporated, and the gender distribution shifted, until by 2004 five of the six most recent appointments were women (and five years later they constitute half the voting members of the department).

It was a process in which I was less a participant than a witness. I had long been oriented more toward the past of anthropology than toward its present problems or its future prospects. When I felt called upon seriously to contemplate its future, as I had in the last essay in *The Ethnographer's Magic*, it was with a cautious restatement of past paradigmatic traditions and of enduring tensions. As the 1990s progressed, however, I came more and more to feel that the anthropology of the 1950s, which I was calling "Anthropology Yesterday," was actually that of the day before, and that in the half century since there had been not one but two major episodes of change in anthropology. The first, a response to the passing of its traditional "colonial situation," was manifest in the "crisis" of the 1960s and in a call for "reinvention," which by the 1990s had in many respects been realized. The second was a response to a global revolution in information and communication. The former phase I had experienced as the passing of a world into which I had been born. The sense of disjunction was much sharper in the later phase, which I experienced as the opening of a new world on whose threshold I might stand, but never actually enter. Unlike a couple of my age mates, who lamented the intellectual enthusiasms of the younger generation as passing theoretical "fashions" and looked forward to the reassertion of an evolving tradition, I began to feel that the "generation gaps" of which I had become acutely aware reflected fundamental changes in the world situation of anthropology. While "paradigmatic traditions" might linger and "eternal tensions" endure in some form, anthropology was changing in irreversible ways (see GS 1992:342–72). And if I could still empathize with the younger generations, as with the Berkeley student radicals in the 1960s, my engrained cosmic pessimism, intensified by intimations of mortality, made me feel ever more marginal (and even irrelevant) to the discipline whose history I had made my life's work.

Biography in an Autobiographical Context

In December 1995 I sent off an application to the Wenner-Gren Foundation requesting support for a study of what I was still calling "Anthropology Yesterday"—a play on the title of the landmark evaluative symposium ("Anthropology Today") sponsored by the Foundation in 1952. Having just seen *After Tylor* through publication and finally sending off the manuscript for the eighth volume of the *History of Anthropology* series, I had decided, in the context of the series of "intergenerational conversations," to turn to the anthropology of the post–World War II period in the United States. The "underlying assumption" was that this was a critical moment in the formation of the anthropology of the later twentieth century, which "to a considerable extent may be seen as a re-action against the anthropology of the 1950s"—and that its "historical significance has been somewhat obscured by this reaction, which has contributed to an historically unnuanced and stereotypic view, mani-fest among my students as amazement that Clyde Kluckhohn could be at one and the same time quantitative and reflexive in ethnographic outlook"–not to mention a "willing servant of the national security state." My goal, described as "refamiliarization" (in contrast to the re-cently fashionable notion of "defamiliarization"), was to "re-present," insofar as possible, "the way things were"—neither to "recuperate" nor "vindicate," but to re-appreciate the "contextual complexity of the pe-riod, in a manner that I hope may be seen as valuable by both defenders (a dying breed) and critics alike." Lying "at the ever-advancing bound-ary of memory and history," the period was of particular methodologi-cal interest in providing a "challenging richness" of source materials, written and oral, for a study to which I was especially suited by virtue of my prior research and my marginal situation in the discipline. And inasmuch as it was the period of "my own intellectual formation as an historian of anthropology," it was also of considerable personal auto-biographical interest. Conceiving the project "with mortality in mind," I imagined it as a series of perhaps a dozen biographically focused essays, each treating one or more "particular topics of both historical and present resonance—e.g., universalism/relativism, in the case of Kluckhohn." If all went well, the essays would articulate in a single volume, as a series of "transparent overlays" (on later thought, a some-what mushy metaphor); if not, they might be "separately published as I went along." To augment this proposal, I applied to the Dibner Institute for the History of Science and Technology in Cambridge (where many relevant research materials were located) for a three-month fellowship starting January 1, 1997.

Once again the "Anthropology Yesterday" project proved to be another in which the reach of my historical imagination exceeded my historiographical grasp—frustrated this time by the threat of mortality, when after years of wolf cries, my hypochondria was rewarded by a diagnosis of colon cancer. Two weeks later (during which I took what I imagined might be a last trip to California to visit children and grandchildren), I was hospitalized for ten days in late June 1996 for a

Christmas Day 1996, at the home of Myron and Ingrid Stocking in Minneapolis, as Carol tried on the nurse's cap with gold halo that I created in appreciation of the 24/7 care she gave during the months after my cancer surgery in July 1996.

hemicolectomy, and a month later for another week due to post-operative infection. For the next year I was on chemotherapy, during which there were two scares of possible lymph node or liver involvement. Throughout, Carol was my personal Florence Nightingale (literally waking up at night every time I did, which was frequently).

It was a year of psychological ups and downs, with periods of depression when I felt "pregnant with death" and could hope at best for "serene resignation." But the depressions were usually short, and by December 1996 I had managed to reengage research—which Carol encouraged me to think of not as "terminal project" or "end game," but rather as "the late show." Because I could not comfortably travel, I chose Sol Tax as the subject of the first biographical essay, and beginning with an hour a day, I started serious research in the large body of his manuscripts nearby in the Regenstein Library. By early January 1997, I had also begun to run again (having abandoned it three years previously due to a foot injury), and by that September I was able to run in a five-kilometer race, without breaking along the way for walks or rest stops. My spirits were further lifted two months later by an all-day

Waving to Carol on the sidelines as I passed by in a rainy day 5K race shortly after I resumed running once my year of chemotherapy was over. Neither one of us can now remember the sponsorship of the race.

symposium at the American Anthropological Association, organized by my students Ira Bashkow and Matti Bunzl, devoted to papers honoring my work. And in the last days of 1997, I traveled to Cambridge to take up the Dibner Fellowship, which I had previously arranged to postpone. Over the next three months, my scholarly routine was broken only by brief visits to my daughter Becky and her family in Westboro, and by several weekend visits by Carol or to her in Chicago. By the end of my Dibner stay, I had managed to write a draft of a Tax essay (and a much shorter draft of the present essay), in addition to many hours of research at Harvard in the papers of Clyde Kluckhohn.

Although I still then had in mind a volume of a dozen essays, over the months after my return to Chicago I was forced to revise this plan. In revisiting the Tax papers, I discovered a file in which near the end of his life Tax reflected on his Jewish identity. Along with other files not previously consulted, this led me to reengage what I had thought was an almost finished essay, but which ended up taking another year—and close to a hundred pages in its later published form (GS 2000). At such a length of words and time, the rest of the twelve essays would have taken at least a decade to complete and a very fat volume to publish, and by the end of July 1998, I decided to "scale back."

Twenty years previously, while working on a short biographical essay on Robert Redfield, I had discovered in his papers copies of materials collected by Anne Roe in 1950 for a study of the psychological characteristics of elite scientists. Eight of her subjects were leading figures in post–World War II anthropology, with each of whom she conducted an extended life history interview and a series of psychological tests (Roe 1953). In addition to Redfield, the eight included several others I had in mind as subjects of biographical essays, and in 1999 the original materials for all save one were to be open for research at the American Philosophical Society. Given five more years, I thought I could write a series of shorter case studies than the Tax essay, which, failing the completion of "Anthropology Yesterday," would still make a book, to be entitled "Anne Roe's Anthropologists." The logical case to begin with was Kluckhohn, in whose papers I had previously done extensive research, and who as a participant in government science illustrated a major theme of the Cold War period. However, my own septuagenarian autobiographical interest won out over that of cultural and political context. I chose instead another of Roe's cases: A. I. Hallowell, without whose guidance and help I might not have become an historian of anthropology.

After drafting a short introductory essay on Roe and her study, I began work on Hallowell. This essay was not published until five years later, in the tenth volume of the *History of Anthropology* series, which was revived by Richard Handler after my hemicolectomy. In the interim I had been distracted by yet another project. Worrying about mortality or superannuation during another decade-long interval between authored (as opposed to edited) books, early in 1999 I proposed to Betty Steinberg that the University of Wisconsin Press publish another volume of my essays. In addition to the still unpublished Huxley lecture, it would include a number of other "occasional" pieces, each with new introductory material to mark both its occasion and its place in the evolution of my work. It took some effort to realize the four-part structure I envisioned (Boasian Culturalism, British Evolutionaries, Institutions in National Traditions, and what I called "Mesocosmic Reflections"), and there was a last-minute title change to highlight the underlying theme of anthropology itself as a discipline "delimited" by the gap between the reach of its inspiration and the grasp of its realization. Even so, the

Members of "My Last Class" who participated in the Alivio y Salud Run for Health on May 21, 2000: (left to right) Mayanthi Fernando, Byron Hamann, Thomas Guthrie, Andrew Graan, Rafael Boglio, and Yarimar Bonilla. I later received a medal in the mail for finishing third in the senior division, which must have been because there were only three over-seventy runners in the race. In the end, it proved not to be my last class, for I taught several more times in the immediately subsequent years. But with increasing leg pains and the aggravation of an episodically painful arthritis of my neck, it was my last race.

time between conception and publication was the shortest of any of my books (GS 2001a).

Delimiting Anthropology was dedicated to "the members of my seminar 'Anthropology Yesterday', Spring 2000, and all the other students, since 1960, who have made a difference." That seminar was my very last class before full retirement and was more multicultural in personnel and more computer-networked than any I had previously given. But the spirit was very high, and on the last Saturday a group of us went to the Pilsen community for a five-kilometer race, in which five of us ran, and all of the class came to our apartment afterward for brunch.

In the course catalogue, the class was described as "The Contextual-ization of Anthropological Knowledge: Anthropology Yesterday," fo-cusing on American anthropology in the early Cold War period. The underlying assumption was that "later anthropology had developed . . . in reaction to that of the 1950s and 1960s"—a decade of crisis both in anthropology and in my own intellectual formation. In the introductory lecture, which I called "Glimpses into My Own Black Box," I introduced the theme of "contextualization as a genre" and indicated that the lec-tures would be informal and interruptions encouraged. The final class was an open discussion of the course, during which it was suggested that the issue of contextualization was relevant not only to the anthro-pology of the past, but also to an anthropological understanding of the present as well as to action in the future. I agreed that these were legiti-mate and important anthropological issues, but expressed some con-cern about the danger of "lecturing the past." At the end of the meeting, the class presented me with a trophy engraved "Anthropology Yester-day, Anthropology Tomorrow: With Gratitude, Class of 2000," a text proposed by Yarimar Bonilla and Andrew Graan, both of whom were at the race.

Some months after the class, Carol was asked by a friend, "What does George do, now that he's retired?" To which she quipped, "Well, it gives him a lot more time for his work." The dynamic of that work was revealed by an anecdote she had previously recalled about the husband of a friend, who had done research in a postcolonial "new nation." Out walking one Sunday morning, he encountered an old African man sweeping the steps of the now deserted British administrative building where he had once been janitor. Asked why, although no longer paid, he still swept, the old man answered, "It's what I do." Writing (includ-ing the prior research and the subsequent shepherding of written words through publication) is what I do to maintain my intellectual being, and if it was no longer a careerist obsession, it was still my de-fault occupation, kept up to keep my "self" alive. So after proofing and indexing the Tax essay and finishing the selection introductions for *Delimiting Anthropology*, in the fall of 2000 I reengaged "Anne Roe's Anthropologists."

Although I no longer had much hope that it would actually be a step toward "Anthropology Yesterday," I kept working away on the Hal-lowell essay, sometimes spending an hour searching my aging mind, my disorganized notes, my crowded bookshelves, and my thesaurus for a few right words—feeling very lucky to manage two hundred of them in the intermittent efforts of a single day. There were minor distractions—including the weekly meetings of a drinking group I thought of as "the four old farts"—as well as major ones, including the prolonged and closely witnessed dying of one of the drinking quartet.

In the interim a serious interpretive problem had arisen: the discovery of Hallowell's homicidal adopted son, who as a teenager in the late 1930s had got into serious trouble, climaxing in a running gun battle with the police. Upon his release from prison in 1947 there was a similar chase, in which young Hallowell actually killed two policemen. Fifteen years later, after his sentence was commuted, he killed his adoptive mother with five blows from a claw hammer and subsequently spent the rest of his life in prison. When I sent a draft of the essay to Murray Murphey, he was sharply critical of the suggestion that the son's tragic history was important for a fully contextualized interpretation of Hallowell's evolutionary thought. Against this, Murray insisted that it was irrelevant to the scientific content of his anthropology and would be taken by my readers as mono-causal rather than multicontextual. The debate between us continued until March 2001, by which time I had inserted into the manuscript, with Murray's approval, a section summarizing our discussion, in which I quoted him extensively—but gave myself the last word (GS 2004:232–36). Even then, that ancient logician Zeno, in his whimsical paradoxical fashion, kept lengthening the race to a conclusion, and kept on doing so for several months, until I finally fooled him by leaping across yet one more half-way gap and declaring the essay done.

By that time, however, I had abandoned "Anne Roe's Anthropologists" as such and thought of a new way of framing a reduced set of five biographical essays: Hallowell as a disengaged "anthropologists' anthropologist"; Kluckhohn as an engaged government anthropologist; Tax as an engaged liberal anthropologist; Dell Hymes's *Reinventing Anthropology* as part of an emerging radical critique of traditional anthropology; and my "Black Box" essay as reflexive autobiographical contextualization. With two of these published and one drafted, another two essays would fill a book that might be a respectable stand-in for the ill-fated "Anthropology Yesterday." To this end, I began serious work on a Kluckhohn essay, portions of which I presented to a small post-retirement seminar in the spring quarter of 2001.

Once again, however, the biographical project underwent transformation the following summer. Going through some old student files for an essay idea I had about "exclusionary processes" in 1950s anthropology that marginalized women, African and Native Americans, gays and radicals, I rediscovered the long neglected file of Robert Gelston Armstrong. Suddenly, it occurred to me that he made a natural pairing with Kluckhohn: the one "a servant of the national security state," the other a victim of McCarthyism—both of them, as it happened, gay men. And in addressing Armstrong's "unfinished business" I might also be readdressing some of my own. So I enlarged by one my reduced cast of 1950s anthropologists and decided to work on two of them at once: Kluckhohn in the mornings, Armstrong in the afternoons. By September 9, however, it was Armstrong who preoccupied me: "there is a sense in which I really live in his life, and find myself thinking about the events in his life more than the events in my own—or in another sense, that the two have merged." Two days later came the horror of September 11, which side-tracked me for several weeks. During that time I thought a lot about the limits of empathic understanding, and about the personal and group identities involved and their embodying pronouns—"the 'We,' the 'I,' and the 'They'"—which, one morning in the shower, I imagined might be the title of yet another unwritten book. But after a few further days of watching CNN, I returned to work on Kluckhohn and Armstrong, who had been lurking in the background of my thinking all the time.

At first the emphasis was on Kluckhohn, until I hit a writer's block in February 2002, after seventy pages that got him only through his collegiate years. So then I turned back full-time to Armstrong, on whom I continued to work intermittently through a year of health problems as severe as those of 1996, including prostate cancer and an abdominal aneurism. But despite worries that my scholarly career might end with yet another unfinished manuscript, I was finally able to reengage the Armstrong essay in mid-July 2003 and by August 20 to declare it finished. Once again, however, Zeno continued to demand revisions, and it was not until February 2004 that I printed out the full 220 pages and shipped them off to Richard Handler, who assured me that there would be room enough for such a king-sized "essay" in the eleventh volume of the *History of Anthropology* series (2006).

With the Armstrong essay off my desk, I resumed work on Kluckhohn, and at the urging of colleagues in the history of science, seconded by the chair in anthropology, put my name in the hopper for selection as one of the university's candidates for a fellowship under a recently established Mellon Foundation program for emeritus scholars. To this end I offered a frank review of the devolution of my "Anthropology

Yesterday" project, in the context of its relation to all my prior work, with a best-case scenario for its completion as a series of essays, in the hope that they might have "a certain coherence in terms of the later development of the Boasian tradition in American anthropology—as well as significant relations to the themes of the early Cold War."

By the end of 2005, the first year of my Mellon Fellowship, it had, however, become painfully evident that there was no way I could realize the "best-case scenario" of the original application, and in writing the required midterm progress evaluation, I offered an overly frank detailing of reasons for this failure. While there had been no further life-threatening health problems, there had been various distracting minor ones, as well as a noticeable acceleration of physical and mental deterioration—including kinesic incompetence and forgetfulness of computer commands, further complicated by two extended episodes of computer failure. Even more to the point, perhaps, was the tendency for "individual components of the project to grow out of hand" as the result of a "late life self-indulgence of an interest in individual human biography"—initially, in the case of Robert Armstrong, but even more so in the case of Clyde Kluckhohn. Working in a "painfully slow" fashion, I had produced over two hundred pages of what I still refused to call a "biography in the full sense," but was clearly well beyond the limits of an essay, and must at least be called "a biographical monograph."

As then reconceptualized, "Reflections in the Mirror of a Man: Clyde Kluckhohn and Mid-Twentieth Century American Anthropology" was to consist of four parts, each composed of several chapters. Of these, two now exist in draft: "Searching for a Shining Something: The Road to Anthropology, 1905-36" and "From Marginality to Centrality in Later Boasian Anthropology, 1936-47." The other two ("Cultural Relativism and Universal Values in the Cold War Period, 1947-55" and "The Darkening Years, 1956-60") will require more research and may themselves yet subdivide. The pessimist in me fears that this is likely to end up as the last of my "unfinished books"; the optimist has not yet abandoned hope that I may be around to see it published. For the present, it continues to sustain my intellect, whether as "end game," "late show," or simply as a folly of my old age.

TWO

Historiographical Reflections

Inside an Historian's Study:
The "Micro-technology" of a "Bottom-up" Historicism

Early in my career, while teaching History 101 at Berkeley, I was much affected by Marc Bloch's comment, in *The Historian's Craft*, about "the curious modesty which, as soon as we are outside the study, seems to forbid us to expose the honest groping of our methods before a profane public" (1953:87). In that spirit, I once imagined a case study in which, from the moment of conception of a project until the day of its realization in print, an historian might keep a systematic diary of its "honest groping"—a daily record of every new idea, every problem of method, every interpretive insight, every painful revision, as they occurred. I quickly realized, however, that such a methodological diary, even if correlated temporally with the more conventional components of the particular research project (the primary and secondary sources consulted, both published and archival), would be unlikely to illuminate all its generative or constraining influences—unless it were somehow also combined with a diary of other aspects of my life, thought, and emotions. And whatever the general historiographical utility such a unique and unlikely record might have, it would have been virtually impossible for me to create, given the sometimes unsystematic way I take my notes and my failure to date them.

Even so, there is perhaps something to be gained, in understanding my output as an historian, from an attempt to "expose the honest groping" of the methods that produced it. Written years later, rather than as a case study of the groping in process, this account will necessarily have a certain "presentist" aspect. Whereas in the preceding "Autobiographical Recollections" I tried to re-present my life in the way I experienced it at the time, these "Historiographical Reflections" may draw out certain implications of which I may not have been consciously aware and retrospectively formulate idealized principles that I did not in fact systematically practice.

To begin with, it should be reemphasized that what happens in the "historian's study" cannot be understood in isolation from an historian's relation to the world outside, or from the inner tendencies of his or her personality or character, inasmuch as it is those prior life experiences and psychological predispositions that may lead an historian to pursue one project rather than another, and to pursue it in a particular way. In my own case, it may be helpful to readers to review briefly some of the major themes of Part 1. These include a perfectionist achievement motivation ingrained by my parents; the inherited and renewable privileges of a middle-class academic liberal upbringing; the rejection of religious belief and subsequent embrace of a dogmatic political faith; seven years in the working class in Massachusetts (and other briefer episodes of cultural alterity); the painful experience of "self-criticism" in the Communist Party's struggle against white chauvinism (an archetype, perhaps, of the present essay); the relativizing disillusion with Communism in the aftermath of the Kruschchev revelations; the attempt in a positivistic program in American Civilization to understand racial thought historically; the mixed success of my quasi-quantitative doctoral dissertation (as a methodological experiment and in effect an anti-paradigm for my later history of anthropology); the experience of a more conventional intellectual history and the development of an historicist scholarly persona at Berkeley, even as my personal marital life was falling apart in a context of political conflict and cultural turmoil; the establishment of a marginal academic identity as historian of anthropology in one of the country's leading departments; the achievement of the status of disciplinary doyen across a widening generation gap in anthropology; and the turn to biography (and autobiography) in the face of impending mortality. It is against the background of these experiences that the generative and constraining contexts of my major projects, both published and abandoned, should be viewed.

Grounded in these relativizing experiences there has also been a commitment to historicism as the governing principle of historical study (see above, footnote 16). First articulated in programmatic terms in 1965 in the editorial essay "On the Limits of 'Presentism' and 'Historicism' in the Historiography of the Behavioral Sciences" (1965c), it has been qualified in various ways over the years, so that what was once a program is now perhaps better characterized as personal credo (1999). I still regard myself as an historicist insofar as I privilege the perspectives of my past subjects, the problems they addressed, and the texts and contexts in which they addressed them, rather than those of the present. Ever since I left the Communist Party, I have been suspicious of a priori theoretical orientations or master narratives. Although I may make use of one meta-theory or another in a pragmatic interpretive way, as a general historiographical principle I try to construct my interpretations inductively from the "bottom up"—from the thinking and behavior of the past historical actors who are my primary subjects, insofar as these are evidentially accessible.

In the discussion that follows I occasionally have something to say about the processes (e.g., personal experience, archival researches, ethnographic fieldwork) by which that evidence is collected. The latter especially is by now the subject of a considerable literature, to which I have contributed on several occasions (1992, 2001a:164). But in what follows, I treat my own "honest groping" as something that takes place within a particular physical site ("the historian's study") and stress that it is essentially a process of writing, based on the analysis and interpretation of texts available to the historian in his or her study. When this essay was first drafted, I thought of the process as "micro-technology." More recently, however, it has seemed more accurate to think of it as "information management"—for two reasons, one of them historical, the other autobiographical. On the one hand, despite the loss or destruction of particular information sources by natural or human disasters (e.g., floods or warfare), the total amount of information available for historical analysis and interpretation has been vastly enlarged in the cultural new age of global computerization and "googlization." On the other, there is my personal experience in the years since my retirement overseeing the disposition of a half-century accumulation of books, photocopies, diaries, notes, and drafts. In recent proto-theoretical musings about "information management," I have imagined it as having four components: the material (the physical or "virtual" embodiment of information); the conceptual (the system of categories in terms of which it is organized or manipulated); the technical (the equipment or processes of that manipulation); and the psychophysical (the physical and mental capacities of the human manipulator)—all four of which change over time.

With these assumptions in mind, I think of my "honest groping" as a decades-long struggle between yearnings for a platonic ideal of categorical ordering and the deeply rooted countervailing forces (inborn, habitual, degenerative) of its disarray—a struggle mediated by an acute and unrelenting self-critical bent. The ordering ideal was archetypically manifest in my doctoral dissertation and is still evident today in citation counts of "influence"—as well as in other categorizations and countings not directly reflected in finished texts. The forces of disarray are manifest in certain deeply rooted mental and motor characteristics (those of a slow reader with a wandering mind, pedestrian imagination, modest analytic ability, unreliable memory, hurried handwriting, and a tendency to untidiness) and in the various note-taking methods that I have used to compensate for them. At one end of my career I recall a "universal" note-taking system that I came across as a graduate student but never actually used (Dow 1924). At the other end there are fantasized but for me mostly unrealized systematic possibilities of computerization and the Internet. In between, in the real world of my scholarship, there are archeological middens and strata of McBee cards, IBM cards, 3 by 5's, 5 by 8's, 8½ by 11's, gathered in boxes or file folders, or dispersed here and there until they find a filing place—not to mention all the underlinings and marginal notations in a rather large professional library, both of books and photocopies. The raw material of my historiography, these notes are rarely typed or systematically entered into a computer, but are initially handwritten in varying degrees of legibility. They may record "facts," or references (often cryptic) to where these raw or secondary materials can be found; or they may be "idea notes" that will impel the actual composition of a narrative or interpretation. Taken together, they form an historically constituted nonsystem of information management that in a project lasting twenty years can cause frustrating and time-consuming problems of composition and documentation.[23]

Within the broad and tentative framework of larger-scale projects (which may be sketchily articulated in grant proposals or in very rough

---

23. Although in the above passage I have put the word "facts" in quotation marks, to acknowledge its epistemologically problematic character, I nevertheless believe that some facts, while in a sense "constructed," are more reliably or compellingly veridical than others—and that on this basis one can make meaningful distinctions between histories and between different historiographical approaches.

outlines of possible chapter topics), these notes record the ideas that carry along (and sometimes detour) a project already in process. While they may occur as I rifle through previously collected materials, they seem often literally to "pop into my brain" at times when it is not straining: rarely in dreams, sometimes in hypnogogic moments between sleep and wakening; more often, in the "brain race" that follows a predawn cup of coffee; or as the free-floating thoughts of an early morning run and in a shower afterward; or during a walk taken later in the day after staring wordlessly at a computer screen for half an hour. For the most part, these ideas manifest themselves initially as fuzzy notions and only become coherent words and sentences after much further mental work. This, in contrast to a recollection of my late colleague Milton Singer, who as a young instructor in the 1930s stuck his head into the open office door of Bertrand Russell, then visiting at the University of Chicago, only to discover the distinguished British philosopher at his desk with pen in hand. When Singer apologized for interrupting his writing, Russell responded: "Oh, I wasn't writing, but simply transcribing material I had composed in my head while walking on the Midway just now." By contrast, the words in which my ideas are eventually articulated are slowly worked and reworked into meaningful sentences, often with the aid of a dictionary or thesaurus (and increasingly, as my mind ages, by associations of alliteration and assonance—not to mention Google or Wikipedia, which I have found helpful [if used *cum granis salis*] in my day-to-day work to clarify or augment notes, check biographical details, locate quotations, etc.).

There are some processes of idea formation to which I have given (or adopted) names. These include the immediately striking items of information ("juicy bits") that I almost instinctively feel must somehow be worked into a coherent narrative argument, or the "revelatory moments" that seem likely to be the basis for a framing structure.[24] Other processes reflect the standards of traditional historiography: the preference for textual as opposed to oral evidence, or the commitment to

---

24. There are some "juicy bits" that fail to fit in. I have a distinct memory that Boas once described himself as "a Jewish German, but not a German Jew." While there is other biographical evidence to sustain this self-identification, I cannot find a source note and am therefore reluctant to use the quote as the basis of an argument. As for "revelatory moments": although a quick Internet search suggests I might have gotten this from my colleague Jim Fernandez, I tend to think of it as my own "independent invention."

chronology as a basic ordering principle, to be overridden only when there are compelling interpretive reasons.

In conjunction with my tendency to think in terms of alternative motives, multiple factors, and ambiguous consequences—all of these grounded in an underlying relativist ambivalence—this anxiously "bottom-up" approach to the construction of interpretation has rhetorical consequences. Sentences thus produced are often long and variously qualified, with polysyllabic adjectives piled up in phrases; clauses joined together by commas, semicolons, dashes, and parentheses; and so many "althoughs" and "howevers" that I once thought of adopting the pen name "Altho Howver." There is no doubt that such a style demands a great deal from the reader, not only by its rhetorical density but also because it is in general fact-heavy and interpretation-light. And there are sometimes topics or themes that seem to me relevant and illuminating, but that are merely hinted at or touched upon so indirectly as to be in effect written "between the lines" for perceptive readers to draw out themselves—in some cases because I am unsure how to knit them seamlessly into the argument in the space available; in others because they seem ethically or evidentially problematic or otherwise arouse anxieties about marginality or authority (cf. Bashkow 1997).

Far from being "reader friendly," my prose may seem to many as rather more labored than crafted. But there is a great deal of laborious craft involved in its construction. There are no "rough drafts" in the customary sense. I try to get every component—whether word, sentence, passage, section, or chapter—"right" before going on to the next in sequence. I am reluctant to accept a formulation that I suspect may be unsatisfactory on the assumption that I can come back to it later—this, although experience has taught me that tentative "rightness" may prove illusory and will later require reworking. But the goal of all this reworking and reworrying is finally to order all the components in such a way that transitions do not seem arbitrary, but have an uncertain a posteriori ineluctability.

Lest that phrase seem oxymoronic, I hasten to explicate its three terms. For me, a narrative interpretation (or argument) may be said to be *a posteriori* insofar as it is not assumed in advance but takes coherent form only in the process of composition. It is *uncertain* insofar as it is offered as suggestively contextual rather than authoritatively causal. (I have upon occasion thought of programming my computer to find and replace all instances of the word or syllable "cause.") But it nevertheless aspires to be *ineluctable*—insofar as after much struggle, I cannot think of a better way of saying it, and a careful reader cannot casually dismiss it.

Writing history in this way is a slow and labor-intensive tinkering, often blocked, and in general is experienced in process as painful or even depressing (especially when I realize that some "juicy bit" or hard-won passage must be abandoned because it does not "work" or "fit" in an emergent structure). To do a craftsmanlike job in these terms is very hard work. But there is a great rush of satisfaction when I finally feel that I have done all I can to get it "right," and can send it off to be published. And there is another rush when, after all the further work of publication,[25] the book or essay finally appears in printed form that I can hold in my hands, and still another rush, a year or two later, when I read the reviews, which with a few exceptions have been quite favorable.

Intellectual Topographies, Concentric Models, Enduring Biases: Some Limitations of a Professed Historicism

Although my goal of "getting it right" may still be in a general sense "historicist," my actual historiographical practice departs from the historicism I advocated in 1965 in quite significant ways. A large number of the words in my hard-wrought interpretive passages are, by intention, not my own, but those of my subjects, either in quotation marks or paraphrase. But with a few exceptions I do not use those words as block quotations—that is to say, in their original textual context—because these usually contain both more and fewer words than are needed to construct an interpretation that will relate them to the authors' words elsewhere. The same might be said of those "juicy bits" that (by processes unspecified) are chosen for careful squeezing in order to extract their potential meanings, as well as the "revelatory moments" of group

---

25. In general, I have played a very active role in the production process of the books I write or edit, including not only proof reading but also selecting illustrations integral to the texts and advising on typeface and jacket design. And ever since I took over the job of indexing when a "professional" botched the index of my first book (until quite recently, when I have become less capable of sustained attention), I have worked for two weeks or more indexing each of them, to facilitate their consultation by readers lacking time or inclination to wade through the complex details of my prose. This active role was mediated by my relationship with Betty Steinberg (chief editor and assistant director of the University of Wisconsin Press) when I began working on the HOA series in 1983 and later on three other books published by UWP (GS 1992, 1995, 2001a). In acknowledgment, I dedicated *After Tylor* to her, with thanks "for her commitment to the crafting of books and her tolerance of authorial idiosyncrasy."

interaction that may be used as framing devices for an essay. The implicit assumption in such cases is that although the surviving words of texts are the starting point of interpretation and the primary evidence for its adequacy, and are presumably intended by their authors (barring misprints, errors of transcription, or the like), they may not be simply or fully intentional reflections of an author's thinking processes or purposes. They may also reflect attitudes or feelings that authors may not deem relevant nor wish to reveal, or of which they may not even be fully aware. Like the words of my own historiography, they may be thought of as the contents of "black boxes" that may be occasionally glimpsed but are unlikely to be systematically scanned. Furthermore, in constructing a contextual interpretation of such textual material, there are always evidential gaps that one must write around or across in a cautiously qualified but responsibly suggestive way.

An historical understanding of an anthropologist's "thinking" is therefore inherently a problematic process. It should always begin with and return to the words in which that thinking is embodied and preserved. To this end, my historiographical ideal (rarely fully achieved) is to write with the original texts near at hand, against which to recheck my selection and juxtaposition of quotations or paraphrases, in order to catch distortions that may have been introduced by me in the lengthy writing process (like those in the rumor chains enacted decades ago on the stage of New Lecture Hall at Harvard). In that process one inevitably goes (however cautiously) behind and beyond the actual words of one's subject. Knowledge (or better yet, understanding) created in this manner can never be rigorously causal but is better thought of as "contextual." Neither can it be unqualifiedly historicist, in the programmatic sense put forward in my essay of 1965. Perhaps, to adapt a phrase of Clifford Geertz (1996), the best that can be said is that it strives to be "experience near to" rather than "experience distant from" the past thought world that it explores.

Since 1965, I have also become aware of other ways in which my own "honest groping" may have been constrained by certain methodological assumptions (ideologically tinged, if not grounded) that were (or became) embedded in my historiography. Sometime in the late 1980s, after reading an essay by Alfred Schutz (1944), I got the idea of an "internal intellectual topography," or mapping of the contents of an individual's mind. Initially, I thought of it in terms of pedagogical utility: sketched upon a blackboard, the representation of my own "internal intellectual topography" might help orient students in a seminar and in the process encourage them to think of their own graduate readings (as well as their subsequent fieldwork experience) as critical episodes in an accumulation of intellectual capital.[26]

Across the top of the blackboard chart were a number of columns extending vertically in time and horizontally in space. On the left was a temporal column for European intellectual history with additional columns for French, German, British, and American anthropology/ social science. On the far right was another column for relevant personal experience, including my years in the Communist Party, and extending downward on the chart and backward in time to the seventeenth century Puritan predawn of my own consciousness. In each column episodes of reading (or experience) were distributed in dated boxes vertically in relation to their place in historical time, varying in size and in cross-hatching to suggest the extent, intensity, and date of my own engagement and its relative importance in my historical thinking. In the wide "American anthropology" vertical column there was a large and loosely cross-hatched horizontal rectangle (dated 1958–60) representing the reading I did for my doctoral dissertation on race in turn-of-the-nineteenth-century American social science. Running up and down through it was a second box (dated 1958–68) darkened to represent a much more intensive reading of the writings of Franz Boas after the completion of my dissertation. In the British column (placed next to the American to suggest their interrelation) there were smaller darkened and dated boxes spaced downward from the early twentieth century back to the late eighteenth century, representing intensive readings of the works of various British writers. With boxes in the other columns treated in a similar (but more schematic) manner, the chart could be read as a mapping of the development of my own historiography. Thus

26. Shortly after I initiated the publication process of the "Black Box" essay by sending the "ultimate" manuscript to the University of Wisconsin Press in January 2010, my research assistant, Debora Heard, in the course of reviewing a listing of documents previously deposited in the university archives, came across a folder indicating that my thinking about "intellectual topographies" did not date from the late 1980s but from the mid-1970s. I spent the next two weeks drafting an essay entitled "Mapping the Terrain of Intellectual History: A Revelatory Moment of 'Honest Groping,'" in which I hoped to insert a copy of the chart described above. Unfortunately, however, efforts to obtain a copy of the chart from students who took the seminar several decades ago proved impossible, as did attempts to re-create the chart from the several sketches rediscovered in the archive, and I am therefore limited to the above description in words.

my intensive reading of Boas, undertaken in the context of prior, more extensive dissertation readings in early American social science, provided a basic comparative reference point for all my later thinking about the history of anthropology. Alternatively, my understanding of the pre-academic history of British anthropology has depended to a considerable extent on reasoning between "observation tower figures" (Kames, Prichard, Tylor et al.) whose works I read intensively in the late 1960s and early 1970s and who still serve as reference points for the interpretation of nineteenth-century anthropologists whose works I have read less systematically.

Although perhaps helpful in thinking about historiographical problems of intellectual biography, for the most part the idea of an "intellectual topography" remained a pedagogical whimsy. But the impulse to conceptualize intellectual processes visually has been more generally manifest in the idea of contextualization in terms of concentric circles of influence. Initially, the model was a simple one, focused on the "works and lives" of individual anthropologists. This reflected a belated reappreciation, toward the end of my dissertation research, of the central importance of Boas's thinking regarding the ideas of race and culture, and of the critical role of his participation in the institutional life of the discipline. In *Race, Culture, and Evolution* this contextual approach was briefly articulated in terms of a movement out from the writings and biography of the individual thinker, through the institutional arenas of a thinker's interaction with others in the same intellectual field, and through these to the world in which they thought and acted—and by which they were in turn molded and modified (GS 1968a:270–72).

In *Victorian Anthropology* (1987), in what I called an attempt at "multiple contextualization," the tripartite concentric contextual model was recast in more complex temporal terms, with a narrowing and then expanding focus. After an introductory "revelatory moment" on the Crystal Palace Exposition of 1851, there was a chapter on the idea of civilization from 1750 to 1830, followed by two chapters on the development of ethnology between 1830 and 1850. The next two chapters treated the idea of progress in civilization/culture in a small group of anthropological writers who were the central figures of the book: one focused on the years immediately prior to the publication of Darwin's *Origin of Species* (1851–58), the second on the decade following (1858–71). Reverting then to the eighteenth century, the forward movement was repeated, first from the point of view of "cultural ideology" (1780–1870) and then from that of "anthropological institutions" (1835–1890), followed by an epilogue matching the "revelatory moment" of the Crystal Palace: "The Extinction of Paleolithic Man." And then, in a conscious modification of my earlier historicism, I attempted a movement forward in time to consider the "historical significance" of Victorian evolutionism in the century after its emergence (xii–xiii, 212–13, passim).

Recently, however, as my interests have became more specifically biographical and therefore preoccupied with the problem of "influence" (which has an inherently "presentist" aspect), the concentric circle model is again in evidence. This time, however, it appears in three-dimensional temporal form, as two cones inverted on a single temporal axis (in the rough form of an hour glass). One cone represents various formative influences converging on the anthropologist as historical subject, the other as influences spreading outward in various channels from the anthropologist as historical actor (GS 2004:238–42).

There are, of course, limitations to the representational possibilities of these visual models, including the failure adequately to incorporate questions that have been central to my historiography: the development of the thinking of a single anthropologist over a life span, including the tensions and contradictions therein, as well as the limitations and problems of documenting influence. It is also an open question how much the models were determinative and how much merely descriptive of my historiography. But the tendency to conceptualize in tripartite concentric terms is evident elsewhere in the present essay. So also, however, is a tendency to think in binary terms between traditional polar ideal types (like those of Boas's "Study of Geography" [1887]) manifest in actual cases along a continuum of blurring boundaries and inner tensions. And sometimes, perhaps, one might find in my work a tendency to think in terms of a sequence of phases, or even in terms of Parsonian four-cell boxes. In this, as in other interpretive contexts, I play an eclectic game of interpretive catch-as-catch-can.[27]

---

27. In going over this text for the umpteenth time, it occurred to me in one of my insomniac brain races that the definition and the boundary relationships of continua and polarities could be thought of as the fundamental problem not only of intellectual history, but of theoretical speculation as well. It is not an idea I will have time or energy to develop, but maybe someone else will—if it hasn't been done already. In my black box, however, it seems like an original thought.

There are, however, certain enduring interpretive biases in my work that have both a methodological and an ideological aspect, insofar as they may be viewed as dependent on my institutional situation and my political evolution, as well as certain psychodynamic predispositions. My appointment in an internationally renowned department of anthropology, although facilitating my access to the institutions and personnel of British anthropology, could also have reinforced a tendency to focus on canonical figures, rather than to pursue neglected paradigmatic mavericks. More to the point, my historiographical style is one that benefits from, if it does not depend on, a privileged institutional position. With a light teaching load, small classes, a generous leave policy, and relatively easy access to grants and fellowships, I have been able to pursue my research interests wherever they may lead, even into the blind alley of a writer's block. If perfectionist anxiety compels me, I am free to spend an hour worrying the words of a single sentence—an indulgence (or hangup) that I could not so easily have allowed myself had I been employed at an institution where there might have been pressure sooner to "cut to the chase," or to choose a meta-chase I could regularly cut to, in order to meet the pressure of "publish or perish."

Lacking such an overriding interpretive orientation, I tend to draw (whether implicitly or explicitly) on an eclectic potpourri of interpretive assumptions, including residues of Marxism, fragments of Freud, snatches, even, of Foucault, as well as assumptions drawn from cultural anthropology and the sociology of science—especially when speculating about black box motives or influences of which past actors may not have been consciously aware. But I do so as interpretive bricoleur rather than as theoretically committed interpretive systematizer, and to the end of understanding the thought and action of the past rather than influencing them in the present.

That said, it is also the case that my interpretive predispositions can be seen as reflections of my own life experience and psychodynamic makeup, predispositions especially relevant to my "terminal project." Insofar as the contents of my own black box affect the substance as well as the form of my understanding of anthropology in the United States during the Cold War period, the critical factors are my suspicion of all meta-narratives, my bias toward complexity, and my insistence on privileging the perspective of actors in the historical past, insofar as we can gain access to it. As a disillusioned, but residually empathic former member of the "Old Left" Communist Party, the most salient master narrative for me is the radical critical perspective that underlies some of the more provocative work so far produced on the anthropology of the Cold War era. Among many anthropologists today, the anthropology of the 1950s tends to be regarded as a pretentiously pseudoscientific enterprise, pursued in terms of various discredited theoretical orientations (structural-functionalism, systems theory, acculturation, modernization, neo-evolutionism) and carried on either willingly or unwittingly in the service or the interests of the Cold War policies of the military-industrial complex or the "national security state." That, at least, is the stereotype that has helped motivate much of my own research.

There is enough of the radical left in me not to dismiss out of hand this meta-narrative perspective, which can be developed in a more serious way than my stereotype suggests, and which raises specific issues of interpretation and evidence that must be given serious consideration. But having once myself accepted and then abandoned an earlier version of a radical meta-narrative, I try to approach the anthropological world of the 1950s not only from a different point of view, but also from a different moment. It is one thing, historiographically, to approach the anthropology of the Cold War from a present point of view that, insofar as it is grounded in the past, adopts the perspective of the late 1960s critics of the Viet Nam War. It is quite another to attempt to recapture the point of view of anthropologists in 1940, and then in 1945, and then in the 1950s, and then in the early 1960s, and then after 1965. It should be needless to say that anthropology and the world in which it was practiced did not look the same to all anthropologists at any one of these points in time, that they did not all act or react in the same manner, and that their views and actions were subject to change over time. And it is by no means to insist that history should or can be written solely in terms of such past perspectives. Men and women often think and act in response to forces or influences they are not aware of or do not fully understand, and some of these are more likely to be available from a different perspective at a later point in time. Though they may not have understood the dynamics of late colonialism or of United States overseas activities in the Cold War in the same terms that are available to us today, post–World War II anthropologists were nonetheless influenced by them. Accepting thus a necessary "presentist" component of historical understanding, I would nevertheless give historiographical priority to perspectives on the past that I still think of as historicist.

In my own work, interpretive predispositions based on prior life experience include, of course, my membership in and disillusion with the Communist Party, which (despite a residue of materialism) left me suspicious of a priori macrocosmic explanatory frameworks. As previous remarks have suggested, there is also my middle-class liberal background, which encouraged an alternative interpretive tendency to privilege individual actors, including (after episodes of my own psychotherapy) the unconscious motives of their actions. Reflecting this same life experience there are unresolved tensions in my own thinking (between relativism and universalism, or between empathic and scientific understanding) that I tend to find in anthropologists I study. And there may be other interpretive predispositions, of which I am not fully aware—as well as those built into the subject matter of my inquiry, including a characteristically Eurocentric standpoint of anthropology itself.

Interesting Questions and Blocked Researches: Notes on Anxiety and Method in My Historiography of Anthropology

Focusing specifically on my own psychodynamic predispositions, there are plenty to choose from among my "Autobiographical Recollections." Many of them, however, can be brought together under a single encompassing rubric: anxiety. In various forms, anxiety has had a lot to do with my historiography: anxiety about competence and method, about identity and marginality, about selfhood and otherness, about authority and influence, about significance and truth—not to mention politics and religion, ethnicity and "race," sex and gender, love and death, and the meaning of it all.

My awareness of "anxiety" as an historiographical category is associated with two epiphanal memories: one, of a conversational exchange, the other of a book; both of them (in the topography of my intellect) dating from the mid-1970s. During my year in Palo Alto at the Center for Advanced Study in the Behavioral Sciences, my then colleague and since friend David Krantz (who is, among other things, an historian of psychology) asked me one day, in his disconcertingly blunt way: "George, what is an interesting question?"—not by way of seeking an example, but rather a general principle underlying all "interesting" questions. Reflecting my then daily conversational experience at an interdisciplinary research center, I was at first inclined to answer in

Members of the 1977 class at the Center for Advanced Study in the Behavioral Sciences, Palo Alto, California, where David Krantz (third row, fourth from left) and I (back row, seventh from left) had mind-expanding conversations on the role of anxiety in social research. Carol also spent the year in Palo Alto, along with her father, who lived with us in our rented home, where we were visited for a month by Lazarov/Roncevic relatives from Belgrade, whom Carol drove on a somewhat stressful tour of several national parks. In her free time, however, she was able to work on her dissertation in an underused office at the Center. (courtesy of the Center for Advanced Study in the Behavioral Sciences)

overly simple terms of disciplinary marginality: a generally "interesting" question must be translatable into the categories or issues of another discipline, and not so technical as to forestall the interest of an intellectual outsider. David's own answer, which I later came to call the "Goldilocks Theory," was rather in terms of the degree of anxiety aroused by any given research topic: if too much or too little, it was unlikely to be pursued because it was considered either too threatening or too boring; just the right amount of anxiety, and one's interest might be aroused and sustained.

Although I recall initially resisting it, I came to appreciate the force of Krantz's answer, especially after reading George Devereux's oddly constructed but seminal *From Anxiety to Method in the Behavioral Sciences*. Recounting over four hundred individual "cases," Devereux offered glimpses into the larger black box of behavioral science, suggesting that human behavioral "data" (a term then eliciting no quotation marks) characteristically aroused anxiety in the individual behavioral scientist, which was warded off by "a counter-transference inspired pseudo-methodology" (1968:xvi–xx, 3–7, passim). Borrowing from Niels Bohr, Devereux discussed behavioral science experiments and observations in terms of the metaphor of a rigidly or loosely held stick bridging the gap between observer and observed—arguing that the former, in the language of William James, produced "knowledge about" and the latter "acquaintance with" types of information (cf. Boas 1887 and GS 1974c:7). I think of my historiography as a loosely held stick, which produces a reasonably reliable and occasionally suggestive "acquaintance with" the thinking of earlier anthropologists, as preserved in their texts, in the context of their life experiences in a past cultural moment—this, as a supplement to (or corrective of) presumed "knowledge about" their thought, construed in relation to the thinking of present anthropologists. Many of the characteristics of my historiography (including the preference for context rather than cause, and the complexly parenthetical although/however sentences) can be thought of as "loose stick" methodological responses to my various anxieties. And insofar as I do value these qualities of my own mind, anxiety can be thought of as facilitative.

But anxieties may also have a seriously inhibiting character, manifest in the difficulty I have in completing, or even undertaking, work on certain topics. When I think about the various books that in my career were blocked for extended periods (*Victorian Anthropology* and *After Tylor*), or partially drafted but left unfinished ("Race and Culture in American Social Science," the history of the Chicago Department of Anthropology, and "Anne Roe's Anthropologists"), or researched and written in part but never seriously undertaken (biographies of Boas and Malinowski and a history of fieldwork), or seriously considered but never pursued (an essay on 1950s modes of marginalization and a book on a half-dozen major early twentieth-century social scientists marginalized by virtue of their violation of cultural sexual norms)—not to mention all those "brain race" ideas recorded on a note slip or two but never pursued—it is clear that in many instances anxiety about the subject matter and my competence to pursue it has played a major inhibiting role in my career as an historian.

In every case of work long blocked, or never finished, or never undertaken, there have been other factors at work than the topic itself. Sometimes there were technical difficulties (including linguistic and ethnographic incompetence). Sometimes doubts arose as to the relative importance of a particular project in the trajectory of my research (in terms of time, energy, and prior effort). Sometimes there were moral or ethical concerns about a particular aspect of the evidence or argument (including especially a sense of obligation to living persons). And behind all these were underlying personality traits dating back to my early familial situation, including a potent achievement motivation counterbalanced by an engrained perfectionism, as well as a tension or ambivalence in my relations to authority, manifest on the one hand in a generally assertive personal style and in several major episodes of confrontation, and on the other in a certain timidity in personal interaction (including a reluctance to "push" my informants into sensitive areas that they might be avoiding).

As the previous account of the fate of the department history indicates, my anxieties increase as my historical interests move closer to the present. While the failure to complete that history was overdetermined, it clearly reflected the fact that the Armstrong case was too close to my own experience, without the same professional outcome. But it reflected also my own long-enduring sense of marginality within the department. Though my colleagues were personal friends, they were also anxiety-arousing figures of authority in the generalized sense that, despite all that I might learn from them through the osmosis of daily participation, they knew more about the recent and present state of anthropology than I did (leading me in seminar discussions to contrast their topographies of intellect, which were more intense at the top of the chart, with my own, which was more intense in the late nineteenth and early twentieth centuries).

A similar anxiety of marginality and authority constrained my relationship to the larger community of professional anthropology, which in the 1970s I had come to regard as the primary audience for my work. Here again, one may see an analogy to my frequently noted concentric contextual model: in moving from the individual through the institutional to the outer "darkness" of the present world, my own anxieties of politics and ideology take on a more potent character, and my historicist posture becomes more difficult to sustain. As a result I have been wary of entering historiographical fields that are inherently and divisively "presentist."

By way of preface to their discussion, I insert here a glimpse into my own black box that I recently experienced about anxiety and historiographical method. My serious thought on this topic occurred at a specific moment in my own development as historian—a moment in the mid-1970s that included my conversations with David Krantz, my reading of George Devereux, and the blockages in my own research, which suggested to me that methodological anxiety was characteristic of historical thought in general. Without abandoning entirely the interpretive utility of that notion, I am inclined now to qualify it somewhat, insofar as it was a projection of my own anxieties and insecurities. There are doubtless many self-confident historians who prefer to live on the interpretive edge, and who are for me a significant reference group, insofar as their views are of a sort that I once shared and still find interesting.

Revelatory Moments Unexplored:
The Mead/Freeman Controversy and the Amplification
of Anxiety in Present History

My anxieties of present history have been sharply manifest in relation to the attack on Margaret Mead by the New Zealand–born Australian anthropologist Derek Freeman. On the basis of his own extensive field-work in Samoa in the early 1940s, and his return in the 1960s, Freeman published in 1983 a critique of Mead's interpretation of Samoan adoles-cence as a trauma-free time of sexual experimentation, arguing that it had been the turning point in the subsequent half-century misdirection of American cultural anthropology into a paradigm of "absolute cul-tural determinism."

From its beginning, I have regarded the Mead/Freeman controversy as involving and illuminating a wide range of questions bearing on the historical constitution of anthropology, as well as its changing present situation and future prospects. The most fundamental of these were the nature of human nature and the range and causes of its varied manifestation—including the tension between (or articulation of) their biological and cultural explanation. But in addition to issues of the goals and the topics of anthropological inquiry, there were also funda-mental questions of anthropological method, including the relations of the ethnographer and the people being studied, not only in terms of the ethnographic process, but also in terms of the ethical obligations im-plicit in it, as well as the scientific status of the information gained by it. Arising out of these issues of subject matter and method were questions of disciplinary boundary definition, both internal (the relation of the "subdisciplines" of anthropology) and external (the relations of anthro-pology to sponsors and audiences in the "world outside"). Included among the latter were questions of the ideological and political implica-tions and the usefulness of anthropological argument—and of the re-sponsibilities of individual anthropologists (and of the discipline as a whole) as actors in the world. Granting that these issues might be other-wise formulated, and more fully explicated, some such range of anxiety-arousing issues seemed to me involved in the Mead/Freeman debate, not only for me, but also for anthropologists in general.

Not surprisingly, the debate quickly generated intellectual passion on both sides. Despite a somewhat ambivalent attitude toward Mead, the American profession for the most part united in its opposition to Freeman, who from that day until his death in 2001 pursued his attack with bulldog tenacity, in further publications (1999) and by air and email from Australia. A few months after his book appeared, it was the subject of a panel at the American Anthropological Association meetings—a panel to which Freeman had not been invited, at which he had no defenders, and which elicited from the floor heated denunciations of him and his book. As invited chair of the session, I suggested that a proposal from the audience to condemn the book as a "poorly written, unscientific, irresponsible and misleading" misrepresentation of "the entire field of anthropology" might better be presented at the association's business meeting—where a motion to that effect was later passed by voice vote.

In this atmosphere, I was disinclined to make public that, as one of several anonymous manuscript reviewers, I had written in favor of the publication of Freeman's book, albeit with some reservations regarding his use of historical texts. Over the next few years, however, I did follow the controversy, compiling a substantial stack of photocopies, with the expectation that I might some day write about it. In 1989, in "The Ethnographic Sensibility of the 1920s and the Dualism of the Anthropological Tradition" (1992:276-341) I referred to it as an illustrative case, but I kept postponing any attempt to treat it at length, and eventually abandoned the project. There were serious problems of ethnographic evidence, which I did not feel competent to evaluate—although I was inclined to think there was merit in Freeman's critique of Mead's methods in what had been her first ethnographic fieldwork. There was the further problem of interpreting motivation, insofar as the issues in dispute had to do with the relations of the sexes in the context of notions about the cultural or biological bases of human nature. On the one hand, it seemed to me evident that Mead's interpretation of Samoa had indeed been affected by ulterior personal and professional commitments. On the other hand, there was gossipy evidence suggesting that the issues involved were not ones Freeman approached in a coolly rational manner (cf. GS 1992:276-80).

The "gossipy evidence" included stories of Freeman's desecration of native statuary in the Sarawak Museum during a visit in 1961, followed by his forced removal from Sarawak. A subsequent account of the actual incident, based in part on an interview in 1992 with Freeman, was included in Judith Heimann's biography of Tom Harrisson (1998), which I evaluated favorably for publication. By this account Freeman had previously clashed with Harrisson, who in 1961 was government ethnologist and curator of the Sarawak Museum. Early in March of that year, Freeman flew into Sarawak determined "to rid Borneo of Tom Harrisson." Upon visiting the museum, Freeman became convinced that it was a veritable "palace of pornography," full of "ithyphallic" and "copulatory" carvings that had not in fact been produced for native ritual purposes but instead were created by natives working for Harrisson. Returning several days later to take pictures of the offending statuary, Freeman went out on the museum lawn and smashed one of the carvings displayed there, ostensibly in order to force attention to the problem of fraudulent pornography. When there was no response to his deliberate provocation, on the last day of his stay in Sarawak Freeman went to Harrisson's house (when he was not at home), took pictures of a number of similar carvings, pried open a locked drawer in search of more evidence, and upon leaving brushed aside two Sarawak police who had responded to a call from Harrisson's servant. Although the exact circumstances of Freeman's departure from Sarawak that afternoon are unclear, it seems that he was accompanied to the airport by a police escort.

In an extended footnote to this passage in the published version of her book, Heimann reproduced an alternate account, offered by Freeman when she sent to him the pre-publication draft. Although the footnote version followed Heimann's original text closely in most respects, there were several significant changes, including the deletion of the police escort to the airport. More to the interpretive point, however, is the inclusion of Freeman's temporally vague reference to his own "cognitive abreaction" while "in the throws of trying to comprehend the actions of Harrisson": "a sudden and deep realization of the inadequacy of the assumptions of contemporary anthropology," which led him "to the development of an evolutionary approach to the study of human behavior" (Heimann 1998:332–35, 443–45).

Whether I would have been able to integrate this incident had it been available to me when I was seriously contemplating an account of the Mead/Freeman episode, I am not sure. In principle I regard such episodes of intense disciplinary controversy as "revelatory moments" when recurring questions about the constitution of anthropology are likely to be actively at issue. I have in fact treated some of these moments and issues in historical context, some extensively, some indirectly, as they arose at various times in the past of anthropology; and there are no doubt things I might say as an historian about their manifestation in present controversies. But there is no denying that in 1983 and again in 1992 anxieties about my disciplinary marginality and interpretive authority (along with issues of method) discouraged me from writing about the controversy in ways that might involve me in a heated debate in which an attempt to historicize a complex historical phenomenon was likely to be attacked from both sides. Although if the Boas medal might have reduced my anxiety of marginality when a similar revelatory controversy arose in 2000 around the activities of Napoleon Chagnon among the Yanomami of Brazil over the previous half century,[28] by that time serious involvement seemed a distraction from what I had come to call my "terminal project"—which of course provokes its own set of anxieties of subject matter, method, ethics, marginality, and authority, as well as those of oedipal nostalgia and fear of mortality.

From the Big Picture to the Biographical Vignette: The Ulterior Historiographical Motives of an Aging Old Historicist

When I was in graduate school at the University of Pennsylvania in the late 1950s, Roy Nichols began his course on "recent" American history by explaining why he would carry it no further than the 1920s: for him, everything after that was "current events." Similarly, the effective stopping point for my own research (from my doctoral dissertation through *After Tylor*) was roughly the moment when I reached the age of twenty-one in 1949. In writing about periods earlier than that, I could treat the past as "another country"; after that, it was the country in which I had lived my professional life, and the events, if no longer "current," were nevertheless in various ways entangled with my own personal history and its attendant anxieties. Although soothed somewhat by my disciplinary status, these anxieties were still strong enough in the mid-1990s to evoke a certain historiographical caution. Ever since Margaret Mead

---

28. For recent references to both the Mead/Freeman and the Yanomami controversies, a convenient source is the Public Anthropology website: http://www.publicanthropology .org.

(1970), in an otherwise favorable review of *Race, Culture, and Evolution*, was critical of its last chapter (which overlapped her own days as a graduate student), I have been sensitive to an inverse temporal correlation between anxiety and authority in my history of anthropology: the closer to the present, the greater my anxiety and the more problematic my authority. For me to presume to study "anthropology yesterday" was thus to lay my work open to critique by those who felt they had an actor's knowledge of the postwar period. Others, who may not have "been there," were likely to think of "anthropology yesterday" in terms of subsequent postcolonial critique—an approach that easily lends itself to stereotypification. For me, however, the suspension of prior belief (one's own) and of disbelief (in the beliefs of others) is the historiographical analogue of the ethnographer's stance on entering the field, and as such is a necessary prerequisite for the empathic and complex re-familiarization that is the goal of my historicism, in the case of past anthropologists as well as of the peoples they studied. Many readers of this autobiographical essay will no doubt regard this concern as a distraction from more pressing critical tasks, if not an implicit apology for changing forms of exploitation. Given the enduring residual ambivalence of my disillusionment with my own radical past, anxiety about the likelihood of such a critical reaction may well have been a factor in the conception of my "terminal project" as a series of biographical vignettes, each covering the same historical period through the life of a different figure, rather than attempting a single unified thematic structure for the period as a whole. In contrast to my somewhat self-serving metaphorical whimsy of "layered transparencies" revealing the larger "big picture," this approach could be viewed negatively as shifting to readers a burden of generalization that should have been my own. However, in my more optimistic moments, I prefer to view it positively, as giving readers the freedom to make (or to justify) their own generalizations in relation to a rich and suggestive body of historical specifics.

There were also motivating anxieties of a more pragmatic historiographical sort. Nearing retirement and having survived an operation for colon cancer, the meanings of my own life took on a compelling personal interest, which tended to be generalized to the lives of others and to become also an occasional comparative reference point. Both my liberal background and my radical disillusion already inclined me to focus on the individual, and although methodological anxieties had previously forestalled any attempt at full-fledged biography, biographical "vignettes" had the advantage that they could be published prior to the moment of my incapacitation or demise. And for a politically disillusioned old historicist like myself, mortality itself might even be regarded as historiographically advantageous insofar as the study of an individual life completed (in contrast to a disciplinary past still open to the future) might encourage a focus on the "wasness" of things, rather than what they might yet be changed to be—about which my anxieties manifest themselves as an extreme and generalized pessimism.

Similarly, the choice of candidates for biographical treatment may also have had both ulterior and pragmatic historiographical motives. The dozen original candidates were roughly of the generation of my own parents, and in studying them I was well aware of what might be called "oedipal nostalgia" as a motivating factor. It was also the case that only two of them (Margaret Mead and Cora Dubois) were women, neither of whom survived the subsequent winnowing. In my more self-doubting moments I wonder if this might reflect deeply rooted gender anxieties of my own. There were, however, other grounds for their exclusion, including the reality of male dominance in post–World War II anthropology—as reflected in Anne Roe's exclusion of women from her study of elite scientists. Perhaps more to the point is the fact that each of the male anthropologists included was connected with me, or seemed like me, in some way that might make them more easily recipients of my empathic understanding: Tax as long-time colleague, Hallowell as mentor, Armstrong as disillusioned Communist, Kluckhohn as worrier of cultural relativism and universal values—Hymes, although a long-time colleague and personal friend, was excluded as he was then still alive. That sense of specific empathic connection, however, is itself anxiety ridden, insofar as it implies an ethical obligation not only to the departed subject but also to living individuals, known or potentially known to me, who could be affected by facts I might reveal or interpretations I might offer regarding someone to whom they were once psychologically close.

Although such worries have constrained my "terminal project" in various ways (some specified, others implied, others only hinted), these anxieties have for the most part remained within the Goldilocks range. There is, however, another worry the effects of which are evident both structurally and substantively in the essays I have written or am currently working on—namely, the anxiety aroused by the opinion of more than one colleague that I am wasting my historiographical efforts on minor figures of doubtful historical and anthropological importance. Rather than writing the historical magnum opus that might have climaxed my career, I am spending my late life writing about an "atheoretical" global anthropological entrepreneur, a prophet of dubious honor in his own department (Tax); about a Boasian who managed to combine what some would regard as two retrospectively questionable projects, culture and personality and cultural evolutionism (Hallowell); about a little known victim of McCarthyism who abandoned serious social anthropological issues for Boasian particularism (Armstrong); and about an anthropological dilettante of dubious subsequent influence, who was compromised by his involvement in governmental anthropology (Kluckhohn). None of them (save perhaps Tax, if I had wished to provoke) would have made the very short list of "world historical" anthropologists (including James G. Frazer) I once tried to compile for a course on the impact of anthropology in the world beyond the academic discipline.

It is thus no accident that each of the essays so far completed concludes with an extended consideration of the "influence" of its subject, along with comments on the problem of "influence" in intellectual history. The fact that the general tenor of these comments has been to diminish the current disciplinary influence of the subjects, while insisting on their importance in understanding the broader history of anthropology, suggests that behind this concern with influence may lurk yet another "ulterior motive." My colleague Ray Fogelson suggested that in the case of Hallowell, it may have reflected an unconscious oedipal need to slay an intellectual father. Pursuing instead the hour glass metaphor, it might be that my recent concern with "influence" is a displacement of my own "anxiety of influence" from the "influences upon" my historiography to the "influences of" the historical work that I have produced. Be that as it may, there is no denying that I have become concerned with my own influence in a different way as an aging historicist doyen than when I was a young historicist rebel.

The Problematic Character of Influence:
The "Gatekeeper" and a "New" History of Anthropology

Although I do not recall worrying about "influence" as such in the early stages of my career, there were both pragmatic and psychological reasons for wanting to make my way in the academic world, and to that end being concerned with the perceived value of my work and with encouraging work along similar historiographical lines. While such concerns are consistent with my engrained perfectionism and achievement motivation, it seems evident retrospectively that they can easily be translated into a generalized and inherently competitive desire for "influence." And however conscious that desire, it would be false modesty to deny that my work has had significant influence both on the way the history of anthropology has been written and the standards by which it is judged—or that on the whole I think this has been (or was at the time) for the good, and I am gratified to have had it.

Viewed in less specifically personal terms, however, there is perhaps a general historiographical point to be made, insofar as personal experience may be illustrative of the contingent character of "influence," both as phenomenon and process. Beyond (or beneath) its dependence on the personal characteristics and cultural context of the author, it is conditioned by the specific influences by which his or her thought has been formed, the institutional context in which it has been developed, and the polemical or critical context into which it has been received. Furthermore, such influence is in most cases limited in range and fleeting in duration. In relatively few instances it may be more extensive and more durable—if not continuous, then recurrent or recoverable, insofar as ideas formulated in one time and place may be found generative or usable in different ideational frameworks in other times and places—a process echoing such traditional anthropological notions as diffusion, independent invention, and acculturation.

Be all this as it may, it is evident that in my own case influence has been heavily dependent on having been "in the right place at the right time." This in turn depended in part on inherited academic privilege: my father's status as economist and his prior acquaintance with Thomas Cochran, Clark Kerr, and Edward Levi; and on my own connections established along the way. Most notable among these were Hallowell, who in 1962 gave me a prominent role on the newly established history of anthropology stage, and Dell Hymes, who after writing a rave review of the 1962 conference went on to facilitate my career in various ways, including invitations to several other important conferences. Contingency (fortunate and unfortunate) played a role also in my moving from Berkeley to Chicago, which might not have happened had my first marriage not fallen apart. And from Chicago, long a major node in the institutional network of the social sciences, the connections ran in various directions, including centers for advanced study east and west, and various channels of foundation support. My scholarly life might have been very different without such links to academic personnel and institutions.

It might also have been different if I had come upon the scene at a different time. I got my PhD when academic history was expanding into new areal and topical niches, and the passing of generations and paradigms in anthropology was encouraging a new look at its past. In 1960, moreover, the history of anthropology was a very small scholarly pond, and all the easier for the first one in to grow into a big fish. By 1969, when I arrived in Chicago, I had published articles on the major founding figure of American anthropology (Boas), its central concept (culture), and the early history of the national organization of anthropology in the United States (1965b, 1966a, 1960b) as well as on its history in Great Britain (1963) and in France (1964a). Beyond these there was a manifesto on how to write the history of anthropology (1965c), a survey of the emergence of the field (1966b), and a sharply critical review of an ambitious attempt to write a general history on different principles (GS 1968c; Harris 1968). With the move to Chicago and the subsequent publication of *Race, Culture, and Evolution* (GS 1968a), an intellectual and institutional basis for "influence" was well established.

Since then I have played a very active role as book reviewer, academic referee, and editor of two important serial publications in the field: the biannual *History of Anthropology Newsletter* (1983-96), which has had a substantial individual, institutional, and overseas circulation, and the annual volume series *History of Anthropology*, each one of which is still in print. And despite extended writer's blocks and unfinished books, there are sixteen of them that bear my name on the title page (five as author, eleven as editor)—most of them still in print and on several occasions spoken of as setting a standard for the history of anthropology. All that granted, there is more to be said about influence and its close congener, authority, in my historiography of anthropology.

My own problems with "authority" have been to a large extent self-reflexive: doubts about my own competence as author, about the value of my work, and about its reception by figures of authority. I still read (or postpone reading) reviews with a certain ambivalent perfectionist apprehension—on the one hand, fearful that a critic may discover flaws either already known (or yet unknown) to me, or alternatively, may embarrass me with praise I yearn for but do not deserve. But there have also been complaints, implicit or explicit, of a more far-reaching sort. The charge that my work is anecdotal and atheoretical—preoccupied with the trivia of historical particularity—though anxiety provoking, is one with which I am prepared to live (and die), an unrepentant "old historicist" to the bitter end.[29] More serious is the charge that I have been a "gatekeeper" to the field, discouraging certain types of research, to the detriment of a seriously "anthropological" or a politically "relevant" inquiry.

An early version of the "gatekeeper" criticism was argued back in 1986 in response to the first volume in the *History of Anthropology* series. Reading it in the light of my 1965 manifesto, a French-Belgian sociological critic complained that there was no "organizing vision" or "theoretical problematic" in the volume, which was simply a series of "empirical" biographical accounts by marginal anthropologists and aspiring young historians, forced by the American academic system to "publish or perish." Granting that it might be unfair to extrapolate from the first volume, he held out hope for the future: *"attendons les suivants"* (Winkin 1986). Two decades later, however, there are those who complain that my critique of presentism "helped to establish a dominant American historicist school" whose "inattentiveness to political economy has led to sizable blind spots in anthropology's understanding of itself" (Price 2004:342).

As to the general question of my role as "gatekeeper" (insofar as it implies a conscious effort on my part, rather than the "influence" of my work): there are no doubt aspects of my scholarly activity that might be marshaled as evidence for the allegation, including the hundred plus book reviews that I have published in some thirty-five journals, as well as an equal number of manuscript evaluations for professional journals and academic presses, and a substantial number of evaluations of academic personnel for hiring and promotion. Rather than go through professional files now in transit to the university archives, which might cast further light in each of these areas, I focus here on my role as editor of the first eight volumes of the *History of Anthropology* (HOA) series as the most convenient indicator of what I would like to think is the general character of my influence.

29. At a symposium in my honor in 1998, Clifford Geertz dampened his ritual praise by predicting my work might eventuate in four volumes on "Anthropology in Northeast Scotland, 1921–22," while he was moving toward a twelve-page essay on "The Foundations of Culture, Society, and Personality"—adding that it was unfortunate I had not kept up with recent historiographical trends, as exemplified in the work of Natalie Zemon Davis (who, as it happens, is my former sister-in-law, whose work I occasionally read, although apparently without real effect).

It is true that the series differed in significant ways from most anthropological or historical journals—among them the fact that it was not "peer-reviewed." As founding editor, I selected the eight members of the editorial board, equally divided among historians and anthropologists, two of them women, and all of them serious contributors to the history of anthropology, chosen to represent each of the "four fields," as well as a range of academic institutions and historiographical orientations. Although I recall only one time when we met as a group, there was occasional postal discussion of general policy matters and volume themes, as well as to get "second opinions" or suggestions of an appropriate outside reader for a particular manuscript. But for practical purposes, most of the editorial decisions were ultimately my own—two of the most difficult being the rejection of manuscripts solicited from Edmund Leach and Ashley Montagu that were put together more casually than I had hoped.

In general, however, the editorial problem was not how to select the best from a surfeit of papers. In a field then still sparsely populated, the problem was rather how to fill each volume with high-quality papers around a common theme. While the original series introduction allowed for occasional volumes of "miscellaneous studies," the thematically unified annual volume format was from the beginning the distinctive feature of the series. But if this had the advantage of giving each volume the sustained scholarly weight of a book, it made it virtually impossible to build up a backlog of publishable essays. Each volume had to be created more or less from scratch, and the major editorial problem was how to rustle up (or to spruce up) a group of publishable papers closely enough related that they could be given a kind of post hoc thematic unity in an introductory essay. These introductions regularly included mention of neglected topics that might be pursued in future study. As a perfectionist editor adept at neither multitasking nor delegation, I found the annual volume schedule difficult to maintain, and after the first four volumes appeared on schedule, the second quartet took another decade.

In this situation of thematic scarcity, I tended to fall back on people whose prior work and current projects suggested they might offer something that would fit into a roughly thematic volume of high quality. Thus twenty-three of the sixty-one articles in the eight volumes I edited were by eight authors who contributed more than one article (including seven of my own). Of the total forty-six individual authors, more than half were people previously known to me, including a baker's dozen of past or present students, another half dozen members of the editorial board, and a like number of colleagues or professional acquaintances. Slightly less than half of the papers published required only nominal or slight editorial input. For the rest, however, my editorial effort (sometimes considerable) was an attempt, by constructive criticism and active suggestion, to draw out from the author's draft a coherent narrative or argument consistent both with the empirical material it contained and with the author's interpretive intent. In general, it was an effort acknowledged appreciatively by authors, and only once resisted, in the case of a 230-page manuscript I had twice drastically shortened. When it came back a third time with new additions, I insisted that it be published as previously edited.

Whether these admittedly rather personalistic editorial practices justify a recent anonymous Internet reference to "the blindspots inflicted by George W. Stocking, Jr. and his mob" as an attempt by "anthropology's historical gatekeepers" to "shield us from knowing" about "political and economic factors" in the historical development of anthropology is a matter that seriously interested readers may judge for themselves (see review at http://www.amazon.com/gp/product/1859734944). In doing so, however, it may be helpful to keep in mind certain other considerations—a term I use here instead of "facts," since some of them will be offered as recollections or impressions of intent. To begin with, I would suggest that at least half of the original members of the editorial board thought of themselves as politically "radical" and intellectually influenced by Marxism, and I do not recall any of them ever suggesting that the series played such a gatekeeping role. As to the actual volume content, I would point to the essays in the volume on "Colonial Situations" (HOA7 1991) or those on race in "Bones, Bodies, Behavior" (HOA5 1988), as well as occasional essays in other volumes, including my own essay on Rockefeller funding in anthropology (1985), which was offered as a study in "the political economy of anthropological research."

Some "gatekeeper" critics, it may be assumed, will not be mollified by mention of the Rockefeller essay, since the issue for them is not simply a failure to deal with certain topics, but a failure to deal with them from a Marxist (or otherwise radical) point of view, and thereby to forestall certain conclusions. Specifically, in the case of Rockefeller anthropology, that the "interests of these particular robber barons are not found to have promulgated their particular 'ulterior corporate or class interest' in selecting particular anthropological research projects to fund" (Price

2004:380). In self-defense, I would note that the actual context of the five words of mine here (mis)quoted is more complex than this excerpt suggests, and includes a footnote specifying, among several other limitations of my analysis, "the fact that records of declined grants were not preserved by the Rockefeller Foundation" (GS 1985:133). As far as "gatekeeping" is concerned, I would note that in discussing limitations of the volume, I specifically indicated that "we would have liked to have an article reflecting more directly the modern radical perspective on all these issues" (HOA3 1985:13).

More generally, I would note that by the time the series was founded, I had become much more sensitive to the variety of anxieties that may direct historical inquiry along quite different substantive, methodological, epistemological, and ideological lines. Echoing Chairman Mao, I began to think of many flowers blooming in the garden of history—although not with the Machiavellian intent of weeding them out as they broke the earth. I do not recall ever having rejected an essay on the grounds that it pursued an interpretive agenda other than my own. It is possible, of course, that this may reflect either my own self-deception or a self-selection on the part of authors who preferred to submit their work to explicitly radical journals, or who mistakenly anticipated rejection due to a presumed bias against radical interpretation. There was, of course, a frank bias in favor of "studies grounded in concrete historical research." Enunciated in the introduction to the first volume, that bias has indeed been a distinctive feature of the series, but always with the hope it would "rise well above anecdotal antiquarianism to contribute to the critical understanding of general issues of serious current anthropological concern" (HOA1 1983:6). Since my retirement as editor in 1996, that goal is still manifest, but with a shift in emphasis suggested by the title of the first volume under the editorship of Richard Handler: *Excluded Ancestors, Inventible Traditions: Essays toward a More Inclusive History of Anthropology* (HOA9 2000).

That I should have taken this much trouble to respond to the gatekeeping charge is, of course, testimony to the continuing potency of my own "anxieties of influence" a decade after having received the American Anthropological Association's Franz Boas Exemplary Service Award for "forcing us to take a closer and more critical look at the historical forces that have shaped anthropology and the challenges the discipline continues to face." Since then, there have in fact been a number of books published in the history of anthropology based on extensive archival and oral historical research, many of them included in the recently established monograph series of "Critical Studies in the History of Anthropology." Ignoring the implicit adjectival dig, I would like to think that these "critical" studies (several of them written from a radical point of view) may not only be a response to presumed interpretive inadequacies of the *History of Anthropology* series, but more positively, may also reflect the emphasis on carefully crafted and empirically grounded historical research that was its founding motive and guiding editorial principle—as well as the growth of the field since the founding of the series a quarter century ago.[30]

Doing "Good Work":
Thoughts on the Craft of One Historian

As aspiring anthropologists, the members of my seminars on "Anthropology Yesterday" were interested in the past of anthropology less for itself than as a way of orienting themselves toward its future—as well as to their own future careers. With that tension still in mind, the dedicatory page of *Delimiting Anthropology* contained two epigraphs: one from Robert Browning: "Ah, that a man's reach should exceed his grasp, / Or what's a heaven for?"; the other from a fortune cookie I had opened two months before, qualifying Browning's exhortation: "Let your ambitions further, not overshadow, your accomplishments." Along with the book's title, these epigraphs were intended to suggest a range of meanings, on the one hand about anthropology as a discipline, but more specifically about my career as its historian (GS 2001a:v). Looking back as I near its end, that career seems to me to have been structured by the tension between reach and grasp, and a continuing attempt to reduce that tension and its associated anxieties by a commitment to my own version of Marc Bloch's "historian's craft": doing "good work."

Perhaps because so much of my work has been devoted to the problem of "influence" and to the influence of my own work, as well as to the related problems of "creativity" and the gap between "reach and grasp"

---

30. Since this passage was first drafted, the new monograph series, co-edited by Regna Darnell and Stephen Murray (published by the University of Nebraska Press), has been augmented by the first two volumes of an annual series entitled *Histories of Anthropology Annual*, co-edited by Darnell and Fred Gleach. In 2005, Darnell's contributions to the history of American anthropology were acknowledged by the AAA's Franz Boas Award.

as general human problems, a more general interest in "creativity" has become a background interest of my own.

Although I was not ungifted by birth and breeding, there were serious limitations to my enculturative experience, which in addition to my mother's *kulturkampf* of the 1930s included my father's equally formative poetic tastes, expressed in paying us a penny a line to memorize such virtue-strengthening pieces as Henley's "Invictus" and Kipling's "If." Despite my birth in Berlin and extended stays in Mexico and Spain, I remained in many respects a provincial Texan, still in the 1940s a bit exotic to my New York high school classmates, only lightly polished by four academically desultory years at Harvard, and then deliberately unpolished during seven more years as a Communist Party industrial colonizer. Valuable as that experience may have been in many ways, it was time away from a more conventional scholarly apprenticeship. Nor was this deficiency eliminated by my subsequent graduate training, rushed to completion in four years and diluted by an arguably dilettantish sampling of social science courses. So it was that in addition to enduring anxieties of disciplinary marginality, I have always felt that I was playing cultural catch-up as an historical scholar.

There were, of course, countervailing strengths, some of them paradoxically enhanced by my seven years in the Communist Party, especially insofar as the process of my disillusion contributed to my sense of the complexity of human motivation and of historical processes. In intimate personal life I fight a tendency to be judgmental, but in my scholarship my general impulse is to see the other side of an issue and its basis in different cognitive assumptions, cultural values, and life experiences. That, of course, has been historically a distinctive feature of modern ethnographic anthropology, which I have never practiced in the present but try hard to emulate in visiting the past of anthropology. In a similarly paradoxical manner, party episodes of "criticism and self-criticism" sharpened my deeply engrained Puritanical tendency to be critical of my own motives and behavior. My brother Myron, a psychoanalyst, contrasted his makeup as passionate and mine as obsessive—a dichotomy whose terms I passionately resist—although I do acknowledge a deeply rooted perfectionist need to worry things until I think I have got them as "right" as I am able to. Sometimes literally counterproductive, insofar as it may contribute to writing blockages, this radically self-critical tendency, applied to everything I write and by extension to anything I edit, is perhaps the most important ingredient in my personal version of the "historian's craft."

In this context, what is most striking about my work is the number of times that some large project was put aside (contemplated but not pursued, begun and abandoned, or blocked and redefined) in favor of something smaller and more manageable. Critics (my doubting self sometimes included) might say that instead of the "big picture" on a single canvas, I have in the end managed only a series of "vignettes" strung together in various ways. It is true that while I have imagined more ambitious ventures in grant applications, I have never seriously undertaken to paint on a single canvas a comprehensive view of the detail and sweep of centuries in the history of anthropology in all its various aspects. That said, there have been two books that after long blockages were eventually completed in coherently integral frameworks, ambitious and weighty enough in scope and detail that they may be called "big" (GS 1987, 1995). And insofar as others of my self-authored books might be called "collected vignettes," this does not imply an abandonment of my deeply engrained perfectionist principles so much as their refocusing (in terms of scale) and redefinition (in terms of process). If I could not be an historical artist painting on a large canvas, I would strive to be a conscientious historical craftsman, producing "vignettes" of high quality—and perhaps even another volume meriting the appellation of "big book."

That said, there is one more set of issues that is relevant here: my changing relation to anthropologists and to anthropology. Since my retirement in June of 2000, I have felt increasingly an outsider to the discipline. My contact with graduate students has dwindled to the point where recent cohorts are with few exceptions no more than nameless faces. I still retain an office and attend most departmental meetings, along with several others of the nonvoting emeriti. But by unspoken custom we sit in the back of the room, separated from the active and voting members not only by physical space and creeping deafness, but also by several decades of anthropology now receding rapidly into the realm of history, if not of myth.

These local feelings of superannuation are intensified nationally by frequent unfamiliarity even with the names of the candidates and elected officers of the American Anthropological Association, as well as of presenters of papers at the annual meetings. And although the topics of current anthropological discourse challenge my interest and are in a general way intelligible to me, the vocabulary in which they are discussed is one I do not customarily use; while I can (sometimes with difficulty) understand the language, I do not speak it, nor am I in total agreement with what I read or hear (since in some respects I remain, however ambivalently, a bit of a positivist neo-evolutionist).

In my more depressive moments, I have come to think of such processes as "islanding"—a word in the Oxford English Dictionary, but which I associate with John Updike, although I seem to have misplaced the reference. Donne's "no man is an island" to the contrary notwithstanding, there are members of some social categories who can become "islanded"—including (in modern Western culture) those consigned to mental institutions. As used here, it will refer to the cumulative effect of a wide range of forces that may impact an aging person, including not only those of physical and mental decay, but also the cultural changes associated with the rapidly advancing technology of the information revolution. In my own case they also include adaptations to the economic crisis—among them recently the use of smaller print and slicker pages, which make it harder to read the sources that connect me to the world. Even more recently they include a minor driving accident, with very little damage, which I was willing to blame on Toyota, but which Carol regarded as grounds for grounding me permanently. I would not suggest that "islanding" is universal among my anthropological age-mates: there are no doubt some who manage to stay afloat in the anthropological mainstream, as well as others on islands more frequently visited than my own. Metaphorically, my island is a "desert island"—visited perhaps by family and intimate friends, but cut off from contact with the contemporary world of anthropology.

Increasingly, I experience my relation to that world as obsolescence shading into irrelevance. Although still mostly favorable, references to my work seem often purely formalistic or honorific, and are frequently omitted in favor of current writers on the same topics, whose work I sometimes regard as dependent on or duplicative of my own. The problem, however, is larger than *amour-propre*. Personal alienation shades into historical interpretation. Since retirement I am more inclined to think of changes in anthropology as disjunctive rather than developmental, and the differences between "anthropology yesterday" and a postmillennial "anthropology today" as more fundamental than notions of paradigm change or pendulum swing or theoretical fashion (or, for that matter, intellectual progress) can easily encompass. The last half century has witnessed destabilizing changes in the character and circumstances of anthropology's human subject matter, of its personnel, of its methods, of its institutional, political, cultural, and global context, that have operated with transformative force. There may be a certain "species" similarity, consistent with a degree of myth-historical continuity, but in fundamental ways the discipline (if that term continues applicable) will never be the same again.

Assuming for the moment that the larger world in which anthropology exists will itself survive, my optimistic alter ego inclines me to think that institutions and a tradition called "anthropological" may continue to exist for some time to come. If so, it is likely that the desire and the project of connecting such a knowledge form to an historical tradition may also survive, whether for purposes of legitimation or validation, or simply for the satisfaction of historical curiosity or historical understanding. And within the community of practitioners and audiences of such a project, there may be some who will appreciate a history that aspires to offer a richly grounded, diversely empathic, and complexly articulated re-presentation (or re-familiarization) of the "different country" of a past anthropological world.

Against this, my pessimistic alter ego might suggest that this hope is simply an aging atheist's attempt to fan a few flickering fantasy flames of "influence" against the fast-descending darkness and nihilistic certainty of mortality. Perhaps they both might recall the words of a long-time comrade and dear friend, for whom it was a high compliment to say "you do good work"—and agree that over the years I have produced a substantial body of "good work." With luck, I hope to persist in working on the history of anthropology in the manner to which I have become accustomed and is now too late to change, and continue to produce "good work" for yet a while.

THREE

Octogenarian Afterthoughts

"Fragments Shored against My Ruins"

Further Steps down a Pyramid of Deterioration

Although the last several pages were drafted during the copyediting phase in 2010, the preceding section ("Doing 'Good Work'") was first drafted some time in 2000. Since then, there have been significant changes in my life and work situation—changes I have experienced not as steady decline, but as steps down a pyramid of deterioration. A very big step occurred in June of 2006, when I was in Malibu attending the high school graduation of my grandson Noah. It was an unusually hot afternoon, and before it was over I briefly passed out and was later taken to an emergency room on the other side of the Santa Monica Mountains. It was ten days—during which I had empty time to ponder the hierarchical miscommunication of information in hospitals—before I was released with a diagnosis of "atrial fibrillation." Since then my blood has been drawn monthly to check medications—and to remind me of my heart condition. During 2006 there was also a series of age-appropriate physical problems: arthritis, gout, symptoms of glaucoma, wobbly walking that quickly tired me out, as well as a bad fall that left me immobilized for two weeks and cane-dependent during an extended period of rehab—and still today for any long walk. Recently, I have had great trouble with any activity that involves bending to the floor—which makes it hard for me to look on lower shelves or to pick up the many things I drop in the course of a day. Along with persisting aftermaths of prior cancer episodes, all of this has made research much harder to manage, especially if it involves travel.

There have also been more specifically work-related problems— some old, some new, but taken together, increasingly bothersome: short- and long-term memory loss, frequent misreading of punctuation marks and words,[31] inability to locate research materials in plain sight on my desk, dead-end computer detours from hitting wrong keys, and frequent panicky brain freeze while staring at the screen of my computer— as well as nightly insomnia after the first three or four hours of sleep, which I try to fill with work-related reading, scribbling idea notes that often later prove illegible, or turning instead to soothing classical music on public radio. When I do get back to sleep, I very often (perhaps due to medication?) have long and vivid narrative dreams, which when I am able to remember them seem work related.

Over the last several years I have had a series of very devoted re- search assistants who, beyond normal research functions, have been my personal home computer techs, trouble shooting by phone and e-mail, or working with me at my apartment, which has become my primary worksite. Acting as advisers on the purchase of new equipment (a bigger screen, better lighting, a voice recorder, new programs, for which they have provided personalized tutorials), they have worked hard to en- hance my failing faculties. But they have not yet figured out a way to keep me from misreading words or hitting wrong keys. To make matters worse, the one mental faculty surviving this general deterioration is the one for critical evaluation—now directed primarily against my own work.

Beyond the department the processes of superannuation and mar- ginalization in the discipline at large have speeded up in the last decade.

---

31. Misreading can sometimes lead to humorous and symbolically significant results— as when (while perusing the *New York Times* one recent morning) I broke out laughing when I misread "experimental" as "experiential"—and on further thought realized that the slippage was not Freudian so much as Boasian. Recalling my earlier footnote on polarities and continua (above, p. 153), I came up with a number of other intellectual boundary issues that could be posed in similar terms, including not only Boas's between "physicist vs. historian" and "laws vs. phenomena," but also one between "epigram vs. enigma" that I came across in the *New Yorker* one morning in a review essay on recent work on the history of Christology—where, as in many other cases, it is a polar opposition sometimes blurred. The latter possibility in the case of my own historiographical thinking is the opposition between "provocative vs. evocative."

Despite an annual session in my name at the American Anthropological Association meeting, critiques of my work seem more often manifest. A major source for these critiques has been the work of David Price, who was briefly my student while earning an MA from our department in 1985. After receiving a PhD in archeology at the University of Florida in 1995, Price embarked on a study of Cold War anthropology, in which he is now recognized as a leading figure (Price 2004, 2008). Price has been extremely generous in sharing with me (and with students I have referred to him) his wide-ranging knowledge of research sources and current work, but there is no denying that we differ significantly in our historiographical assumptions (see above, pp. 169–73) and that he has been and continues to be a generative figure in recent critiques of my failings.

Another such figure, but with a somewhat different critical agenda, has been Peter T. Suzuki (my exact contemporary), who was an internee in Japanese relocation centers when I was in the Lincoln School on my way to Harvard. By the time I returned to graduate school in 1956 he had studied anthropology at Columbia, Yale, and at Leiden (in Holland)—from which he received his PhD in 1959 for a dissertation on "The Religious System and Culture of the Nias, [of] Indonesia." Over the next quarter century, he did ethnographic and linguistic research among Turkish peasants undergoing urbanization in Istanbul and in Germany, and as participant observer of jitney cabs in Omaha, Nebraska, where he was for many years a member of the faculty of the University of Nebraska, and carried on research among several Native American groups. In the late 1970s, Suzuki began to work on topics related to his internment experience, and since then has carried on a continuing critique of the role of "establishment anthropologists" in the camps and in their subsequent historiography (Suzuki 1976, 1980, 1981, 1986, 2009, in which my name figures prominently).

I say "my name" because the only specific reference to my work is to a single short sentence in a seventy-five page essay entitled "Thoughts toward a History of the Interwar Years" first published in 1976 as the introduction to a collection of papers called *American Anthropology, 1921–1945*. Embedded there in a paragraph about the involvement of anthropologists in World War II, the offending sentence is a small part of a nine-page discussion of a more general transition from "Cultural Critique to Applied Anthropology" in the interwar period. Slightly misquoted in the volume of my essays consulted by Suzuki, it reads there as follows: "John Embree, John Provinse, and other[s] were involved in the analysis of troubled communities of forcibly evacuated Japanese for the War Relocation Authority" (GS 1992:165). Wrenched from this context, that single sentence has been offered as evidence of my failures (if not sins) as an historian of American anthropology—and I have no doubt that the publication of the present "exercise in self-deconstruction," with its anxious commentaries on books unfinished and projects not undertaken, will provide truckloads of grist for the mills of criticism.

These mills now grind at a much faster rate than they did when I became an historian of anthropology in 1960. In the decades since, the "information revolution" has precipitated major changes in the world of anthropological scholarship—in its technology, its temporality, and in the size and character of its community. In the last decade the rate and scope of these changes have had an impact even on informational luddites like myself, who despite their resistance to direct participation, may nevertheless become involved as subjects of discourse in the "blogosphere" (it's in the OED)—as I recently discovered myself (see http://savageminds.org/2005/05/19/anthropologists-as-counter-insurgents).

While arguments can be offered for blogging as a democratization of human knowledge, my own experience suggests that, like many other advances in that realm, it is a double-edged sword. That said, it is also the case that once wielded, it is unlikely to be put down—until surpassed by another, sharper one. The general point, however, is worth encapsulating: changes in the world "outside" of anthropology, whether cumulative or catastrophic, reverberate within; in contrast, my basic historical orientation remains much the same—as does my general pessimism about the not too distant future in which my work as an historian of anthropology may yet be carried on.

In a prior draft of this material, written several years ago when I was trying to muster optimism about the years (or months) to come, I offered the possibility of a somewhat different future, which I recall now as yet another illustration of the tensions in my own outlook, and of the way the balance between these tensions responds to changes in my own psychological state and in the world "outside."

That said, it nevertheless seems likely that institutions and a tradition called "anthropological" will continue to exist, if only by disciplinary inertia, for some time to come. So also will the desire and the project of connecting the current knowledge form and the historical tradition, whether for purposes of legitimation, validation, or critique—or simply for the satisfaction of historical curiosity by historical understanding (if such an activity may be called "simple"). And within the community of practitioners and audiences of that project, I may perhaps hope that my works may retain a certain relevance for yet a while. If anxiety is the generator of interest, one may hope that readers with different anxieties and interests may find grist for their own mills of understanding and action in the present world.

There have been occasional exhilarative moments that reinforce that hope. One of the comments I prize most about my work was that of a reviewer who praised my "ability to breathe life into the dead" and to "capture the human dimension of anthropology's past" (Munson 1996). Another was when a student of Boas said to me "you gave us back Boas"—although my own remembered intention had been simply to try to understand Boas in historical context.[32] And while I am personally inclined to think that there may be losses as well as gains to anthropological understanding with the abandonment of the "four-field" tradition, it is pleasantly surprising when advocates of its disarticulation find support for their position in my short essay, published years before in an obscure venue, which referred to anthropological institutions as "guardians of the sacred bundle" (Segal and Yanigisako 2005; cf. GS 1988). At a more mundane level, whether or not it provokes or resolves anxieties, my work does so far continue to have some useful referential value for anthropologists and other readers of various interpretive persuasions.

In the several years since those words were written, changes in my own psychophysical state and in the state of the world "outside" have made it increasingly difficult to maintain the appearance of an optimistic outlook upon the future. The general point, however, is worth considering: although changes in the world "outside" of anthropology, whether cumulative or catastrophic, reverberate within, my basic historiographic orientation remains much the same—as does my general pessimism about the world's future.

---

32. There are those, however, who question my interpretation of Boas, including Quetzil Castañeda, who focuses on the issue of "influence" in specific relation to the history of anthropology in Mexico, but with comments on "Stocking's arguments for the conceptual unity of the Boasian 'tradition' and 'paradigm'" (Castañeda 2003:235).

The personal psychological result of all this is that depression, once intermittent, has for some time been my underlying psychological state—a quicksand sinkhole liable to drag me down at the slightest blockage in my work, making it extremely difficult to pursue my "terminal project" in a consistent manner. I am now finally on the verge of finishing this essay and will do my best also to keep work going on the Kluckhohn monograph, which might still be a significant contribution. However, it seems more likely that it will be my last "unfinished book," taking its place among other materials deposited in the Regenstein Library's Special Collections Research Center.

Increasingly doubtful of my ability to "do good work," I began to ask myself, "Why bother? Who really cares? Why not give up trying?" Instead, I could spend my remaining time (probably better measured in months than in years) listening to music I find soothing or invigorating, while perusing periodicals (most of them emanating from New York) that keep me somewhat abreast of current intellectual issues— and of national and global political developments, depressing though they may be. Or I could immerse myself in readings that take me into other historical or cultural worlds—or otherwise cast light upon the peaks and paradoxes of cultural or individual human creativity. Or I might simply lounge before a TV screen watching sporting events, science shows, historical re-creations, and Netflix—or searching the Internet for any topic that arouses my casual curiosity. All of which I do already, when unable to focus on "my work." Upon occasion, if her topic engages my interest, I watch Oprah, the most influential of the African American pop culture multimillionaires who have changed the world in which we live today. If all else fails, I might even work out on my exercycle.

Conjuring a Readership:
Yet Another Try at Influence

An epiphanal moment occurred in December 2007 when I received one of the most conscientiously constructive critiques I have ever experienced: a reading of what was then ostensibly a final draft of this essay, offered by my erstwhile student, dear friend, and wonderfully creative colleague in the history of anthropology, Ira Bashkow. Not only did it provoke me to write two new sections for the present version ("Divergent Family Histories within a WASP Tradition" and "Imagining a Future with Wilhelmina Davis") and to make numerous minor changes in response to his line-by-line comments, but I also felt compelled to deal with a more general question he raised: "In the end, one issue the essay doesn't really clarify is *why you wrote it*." Listing "constituencies" it might be addressing, Ira suggested that on the whole, it seemed to "conjure" its readership "as a composite audience that encompasses and also transcends them all":

So is it addressed in fact to your posterity, history, legacy, influence (all these are terms we give to ways in which some part of us may carry on beyond our lives' immediate confines)? Or perhaps "merely" (as if that were just something small) to your own profound sense of being observed and judged by others, a nonspecific chorus of others, a general public that is touched by your work and that cares about your merit? In some ways it's as if you were writing *for* (and not just about) your "black box."

Although I was at first somewhat put off by Ira's comments, they did inspire me to have another try at the issue of "influence" in the most general terms—only to find myself reiterating much that I had already said in the main text. Focusing instead on the possible influence of the "Black Box" essay itself, I began by following up an incidental biblio-graphic suggestion of Ira's: Jeremy Popkin's *History, Historians, and Autobiography*. Among the roughly three hundred books and articles Popkin listed as "Historians' Autobiographical Publications" (2005:69; cf. 307–22)—of which I have read only a few—there seems not to be one that by its title or Popkin's discussion would be what this essay attempts to be: "An Exercise in Self-Deconstruction."[33] Whether it is published before or after my demise, it seems likely that, whatever its flaws, its audience might include quite a few historians, anthropolo-gists, sociologists of science, and even literary theorists. Although a substantial number of these might be critical or even dismissive, the efforts of the last fifteen years would at least have provoked some thought.

Turning from the possible future influence of an essay written at the end of my career to the actual influence of one published at the

33. Searching the Internet for that phrase did produce one reference, in a film review: "What follows is either an exercise in self-deconstruction or a lesson in how not to write an ending; with *Limbo*, Sayles shows how high, and low, he can go . . . not to write an ending" (http://weeklywire.com/ww/06-07-99/boston_movies_clips.html).

With Ira Bashkow on the beach of Lake Michigan in May 1999, at the last of the student parties at our summer place in Beverly Shores—which was then in the process of being sold. Ira had just returned from fieldwork in two regions of Papua New Guinea and had begun work on his doctoral dissertation on the image of "the white man," which as subsequently published won the Victor Turner Prize for Ethnographic Writing. He is now associate professor of anthropology at the University of Virginia and (among other interests) works with his wife, Lise Dobrin (a linguistic anthropologist), on topics in the history of anthropology, including the controversy between Reo Fortune and Margaret Mead on the cultural personality of the Mountain Arapesh (see Bashkow 2006; Bashkow and Dobrin 2010).

beginning, consider again the 1965 editorial on "presentism and historicism." Although my own position has since evolved, there is evidence to suggest that subsequent historical study of the social sciences has been significantly influenced either directly or indirectly (whether for better or worse) by the issues it raised. While there are prior usages of both terms separately, searches so far undertaken indicate that the linked phrase was not used before 1965. And while the failure of some subsequent discussions to cite it could be simply an instance of the bibliographic amnesia that accompanies the forward march of disciplinary "progress," I prefer to think that it is an indication of the timeliness of the original linkage and the dispersion of its influence. Trying yet another approach, I drafted several more paragraphs, but it soon struck me that, except for a sentence here and there, I was once again repeating myself. And if I am bored, others will certainly be. So "enough already!"

Reconceptualizing Historicism: "Handling the Rich Complexities of the Lives of Others"

Putting aside, insofar as that seems psychologically possible, the question of influence, there is another issue that has preoccupied me recently that may be fruitful historiographically: "handling the rich complexities of the lives of others." As I recollect its genesis, the phrase harks back to Jack Nicholson's courtroom confrontation with Tom Cruise in *A Few Good Men*: "You can't handle the truth!" By a series of intervening associations, additions, and emendations I managed to transform Nicholson's volcanic outburst into an historiographic mantra—a retrospective characterization of the historicism I have sought to practice since the 1960s. As re-presented here, these emendations draw heavily on an early morning conversation with my wife Carol that made me consider the selection and implications of each word of the mantra.[34]

Rejecting the notion of a single "truth," the mantra nevertheless leaves open the possibility that some historical interpretations may

---

34. Belatedly, it occurs to me that my "historicism" has been developed primarily in relation to textually based inquiries, and its extension to archeology and physical anthropology would require more systematic discussion than I have time or energy to undertake at this late point.

offer understandings that seem to me more fruitful than others. It also requires a particular reading of "handle": one that emphasizes not only the psychological state of the historian but also the delicacy and richness of the subjects of interpretation. If I recall correctly, when I first began to use it, it was phrased differently: "Handling the rich complexity of human life." In the interim the final phrase was recast to eliminate evolutionary implications, and the words "complexity" and "life" were pluralized—thereby encouraging a shift to cultural plurality and relativism. Plurality may also, however, imply a focus on individual cases and by extension a biographical approach. Granted this emphasis may be historiographically problematic, it has long been a major theme in my own work, which for the most part has centered on the lives of individuals. But in my dotage this focus has narrowed, as I look back on my own life and the meanings thereof, and on the relationships that have made a difference: those with parents, siblings, wives, progeny, in-laws, students, colleagues, as well as the figures who are the primary subjects of my historical inquiry. For each of these, the interpretive problem may be formulated as "handling the rich complexities of the lives of others."

As a frankly egocentric projection of my terminal life situation, this reconceptualization of my historicism involves an implicit modification of the "concentric circles" approach that for decades has served as a model of and for my historiography. This, specifically as these relate to the future conditions of the world (national, international, global, cosmic), about which I am increasingly pessimistic, with little or no hope that anything I may do, alone or in concert with others, will prevent catastrophic changes. With Carol I share these pessimistic feelings more than I should. In the circles beyond—siblings, students, and progeny—I try hard to maintain a more optimistic outlook.

In April 2008, when my brother Myron in Minneapolis had a seriously incapacitating stroke that left him unable to speak but still able to listen to phone calls, I tried to tell him jokes I found on the Internet, in the hope that the therapeutic impulse of laughter might run along different neural tracks than the impulses that govern movement. Over time, however, he progressed to the point that we could actually carry on short conversations about his prospects of recovery, or about the elections, or about his plans to renew his work on "The Herne Chronicles"—an autobiographical roman à clef on which he had begun work some years before.

I also try to put aside my pessimism about the coming decades in the case of the few students with whom I am still in regular contact who are planning fieldwork, or writing up dissertations, or seeking jobs. Though reading manuscripts and writing letters has become a strain on my mental capacities, I try my best to offer constructive advice and support for projects of a postclassical, postcolonial, postmillennial (post-Stocking?) character.

The attitudinal shift is perhaps most striking in the case of my own ten richly talented grandparental progeny, whose voyages of self-discovery have given me so much vicarious pleasure. Were there space enough and time to write about the changing complexities of their lives I would have to meet the challenge of doing so in a manner that did not violate their concerns with privacy or discourage their dreams of the future—putting aside my global pessimism and abandoning myself momentarily to proud grandparental optimism.

Missing from the sequence above are my own children, who in the writing of this essay have presented several historiographical problems worthy of some comment. The account of their Berkeley experience in the paragraph describing them as among "the luckier ones" (see p. 84) is the end result of considerable negotiation. After reading the penultimate version of this essay, my daughter Melissa was concerned that its only treatment of my children as a group was in a footnote. To remedy this defect, I went back to my correspondence from the Berkeley period and, fascinated by its richness, drafted what I called "Melissa's Addendum"—which included among its many "juicy bits" her childhood aspiration to be a "star of stage, screen, and radio"—and who in her early teens played roles in two well-reviewed motion pictures. Becky, however, worried about privacy and informed consent in the new age of Facebook and Internet searches, objected to "Melissa's Addendum." When I discussed the issue with Melissa, she gracefully agreed to the present version. Although I have not again referred every one of the references still in the text to the children concerned, on the basis of recent exchanges I have reason to think that they will not be disturbed by them. Some readers of this paragraph may perhaps catch resonances of the previously discussed problems of writing a history of the present—as well as those of ethnographic fieldwork. But despite such limitations to any attempt to understand "the rich complexities of the lives of others," it remains in a general way the mantra of my historicism.

Office in a Storeroom:
Trashing the Icons of a Scholarly Life

As far as my own life is concerned, there has been a development, largely self-inflicted, that has been more depressing than enriching. In a fit of social responsibility, early in 2008 I volunteered to give up my large office on the second floor of Haskell Hall at the end of that calendar year. By that time, I would have entered my eighty-first year and my Mellon grant would have expired, and it did not seem to me appropriate to hold on to a prime piece of departmental real estate when it might be given to one of the half-dozen recent or prospective faculty appointees who would be much more involved in the activities of the department. Better that I should find some smaller space in Haskell for my occasional use.

When negotiations for the move began in October 2008, I was thinking in terms of a space on the second or third floor, but in response to Carol's worries that I might tumble down two flights of stairs, as well as my own need to be near a water fountain and a men's room, we decided that I should move down to the first floor. In the absence of free office space there, in June 2009 it was agreed that I might have a corner of the storeroom next to the faculty meeting room. Although the major portion of my new "office" was already filled by file cabinets of past student records and shelves of faculty and course catalogs, there was room under a window to create a cozy *pied-à-terre*, into which could be crowded a desk, two bookcases, and five file drawers—as well as a computer connection and a telephone.

Clearing out my old office and filling the new one, however, was a much more difficult problem than anticipated. By this time arrangements had already been made to deposit a major portion of my files into the university archives, but the actual packing and conveying of the first sixteen boxes required a lot of work, and there were many more research materials crammed into the new space, or otherwise disposed of. My old office had been jammed with several thousand books in a maze of bookcases created over the years from the discards of remodeled offices, which left only a narrow alley between the door and the windowed area in which I had consulted with students and carried on my scholarly work. In preparation for the move downstairs, over two thousand books were hauled away by second-hand dealers or given to colleagues and students. Left behind, however, were another thousand in which the dealers were not interested and more than a hundred

"Worrying a Word"—taken in my home office with my research assistant Debora Heard in June 2010. We were reviewing a passage in the copyedited typescript of this book, with the hope that the job could be completed before her then impending departure for Oxford University, where she would be doing archival research for a doctoral dissertation on religious manifestations of political organization and subjectivity within the ancient African state of Kush. In this phase she is analyzing the records of European archeologists who have excavated major Nubian temples from the Napatan and Meroitic periods. What I will do without her assistance was then a problem that had not yet been solved.

inscribed by their authors, some with fulsome acknowledgments—as well as reprints and books remaining on the freebie giveaway shelves outside my office door. There were also several dozen dissertations in which I played a significant role, almost all of them either published or in the library or preserved on microfilm, for which the only viable disposal solution was either trashing or shredding. The underlying problem, of course, was that changes in information technology were making physical texts obsolescent, if not obsolete: why bother with them when the information is easily available on the Web?

If I had died suddenly, emptying my office would have been handled by others, more efficiently and in a much shorter time—and with less emotional involvement. But for an anxiously obsessive person like my-self, it was quite a challenge. There was a great deal of dithering as to whether a particular book or document could still be useful in whatever scholarship I might manage in the time remaining to me—a triaging I was not willing to delegate to anyone else. To complicate matters it was not one triage but two, since it proceeded in two distinct stages: the removal of materials from one office and the cramming of a portion of them into another much smaller space. Fortunately, on the two mornings a week that I was then able to go from my apartment to Haskell Hall, I had the help of a dedicated and empathic research assistant, Debora Heard, who was pragmatically decisive in suggesting what might be done in particular cases, and who herself carried out much of the physical labor involved. Despite her best efforts, however, she was not able to alleviate the subtler psychological aspects of this process, which for me has been literally life-redefining, physically, emotionally, and symbolically. At the deepest level it represented a trashing of the icons of my scholarly life, which was doubly guilt ridden since I did not plan to make much use of my new sanctuary.

Becoming an Octogenarian and Accentuating the Positive

In December 2008 I composed a seasonal letter to be sent to people I care about most: progeny, siblings, old friends, students, and colleagues. This, in the spirit of Bob Dylan, who as five-year-old Bobbie Zimmerman had sung a song by Johnny Mercer at a Mother's Day celebration:

> You've got to accentuate the positive
> Eliminate the negative
> Latch on to the affirmative
> Don't mess with Mister In-Between
>
> You've got to spread joy up to the maximum
> Bring gloom down to the minimum
> Have faith or pandemonium
> Liable to walk upon the scene

The letter went on to "minimize such unseasonal topics as mental and physical deterioration, major computer breakdowns, office dispossession, financial disaster, international conflict and global warming" and "focus instead on one joyfully affirmative scene: George's 80th birthday celebration." The event was conceived by our California daughters, Melissa and Susan, and scheduled for October 11 because travel in December might be problematic. When the planning was inadvertently revealed to me, I opposed the celebration as costing money that could be put to better use. Finally, however, I relented, on condition that there be plenty of champagne and music. As master of local arrangements, Carol rented a large room in International House with a piano and a bar and hired a caterer—doubling the number of bottles of champagne he suggested. With Rachel's help she arranged for the housing of out-of-town guests—a dozen of whom slept in our apartment in beds or on couches or in sleeping bags. Although there were just over two dozen guests present at the dinner, they consumed all the champagne and a large carrot cake with eighty candles—which with help I managed to blow out in a single prolonged puff. But the highlight of the six-hour evening was the spontaneous program of traditional and original music and song offered by my multitalented extended family. All in all, it was an unforgettably joyous scene—photographed by our daughter-in-law Ari and others, from which I created a collage to hang in our apartment and refresh our memories in the months or years to come.

The event was particularly meaningful insofar as it reflected a new stage in my relationships to my daughters. Although Mina bore the primary burden of their daily care from infancy on, and after 1956 my time and energy were taken up largely by academic work, I did play an important role, both positively and negatively, in their child-rearing. I went with them to museums on weekends, helped put them to bed at night, made up bedtime stories, and tried to answer such big questions as four-year-old Rachel's "What happens when you die"?—to which I suggested that it was "like going to sleep and never waking up," and she worried that "you won't get any breckfesk." But there were also rules and punishments—on very rare occasions spankings (e.g., for biting a sister). When many years later I suggested to my eldest daughter Susan that child-rearing in most cultures required an ultimate deterrent, either psychological or physical, she christened this "the big-bang theory of child-rearing." Although I long ago gave up giving unsolicited advice and have tried with some success to develop a serenely empathic demeanor in our relations, there is still a tendency to recall the more dramatic episodes of the bad old days. Susan once told me that the father to whom she related was not the present me but a remembered authoritarian of her early childhood; by contrast, her sister Becky once complained that I had not forced her to make better choices in her teenage years: "You knew! You knew!" Eventually, I was inspired to coin a maxim: "There is no statute of limitations on the crimes of parenthood"—until my eightieth birthday suggested that while they might not be forgotten,

With Carol at my eightieth birthday celebration, in front of five of our ten grandchildren: (left to right) Samantha Stocking who is now in Chicago studying at DePaul University; Dorian Stocking, who since the party has started work on a futuristic science fiction novel to be entitled "The Mysterious Black Dragons" and projected in a detailed outline to be five hundred pages long, of which he has already written the first one hundred; Isabel Reidy, who recently took the band she had organized on tour in New England and subsequently came to Chicago to enter the School of the Art Institute; her elder sister Madeleine, who at the birthday party had just returned from an arduous and mostly solo bicycle trip from Guatemala to Arizona and who currently busks as a self-taught accordion virtuoso; and Nicky Baltrushes, a talented musician (composer, singer, performer) who at the time of the party was a second year medical student and later made a series of block prints illustrating symbolically the various pathologies studied in one of her classes, which her professor arranged to display outside the lecture hall, and who is now taking a

A multitalented musical trio improvising at the birthday party: (left to right) Melissa, who plays several instruments and since the party has become an accomplished salsa dancer; Tomas, who over the years has been involved in musical groups in the San Francisco Bay Area; Jim Reidy, a computer programmer who has long been active in numerous music groups, including one called The Chicken Chokers that specializes in "old time," a blues group, a zydeco group, a group called Toivo that plays "Finnish and Tex-Mex," and most recently The Rocking Steady Family Band (the first two words are a spoonerism for Stocking-Ready, listed in the OED as an early alternative spelling of "Reidy").

course at the Art Institute of Chicago with the goal of combining medical practice and art. Unable to be present at the party were: Robin Baltrushes, who was busy preparing for her board exams at medical school in Boston and is now a resident at a hospital in the San Francisco Bay Area; Noah Baltrushes, who was studying for undergraduate exams at U.C. Santa Cruz; Silas Reidy, who had left for Germany on a Rotary Club fellowship and is currently a student at SUNY New Paltz; Jesse Ruben, who was busy at his law practice when he wasn't sharing care of our three great-grandchildren while his wife Giulia was at school working toward a PhD in neurophysiology at U.C. Santa Cruz; and Evan Angus Smith, who was off to Peru as chief editor on a film called *Postales*, selected in 2010 as an entry in the Edinburgh Film Festival.

On the laps of my children, in order of age: Susan, Rebecca, Rachel, Melissa, and Tomas, the morning after the birthday celebration. The painting on the left behind them had caught my eye on a New Year's art tour in 2000 of sites around Aix-en-Provence that included a visit to the Saint-Remy convent and mental hospital in which Vincent Van Gogh spent a year shortly before his suicide. When I saw it on the wall outside the gift shop, in a fit of aesthetic enthusiasm I offered to buy it, to which the nuns responded almost ecstatically, explaining that it had been painted by an outpatient betrayed by her lover, who would be overjoyed when they told her that it had been sold. Unfortunately, most of our dinner guests have to be prompted in order to share my enthusiasm, leaving me to ponder with a certain sadness the relativity of artistic judgment.

they could be forgiven. With my death now a more immediate possibility, all my children are more inclined to cut me slack as a beloved elder, and they have each arranged several trips to visit while I am still around. There are issues we tend to shy away from, including some of the episodes of their adolescence, but we talk about a lot of things that have been avoided in the past—including the time when Melissa, while visiting us in Chicago, flushed marijuana down the toilet when I returned unexpectedly to our apartment and buzzed myself in with a bad joke about being an FBI agent. In short, I feel very close to each of them in this final stage of my life, and there are many signs that the feeling is reciprocated.

Myron Stocking in 1995 on the beach at Pauley's Island, South Carolina, during a visit with his eldest son, Ben, and Ben's future wife, Diana Measham. Most recently, she is a world health expert at Bill Gates's home base in Seattle, where Ben, after a decade as a journalist in Hanoi, is now working for the Associated Press. (courtesy of Ingrid Stocking)

I experienced a similar late-life closeness to my brother before his death in 2008. Several days before the eightieth-birthday celebration, I received news that Myron had died in his sleep, seven months after his paralyzing stroke, at a point when it seemed he might actually recover full functionality. Our sibling relationship over the years was in many respects agonistic—most strikingly when, on one of the rare occasions when we fought physically, he suddenly realized that "when I'm big enough to beat you up, we'll be too old to fight." Even so, he was my oldest and closest friend, especially in the last decade of his life, when, against his will, he was several times hospitalized as manic-depressive. As a traditional Freudian psychoanalyst he resisted the new pharmaceutical treatments, as well as the diagnosis itself. He was willing to grant that he was sometimes depressed and sometimes manifested manic behavior, but he was not willing to define himself in these terms, and in our long early morning telephone conversations, I always respected his view. Although thought by some to be a "facilitator," I

experienced our talks as an enrichment, enabling me to recognize similar tendencies in myself and to embrace Myron as an alter ego. Three
days after the birthday celebration, Carol and I flew to Minneapolis
for the funeral, where I gave one of the eulogies and took back to
Hyde Park Myron's cane—still in daily use as a permanent token of his
earthly presence. I have also negotiated with the archivist at the University of Minnesota to establish a collection of his papers, which contain quite fascinating autobiographical and clinical material, including
his analysis of an anthropologist who worked with Somali victims of
genital mutilation.

The Audacity of Hope and
the Politics of Mr. In-between

Although Myron did not live to experience the ecstasy of Barack
Obama's election to the presidency, he had volunteered his services
to the Obama campaign in December 2007. As a skeptical realist, I
was then still for Hilary Clinton and continued to waver even after I
climbed upon "the Obama Bandwagon" at the end of January 2008.
Throughout the campaign, my worries continued: that the Democrats
would "blow it," that Hilary would be a "spoiler," that Obama would
be "swift boated," that he might even be assassinated, that Sarah Palin
might actually appeal to a substantial portion of the electorate, and that
Obama might abandon his liberalism. But in September 2008 I salved
my own inactivist liberal conscience by donating to his campaign
$1,200 from the sale of a portion of my books.

Watching the election results through the night of November 4 was a
whirlwind of emotions: moments of joy, moments of tearful exaltation,
moments also of fear, all of them replayed many times on TV. While it
had clearly been a "world historical event," it also seemed in terms of
timing an accidental one: had the recession manifested itself a month
later, it seems not unlikely that the election might have gone the other
way. At the time, I could not help worrying about its fragility: even
barring assassination, "the management of all the grim realities of the
world . . . would be a much tougher and more compromising process
than momentary exaltation imagines."

For a brief historic moment, his inauguration did inspire a surge of
euphoria even higher than that of the election itself: some two million
people crammed on the Mall beyond the Capitol steps and millions

more watched on television. By this time, however, the dark realities challenging his presidency had exploded in magnitude. Domestically— but with global implications—these involved the interdigitated "trickle down" of a whole series of major economic problems (including financial collapse, business failure, home foreclosure, rising unemployment, consumer retrenchment—not to mention skullduggery to the point of criminality). The result was an almost unprecedented economic "perfect storm"—a reality so desperate as to provoke a crisis in traditional American cultural values, in which a backward-looking notion of the rights and self-interests of the individual against the state was confronted by a forward-looking vision of the welfare of the individual within a social collectivity. Internationally, the post-inaugural situation included not only the difficulties of a rapid withdrawal from Iraq but also the threats posed by failing states in Afghanistan and Pakistan, by the rising state of Iran and the rogue state of North Korea, by the deeply rooted and explosive crises on the Mediterranean shores of the Middle East, and by the continuing threat of terrorism even after years of "war" against it—not to mention the looming threat of global warming. Even before Obama took the oath of office, these problems were overflowing on his plate and nonetheless intractable insofar as they were abandoned leftovers of the policies of the Bush regimes. Furthermore, the timetable for dealing with them was now pushed back at least two years—during which conditions locally and globally might worsen (and did) and greater sacrifices might be (and have been) required among all but the most privileged sectors of the population—including corporation lawyers looking for loopholes in a "bailout plan," venture capitalists seeking products that might be depression proof, business-people marketing their wares as "stimulus packages"—as well as vulture capitalists scamming to enrich themselves by preying on those about to drown.

While there were specific preventive and ameliorative steps that could be taken by action within the executive branch, there were also miscues and missteps (even self-acknowledged "goofs") that played into the hands of ideological opponents of the immediate and longer-run legislative measures that would be required to address the larger issues. In negotiating them Obama has had to deal on the one hand with Republicans who can think only in terms of tax reduction and opposition to "big government," and who regard fresh initiatives of foreign policy as betrayals of national security in the "war on terrorism." And on his left hand, there are the disappointed Democrats committed to a more active government intervention sustained by tax increases for the wealthy—as well as to more radical approaches on many issues of international affairs. It was in this context that I began to think of Obama as "Mr. In-between."

It was only after the inauguration and Obama's first White House press conference that I was inspired to read the two best-selling autobiographical books that demonstrated the extraordinary quality of his mind (Obama 1995, 2006). Wide ranging, sociologically sophisticated, historically grounded, self-critical, and adaptively visionary, he displayed a constellation of mental attributes rare in a political leader. From my own historicist point of view, the most striking was "empathy"— which Obama spoke of as "the heart of my moral code . . . not simply as a call to sympathy or charity, but as something more demanding, a call to stand in somebody else's shoes, and see through their eyes." Discussing it at length, he suggested that empathy was largely an inheritance from his mother, Stanley Ann Dunham. From his own account and from other sources we learn that as a pregnant teenager, she had married Obama's father and namesake in 1961 while they were both students at the University of Hawaii, unaware that he had another wife back in Kenya. Several years after their divorce in 1964, she married again, this time to Lolo Soetero, an Indonesian who worked as a government relations consultant for the Mobil Oil Company, returning with him to Jakarta along with her six-year-old son. After she gave birth to a daughter in 1970, Soetoro's desire for more children ran counter to her hope of pursuing graduate studies, and in 1972 she sent her son back to her parents in Hawaii, returning herself two years later to enter graduate school in anthropology. When she went back to Indonesia to undertake fieldwork in 1977, Obama—by then known as "Barry"—chose to remain with his grandparents until his graduation from high school. By his account, he was "a rebellious teenager," who in his senior year had a kind of empathy epiphany, gradually "awakening" to the realization that by constantly resisting authority, he was "in some way diminishing myself" (Obama 2006:67–69).

Obama's empathy had few limits. Insisting that "no one is exempt from the call to find common ground," he professed an obligation to see the world through George Bush's eyes, "no matter how much I may disagree with him." In the end, however, "a sense of mutual understanding" was not enough: "like any value, empathy must be acted upon." Drawing on his experience as a community organizer in Chicago, Obama argued that the true test of our values was a willingness to pay a price for them in "time, energy, and money." Failing that, we should ask ourselves "whether we truly believe in them at all."

Without going into specific detail on every issue, I would suggest that Obama's two autobiographical volumes, carefully considered, foreshadow both the content and the style of his mode of governance. Although by birth and early experience a multiculturalist, both nationally and internationally, there are fundamental aspects of his ideals that are quite traditionally "American"—in the "beacon on a hill" mode of the "founding fathers" and the "pilgrims." As their titles and subtitles suggest, both books are about "dreams": *Dreams from my Father* is a multicultural "Story of Race and Inheritance"; *The Audacity of Hope* offers a political agenda for "Reclaiming the American Dream." From this point of view, Obama and Bush, as well as FDR and the four presidents on Mount Rushmore, may be said to share a common vision of American exceptionalism.

True, there is literally a world of difference between the ideologies, the goals, and the political practices of Barack Obama and "Dubya" Bush. Obama's attempts to realize his view of the American Dream in legislative terms by negotiation and compromise have been to a great extent stonewalled by those who conceive the American Dream in very different terms, who regard negotiation as a sign of political weakness, and whose resistance is at times implicitly if not overtly racialist. On the other hand, Obama's pragmatic willingness to settle for the "best possible" rather than the ultimately ideal has led him sometimes to accept or adopt positions and policies, legislative, diplomatic, and even military, that are similar or even identical to those of the Bush/Cheney regime—and in all probability inadequate to stave off the disasters facing not only our country but humankind in general. Back in the early months of 2009, when I first drafted this section, I had just enough audacity to hope that Obama's presidency would lay the basis for "a longer and more livable world future" than "my default pessimism will permit." But in the face of recent Democratic electoral setbacks and the resurgence of deep-rooted anti-governmental and anti-"other" tendencies among large groups of American Dreamers—and the consequent likelihood that Obama will be a one-term president—there is not much left of my own "audacity of hope" for the future of the nation or the world. However, for the sake of my progeny I will do what I can to nurture it.

Notes from the Edge of the Abyss:
The Serenity Prayer and Pascal's Wager

In the spring of 2009 I had a surge of optimism and wondered why. Perhaps it was the vernal equinox rebirth of life after a long winter of mourning my brother. Perhaps it was the impending completion of my office transfer, or even of this "Black Box" essay—for there were already signs that I might once again foil Zeno by leaping across to the finish line. Six months later it seems that I am doing that and in the process have accomplished a feat that sixty years ago seemed totally unrealistic and even fifteen years ago rather unlikely: namely, to be living and still functional into the twenty-first century. Having been born in the "twenties" and still alive as we enter the "teens," I have actually accomplished a centenary cycle at the beginning of my eighty-second year. The question thus suggests itself: what will my life be like, what kind of person will I be, in the time that remains to me?

Recently, I have tried to think of the future in terms of the Serenity Prayer—which I vaguely recall as a favorite of my sister Sybil. An Internet search revealed its full text and history, as the work of the distinguished American theologian Reinhold Niebuhr. Composed by Niebuhr in the pre–World War I period, it was subsequently appropriated and popularized by Alcoholics Anonymous and other self-helpers—of whom I have long been one: "grant me the serenity to accept the things I cannot change, courage to change the things I can, and wisdom to know the difference." In keeping with my atheism and pessimism, I think of this not as a prayer but as a behavioral mantra appropriate to the final phase of my life, in both its professional and personal aspects.

Carol cannot avoid my darker fits, and her worldview (though few would guess it from her lively public demeanor) is even darker than mine. She can still quote passages of Shakespeare from memory, including Macbeth's agonized lament that life "is a tale / Told by an idiot, full of sound and fury, / Signifying nothing." But if she does not believe in the Serenity Prayer, she still enjoys sharing with me the occasional solace of a toast attributed to the French poet and diplomat Paul Claudel: "In the brief moment between the crisis and the catastrophe, there is always time for a glass of champagne"—a favorite drink of Carol's, who has always found delight in bursting, sparkling things, including fireworks, twinkling night lights, and even hydrangeas. When there is no longer time left to share with her this sybaritic substitute for the Serenity Prayer, I hope to find the courage to call Pascal's bluff before tumbling into the abyss of nothingness.[35] Compared to all the hundreds of millions of humankind, past and present, my life has been a very lucky one.

35. As a final instance of my oedipal problems as life-shaping factors, I offer this memory of my father. In March of 1973, during my second research trip to England, he came to visit me after my mother's death. When on one occasion he looked the wrong way in crossing a street, I had to grab his arm to pull him back and was struck by how physically strong he still was. Days later, on a hill overlooking Edinburgh, what struck me was the emotional weakness that seemed to overcome him in his grieving, when he asked me if I believed in an afterlife. Although I recall parrying his query out of respect for his sorrow, I could not help but feel that, after a half century as unbeliever, he wondered if he should perhaps accept the terms of Pascal's wager. Instead, he settled for solace and support in a marriage that September to another resident of the retirement home, whom his children could never embrace, but with whom he lived until his death in 1976.

Epilogue

Penelope's Shroud, Zeno's Paradox, and the Closure of the Black Box

Although Carol has served (along with the Internet) as a substitute for my failing memory and has sometimes commented on a problematic passage I have read aloud to her, by her own choice she has never actually read the "Black Box" essay. She has, however, commented on the process of its composition. This, by reference to Homer's Penelope, who during Odysseus's twenty-year absence kept would-be suitors at bay by weaving a shroud for her father-in-law Laertes and each night undoing the work of that day. But since my modifications of this text have mostly been by insertion rather than deletion, I prefer the analogy to Zeno, who kept the race going by the logical manipulation of its length. Having prematurely celebrated with champagne the printing of a "last penultimate version" on May 20, 2009, within two days I opened a file of "Changes since the May 20th printout." A few days later, it occurred to me that to foil Zeno once again by leaping across his half-way gap, I needed a coda (offered here as an epilogue) to make clear why and how the "Black Box" was closing at this point. For a while, I wondered if the ideal moment of completion might be the moment of my own death, leaving to Carol and designated advisers the issues of publication and preservation, of audience and access.

At the end of 2009, however, I was still around, still tinkering with the "Black Box," still worrying about issues raised in its "penultimate version." Some of these related to content (am I more conservative, politically and methodologically, than I have allowed myself to admit?). Others had to do with audience and future disposition: Did I want my children to read this while certain autobiographical topics affecting them remain unresolved? Did I really want the general scholarly world (including my critics) to have this much access to my darker side? Would my black box perhaps be more aptly named Pandora's? Does anyone really care? Will the end of the scholarly world as we know it (whether by global warming or by atomic disaster) come so soon that issues of preservation and access will no longer be relevant? Eventually, however, I decided that to continue to worry about such issues might forestall indefinitely the closure of the "Black Box"—and thus allow Zeno once again to triumph, after more than a decade of my hard work. The only way to foil him was to initiate the process of publication, with the hope that I may still be around and functional enough to see it actually accomplished.

The likelihood of that outcome, however, was compromised by a prior diagnosis of MCI (mild cognitive impairment), for which my primary care physician (PCP) prescribed the then standard medication Aricept, which is marketed as stalling the advance of Alzheimer's. Unfortunately, however, I was extremely susceptible to its side effects, so much so that (in the spirit of my brother Myron) I refused to go ahead with the treatment, hoping that I would somehow manage to see the "Black Box" essay through to publication. It was in this context that an old friend of mine, in touch after many years, reported that she had a similar reaction to Aricept, but had tried "alternative" non-pharmaceutical treatments (among them herbal remedies, Yoga, meditation—and perhaps controlled doses of lithium) that seemed to work for her without side effects. Coincidentally, I also watched two episodes of *The Dr. Oz Show* devoted to "alternative" therapies—many of which he took quite seriously, although translating them into brain-function terms. For a month or so, I was tempted to reject big pharma and go with Dr. Oz and at least part way with my old friend, but I continued to vacillate even after my PCP offered a more recently developed pharmaceutical treatment (the Exelon Patch) that, although more convenient in application, listed a similar array of possible side effects.

Not for the first time in my life, I was faced with an anxiety-charged choice between very different therapeutic options. In the event, I decided to go with the majority vote of those closest to me. My doctor daughter Rebecca, who is always my "second opinion" in medical matters, sided with my PCP—as did two of her sisters and my wife Carol. Despite my deeply rooted (and to my mind quite realistic) pessimism about my own future and that of the world, I have chosen to assume that I will see the "Black Box" essay through publication—and that, in the spirit of the Serenity Prayer and my life-long propensity for

On a walking tour of Vermont in the early 1990s, Carol and I visited the Ben & Jerry's ice cream factory in Waterbury, where we sampled the flavors and purchased this striking T-shirt. Neither of us can remember exactly where or when the picture was taken, but the Cherry Garcia flavor is still available at our local Treasure Island Market.

New Year's resolutions, I will devote my remaining time and energy above all to Carol and my progeny.

To relieve her of the burden of cooking when she comes home tired from work, I will try every week to cook a more-than-one-meal dish, as well as serving as willing sous-chef and dishwasher on those occasions when she is inspired to give a feast for our shrinking circle of intimate friends. For my health and hers, I will join her on early morning or after dinner walks when weather permits. To enrich our evenings, I will spend less time watching TV and more reading aloud to her (which she greatly enjoys)—currently A. S. Byatt's very long but very rich *The Children's Book* and after that something other than the joint comparative reading of R. Crumb's graphic novel version of Genesis and my father's copy of the King James Bible (which I suggested and she summarily rejected). Insofar as I can do so without being a bother, I hope to go with her on local outings and to cultural events, and perhaps again to accompany her on more extended travels. Or if that is not possible, I will accept with good grace her plan for twenty-four-hour paid assistance while she is away or some other means of calling for help during her absence. And in the meantime, I will try to complete the task of clearing our apartment of the numerous remaining relics of my scholarly career.

If I still then have the competence and energy to seek nonscholarly outlets for my creative urges, there are several possibilities. I no longer have the tactile sensitivity required for Christmas stockings or musical instruments, nor the voice for singing, nor the finger control for drawing. A more likely possibility might be one of the small-scale literary ventures that I have worked on in the past: "Memory Archetypes," Haiku, sonnets, limericks—all of which have in common that they are defined by formal requirements that give them a puzzle solving character.

The idea of the "memory archetype" came to me in an early morning brain race in January 2004. Derived from personal experience rather than numerous intellectual historical precursors (e.g., Jung), my archetypes assume that human memory (or at least my own) is by nature highly selective and that in recollecting the past we choose (consciously or unconsciously) aspects with paradigmatic potential in order to give meaning and unity to our behavior, our beliefs and our character. Initially, my plan was to write a one-page archetype daily for a collection I would call "An Aesop's Album of Memory Archetypes." However, more pressing obligations made it difficult to sustain that pace, and I soon put the project aside. When I resumed it two years later, I decided not to limit it to my own experience but to supplement that with the experiences of "significant others" who influenced my being and behavior (notably, my father and my mother), and to allow myself to check dates and events against photographs and documents that over the years had been preserved or happened to come into my possession. Although failing memory may make it difficult for me to resume the project, I could perhaps complete the album for family circulation. Over the years, I have also several times dabbled with various short poetic forms, usually inspired by experiences in which my children were involved. Most recently, there was an album of Haiku (GS 2001b), and in the late 1950s and early 1960s there were sonnets and limericks, a number of which were included in 1962 in a short-lived family magazine we called *Sisyphus*. And of course there have been several attempts (now technologically outmoded) at round robin family newsletters.

To maximize contact with my progeny when mutual visits become difficult to manage, I will try not only to keep in frequent touch by old-fashioned telephone calls, but do my best to learn to use the postmodern means by which they communicate: Facebook, Skype, and texting—as well as to update the outmoded language still in use on my shrinking island. Four of our grandchildren (Evan, Nicky, Isabel, and Samy) are currently settled in Chicago, and we may be able to manage gatherings or outings with them and members of their considerable cousinage who live in the Chicago area or who make it a rest stop in their travels back and forth across the continent.[36]

Insofar as there may still be "world enough and time"—and mental functionality—left over after the publication of this "essay" for the intellectual "work" that has been a driving force in my life, there are various scholarly activities that I might reengage. I could respond more positively to requests for manuscript evaluations, or perhaps accept one of the speaking invitations I have for some time been refusing, or even attend a scholarly meeting outside of Chicago. I might even reengage the Kluckhohn manuscript, which exists now as a draft of two hundred pages, or if that proves too daunting, at least prepare it for publication in abbreviated form. Who knows, perhaps there will be

36. Carol has no relatives in this country; there is no active tradition of cousinage in the Stocking family—unless you count Facebook.

synapses in this old geezer's brain still firing when we learn whether Obama will be more than a one term president—and whether a world will still exist in which he can play a leading role. In the spirit of the "Black Box" itself, I might then try the essay I imagined in one of my recent early morning brain races: "The Unsaid, the Said, the Unsayable: 'Handling the Truth' in Psychological, Cultural, Historical and Scientific Context."

While there are surely more glimpses into my black box that might be gleaned from note slips scattered here and there in file drawer folders or desktop piles, there are corners and crannies that will remain obscure—in some cases because the corners were too dark to penetrate, in others because I could not bring myself to look too closely, in still others because I saw and have chosen not to reveal their contents.

Striving for Perfection and Accepting the Terminal Realities of Life: Final Notes on the Making and Completion of This Book

In an earlier draft of this volume, I composed a rather boring introduction I called "The Making of This Book"—which on second thought I deleted as a distraction from the book itself. To replace it, I then used a brief (and hopefully more readable) essay that had previously served as prologue to "Autobiographical Recollections." With the book now finished, more than a decade in the writing, I am here offering further "afterthoughts" to bring the "Black Box" essay up to date from the time since its previous "Final Closure."

To begin with, it may be helpful to refer again to events prior to July 1, 2010, as well as those in July and early August of that year, which has been perhaps the single most critical period in the production of this book, if not in my whole scholarly and personal life.

Although I wrote a sixty-page draft of the "Black Box" essay in the spring of 1998, it was another ten years before serious planning began for the publication of a draft that by then was twice as long. That possibility was first broached in the late spring of 2007, in an e-mail to me from Gwen Walker, the acquisitions editor of the University of Wisconsin Press, which had been publishing my work for almost fifteen years. She had just had a conversation with Betty Steinberg, who was aware of work I was doing on an autobiographical essay. For a variety of reasons, however, the contract for the present volume was not signed until early in March 2010.

Although by July 1, 2010, these problems seemed close to resolution, what remained was to seal the deal in time to meet the publisher's deadline: the American Anthropological Association meeting of November 2010, at which printed copies (or failing that, page proofs) of the book were to be available for display and sale. Unfortunately, the impending reality of this longed-for moment had the side effect of focusing long-felt mixed emotions. On the one hand, it discouraged any further comments by my wife that my inability to complete the "Black Box" essay was in effect a means of holding death at bay and delaying the time when "revelatory moments" in the book might offend people close to me, including family members and departmental colleagues—as well as providing grist for the mills of critical reviewers in anthropological or other journals. Acknowledging these possibilities, I nevertheless preferred to think that delaying completion would give me time to bring the manuscript closer to perfection.

Perfectionism, expressed in certain virtues realized in achievement and rewarded with success in life (notably those of self-reliance and self-control), is of course an American character trait at least as old as Benjamin Franklin. Whether or not my father actually read *Poor Richard's Almanack* or Franklin's *Autobiography*, he instinctively thought in the same terms, which were also manifest in the child-rearing manual published in the year of my birth: J. B. Watson's *Psychological Care of Infant and Child* (cf. Kell and Aldous 1960).

My mother bought the manual some months before my birth, and it did not simply gather dust on a shelf. The annotations in the copy I inherited in 1960 suggest not only that my parents read it, but that they applied it in their daily child-rearing practices—including not only the draconian cure prescribed for thumb-sucking, which would teach me self-control, but also the holes dug in the back yard, from which I was left to climb out on my own, which would teach me self-reliance. Ultimately, Watson's precepts systematically applied would be the basis for a powerful achievement motive, which went well beyond the army recruiting slogan "be all that you can be." According to my mother's version, even if I was just a garbage man I should strive to be "the best garbage man in the world" (see above, p. 62). In short, I experienced Watsonian child-rearing in a rather extreme form, the permanent marks of which were later evidenced in my own obsessive-compulsive perfectionism (see above, pp. 127, 144, and 154)—which implies not only a need for self-control, but also a need to control the responses of others, including the readers of these "afterthoughts." This pattern, moreover, has been a recurrent theme over the years of my life. Faced with crisis, I am likely to turn to self-analysis and to resolutions as a basis for future action that will result in reward rather than in punishment. Perhaps a residue of my early Protestant upbringing (see above, p. 29), this pattern was strikingly manifest in my response to criticism in the Communist Party's "struggle against white chauvinism." A recent re-reading of my diaries suggests that the pattern was pervasive, especially in the seriousness with which I have approached the annual ritual of making New Year's resolutions (see above, p. 208).

In this context, I came to realize that the "Black Box" essay might be viewed as an amalgamation of three components, Part 1 is autobio-graphical, Part 2 is historiographical, and Part 3 consists of terminal thoughts. Furthermore, in the years since my retirement from teaching, the autobiographical tendency has become dominant in a manner that has created tensions, which are especially evident in the relationship between the main text and the footnotes and illustration captions. Because the project was not conceived or constructed primarily as an auto-biography, there were omissions and gaps concerning important events in my life that were not explicitly historiographical. As a result, I found myself constantly impelled to use the footnotes and captions to introduce what seemed to me to be necessary autobiographical material that did not bear a clear relationship to the historiographical project. To those inclined to dismiss all this as whining about the universal problems of old age, for which there are pharmacological or technological remedies or palliatives, I can only plead a bias against pharmacology due to prior experience with its side effects and a general incompetence coping with technological advances.

During the month of July 2010, such issues contributed to an almost paralyzing stress, marked on the one hand by psychological problems I have had over my lifetime (e.g., my frequent difficulty finishing books), as well as physical problems manifest over the last decade (including gout, the loss of manual dexterity, mobility difficulties, memory lapses, etc.) that had become more intense, as well as cumulative in impact, at a time when I was in a rush to finish the book, in order to meet the deadline for its completion. Among these were chronic insomnia, and even worse, occasional incontinence. The most dramatic problem, how-ever, was a fall on July 8 that bounced me against furniture for ten feet, until I grabbed the back of an easy chair to stabilize myself, causing it instead to fall backward and pin me to the floor, from which I was not able to get up for twenty minutes. In the process of the fall, I suffered a hematoma on my right hip that caused extensive bruising from above my crotch to the tip of my toes, and since then I have been virtually confined to our apartment.

Compounding the crisis was the impending departure of my very helpful research assistant Debora Heard, who boarded a plane for England on July 23. All of this left me seriously depressed and unable to work effectively. Fortunately, however, on the day immediately following Debora's departure, my spirits were uplifted (occasionally rising even to manic moments) by her replacement, Saul Thomas, who was a member of "my last class" ten years ago and my research assistant for the following year. With his help in the two weeks following, we were able to narrow the gap between reach and grasp to a point where I was comfortable sending in the finished manuscript to Adam Mehring, the managing editor of the University of Wisconsin Press, on August 9.

The weeks after Monday August 9 promised to be a somewhat happier period, enriched by visits from each of my children. On that day, my daughter Susan stopped over for a brief visit on her trip west. On August 25 my son Tomas arranged to bring his daughter Samantha to Chicago for her entering orientation at DePaul University on August 28; my daughter Rebecca arrived that same day with her daughter Isabel for the orientation at the School of the Art Institute of Chicago; we also expected Rachel to drive up from Carbondale to attend my children's Aunt Terry's seventieth birthday celebration. To complete the circuit, Melissa was scheduled to stay with me when Carol left on September 8 for a ten-day tour of the sites of Jane Austin's *Pride and Prejudice*. Anticipating the appearance of my book at the AAA meetings in late November, it seemed possible that my spirits and my functionality might remain high until the end of 2010. Although Saul Thomas, in preparation for research in China, finished working for me on August 8, I had by then already engaged another extremely capable and multicultural research assistant, Yaqub Hilal, to work with me in the final stages of the publication of this essay and to pursue the possibilities of publishing some of my research on Clyde Kluckhohn. The three of us met together on August 10 to review the status of the "Black Box" essay, after which I left the room so Saul could brief Yaqub on what it was like to work for me. Two days later I met alone with Yaqub to discuss in more detail the work that we might carry on together prior to January 1, 2011. Before this second meeting, however, I had a major episode of insomniac self-analysis, to the accompaniment of Peter Van De Graaff's music program *Through the Night*. Seven nights a week he draws from a fabulous personal collection of recordings, and from a deep well of knowledge of the lives of their original composers and the circumstances of their creation, in order to elucidate such matters as their reinterpretation in changing cultural contexts, including such "events" as the invention or modification of musical instruments. By leaps of analogy, I often find *Through the Night* very helpful in thinking about my own current work in a very different realm of human creativity. On this occasion it made me think about my work with Yaqub, which I now visualize as divided into two parts. On the one hand, there are the final steps in the publication of my "Black Box" essay and the exploration of further work on Kluckhohn. On the other, there is the possibility of smaller and more manageable future projects, which, should my fears about the critical reception of the "Black Box" essay prove unwarranted and my creative optimism and mental functionality remain strong enough, might sustain serious intellectual activity for at least some months after December 31.

In addition to the future publication of an abbreviated Kluckhohn manuscript (or parts thereof) there is "The Said, the Unsaid, and the Unsayable," which I now envision as having significance not only in my own work, but for anthropology throughout its history and in relation to its present prospects. And there are other topics that have come to mind in moments of creative insomnia, including a paper about students of mine who have not become professional anthropologists (tentatively entitled "Exceptional Cases: Students Who Have Gone on to Stellar Careers in Areas Outside of American Academic Anthropology")— students who may have disappeared from departmental records but with whom I have continuing or recurring personal contact, who have become influential in various different contexts, including the annals of popular culture. In my own case these include Sarah Paretsky (the novelist) and Gabrielle Lyon (executive director of Project Exploration, which helps minority students from Chicago Public Schools to go to college and even to become paleontologists). Other anthropologists may be familiar with similar cases, either present or past, including icons of popular culture such as Kurt Vonnegut and Zora Neale Hurston, going back to Andrew Lang and beyond.

Another possible topic would be my experience of "Ethnographic Tourism"—which was often enriched by kinship or other connections, and would not have been likely without them—in places such as Moscow, Morocco, Japan, and Yugoslavia (see above, pp. 97–99 and 104; GS 1984b), as well as my own experience of being "Lost in Translation," when in 1987 I gave the distinguished lecture at a conference of Spanish anthropologists. Although I had drafted the lecture in

English, it was then translated into Spanish by the conference organizers, who subsequently congratulated me on the excellence of my
Spanish pronunciation—only to leave me isolated from their rapid-fire
luncheon conversation, in which I kept making wrong linguistic turns.
At the end of the day, I politely declined an invitation to join them for
dinner, returning instead to my hotel room, where I collapsed on my
bed exhausted both mentally and physically. And there are a number of
other conferences that left me similarly embarrassed and exhausted. All
of these made me think of my own ethnographic limitations as characteristic of ethnographic anthropology for centuries back (see above,
p. 117; GS 1984b).

While such small-scale scholarly ventures may keep me going for a
while, a time will surely come in the not-too-distant future when I will
no longer be capable even of smaller-scale personal and family projects
(such as a family blog) that, in the spirit of E. M. Forster's "only connect," might keep me for a while in contact with the outside world,
rather than stranded alone on my desert island. And should that become no longer possible, I hope that I will already have managed to get
my affairs in order, so that I and my loved ones may experience my final
demise not as a senescent decline toward total decrepitude and a lingering death, but as the quick result of a "spontaneous evanescence"—
preferably in the form of a fatal stroke, of which there have been quite a
few in my family.[37]

37. The text above neglects what at other points in this essay have been an important
context of my scholarly work: my mental and physical health, in which there have recently
been significant developments—notably, continued short-term memory problems and
a general physical instability. To deal with the former, I have begun the daily use of the
Exelon Patch—so far without any noticeable ill side effects. As to the latter, I have finally
agreed with my wife Carol that I should not be left alone in our apartment and have
accepted her offer to take on all responsibility for the planning of my daily health care so
that there will always be someone with me during the daytime hours. She has hired Amy
Levin, a friend of hers (a specialist in the care of seniors) with whom I get along very well,
and they are planning to find ways to improve my life, starting with a rollator, a rolling
walker with a seat to rest in, and rehab exercises to facilitate outdoor mobility. All of this
on the assumption that I may be around and (within limits) able to function for some time
to come—perhaps even until the 2012 election.

Acknowledgments

In the course of writing this book I have accumulated many debts to institutions and individuals which I would like here to acknowledge—as well as others along the way whose names are lost in failing memory or disorganized notes. The original sixty-page version of the "Black Box" essay/monograph was drafted in the early months of 1998, while I was at the Dibner Institute for the History of Science and Technology at the Massachusetts Institute of Technology. Although the bulk of my scholarly energy in the next seven years was devoted to other projects, including several articles published in the *History of Anthropology* series, the collected essays included in *Delimiting Anthropology*, and an abandoned project on Anne Roe's anthropologists, as well as research on Clyde Kluckhohn (see p. 139 above), by 2005 I had managed to create a 140-page version of the "Black Box." What I have called the "penultimate version," however, was developed during my tenure as a Mellon Foundation Emeritus Fellow (2005–8); the final version printed here includes substantial emendations and additions prompted by Ira Bashkow (see pp. 184–85).

Prior to and since then, my work has been supported by the Lichtstern Fund of the Department of Anthropology at the University of Chicago and by members of its administrative staff, including especially Anne Ch'ien. Along the way I also had a series of research assistants, including Kevin Caffrey, Byron Hamann, Tal Liron, Saul Thomas, Kate Goldfarb, and most recently Nicolas Harkness, Benjamin White, Debora Heard, and Yaqub Hilal—as well as others acknowledged in previous publications.

Although in writing it I relied heavily on my own memories and manuscripts of the period, I was able to take advantage of ten interviews taped by Ira Bashkow and Matti Bunzl, as well as those conducted by Lisa Rubens of the Bancroft Library at Berkeley. For specific memory assistance, I would also like to thank Leonard Ragozin for responding to my inquiry about the "Victory Cantata" he and Curtis Davis wrote for the 1945 graduating class of the Horace Mann–Lincoln School; Steve Wechsler (now Victor Grossman) for making available a draft of his fascinating biographical reminiscences (see Grossman 2003); my long-time friend Sheldon Rothblatt, with whom I carried on extensive correspondence in the later 1960s; and the late Dell Hymes, whose career touched mine at many points. More recently, I have benefited greatly from discussions of the problems of autobiographical memory with my late brother Myron, as well as from his memories of specific events in our lives.

Obviously, the book would not have been possible without my interactions over the last four decades with colleagues in the Department of Anthropology of the University of Chicago, including Robert McCormick Adams, Barney Cohn, Jean and John Comaroff, Jim Fernandez, Raymond Fogelson, Paul Friedrich, John Kelly, Joseph Masco, Marshall Sahlins, David Schneider, Michael Silverstein, and Raymond Smith. So, also, it has benefited from discussions with Chicago historians of the human sciences, including especially Peter Novick and Robert Richards (who has also served as computer consultant on demand). Although most of my earlier debts to colleagues at Berkeley are evident in the text, I should specifically single out Larry Levine, Henry May, Sheldon Rothblatt, Irv Scheiner, Carl Schorske, Kenneth Stampp, and Reginald Zelnik. I should also thank again all those who assisted my research in specific projects mentioned in this book and who were acknowledged therein—as well as others along the way whose names are lost in failing memory or disorganized notes.

In addition to those who contributed to the research process, I wish to thank those who read and commented on various drafts, or portions thereof, including Ira Bashkow, Debora Heard, Murray Murphey, Barbara Rosenkrantz, Sam Schweber, Betty Steinberg, Connie Sutton, and Nikki Keddie—as well as my children: Susan Stocking Baltrushes, Rebecca Stocking, Rachel Louise Stocking, Melissa Stocking Robinson, and Thomas Shepard Stocking. If it were not for Richard Handler's efforts in keeping the *History of Anthropology* series going since he took over as editor, this book (as well as several others of unusual length) might not have been published in its present form, to which he contributed several close readings along the way.

Given the role that my medical history has played in the writing of this book, it seems appropriate to mention some of the doctors who have helped me most: Martin Gorbien who initially diagnosed my colon cancer in 1995; Philip Dobrin who provided me with sage advice; Mitchell Posner and Bruce Gewertz, who performed my surgeries; and my current primary care physician Daniel Brauner. I should also mention Alan Richardson, the last of my psychotherapists, who helped make it possible for me to see my life whole.

And as always, there is Carol, who in the last rush of page-proofing relented her unwillingness to look at the manuscript and, along with Yaqub Hilal, read the complete text, offering many constructive suggestions.

References Cited

Adams, H. 1904. *Mont-Saint-Michel and Chartres*. Washington.

Aron, C. 2006. "Dorothy Lerner Gordon." In *Jewish women: A comprehensive historical encyclopedia*, ed. P. Hyman and D. Ofer. Jerusalem.

Bashkow, I. 1991. The dynamics of rapport in a colonial situation: David Schneider's fieldwork on the islands of Yap. In George W. Stocking, Jr., ed., *Colonial situations: Essays on the contextualization of ethnographic knowledge*. Madison, WI. *History of Anthropology* 7:170–242.

———. 1997. Craft and worry in the historiography of anthropology: George Stocking's style. Paper presented at sessions in honor of GWS. American Anthropological Association Annual Meeting.

———. 2006. *The meaning of whitemen: Race and modernity in the Orokaiva cultural world*. Chicago.

Bashkow, I., M. Bunzl, R. Handler, A. Orta, and D. Rosenblatt. 2004. A new Boasian anthropology: Theory for the twenty-first century. *American Anthropologist* 106(3):433–94.

Bashkow, I., and L. Dobrin. Forthcoming. "The truth in anthropology does not travel first class": Reo Fortune's fateful encounter with Margaret Mead. In *Histories of Anthropology Annual* 6, ed. R. Darnell and F. Gleach. Lincoln, NE.

Bellah, M. 1999. *Tammy: A biography of a young girl*. Berkeley, CA.

———. 2002. *Abby and her sisters: A memoir*. Berkeley, CA.

Bloch, M. 1953. *The historian's craft*. Trans. P. Putnam. New York.

Bloom, H. 1973. *The anxiety of influence: A theory of poetry*. New York.

Boas, F. 1887. The study of geography. *Science* 9:137–41.

———. 1894. Human faculty as determined by race. In GS 1974c:221–42.

Borofsky, R., director. n.d. Center for a Public Anthropology, http://www.publicanthropology.org.

Butterfield, H. 1963. *The Whig interpretation of history*. London.

Castañeda, Q. 2003. Stocking's historiography of influence: The "Story of Boas": Gamio and Redfield at the Cross-"Road to Light." *Critique of Anthropology* 23(3):235–63.

Caulfield, M. 1969. Culture and imperialism: Proposing a new dialectic. In Hymes 1999:182–212.

Cochran, T. et al. 1954. *The social sciences in historical study*. Bulletin 64, Social Science Research Council. New York.

Cohen, M., and E. Nagel. 1934. *An introduction to logic and scientific method.* New York.

Collingwood, R. 1946. *The idea of history.* Oxford.

Creelan, P. 1974. Watsonian behaviorism and the Calvinist conscience. *Journal of the History of the Behavioral Sciences* 10:95–118.

Davis, H. B. 1929. The German labor courts. *Political Science Quarterly* 44:397–420.

———. 1933a. *Labor and steel.* New York.

———. 1933b. *The condition of labor in the American iron and steel industry: Chapters from a longer work, "Labor and steel."* New York.

———. 1940. *Shoes: The workers and the industry.* New York.

———. 1967. *Nationalism and socialism: Marxist and labor theories of nationalism to 1917.* New York.

Davis, H. B., ed. 1976. *The national question: Selected writings by Rosa Luxemburg.* Introduction by H. Davis. New York.

———. 1978. *Toward a Marxist theory of nationalism.* New York.

Davis, H. B., and M. R. Davis. n.d. *Liberalism is not enough.* Privately printed. San Rafael, CA.

De Beauvoir, S. 1952. *The second sex.* Trans. H. Parshley. New York.

Devereux, G. 1968. *From anxiety to method in the behavioral sciences.* The Hague.

Diamond, S. 1992. *Compromised campus: The collaboration of universities with the intelligence community, 1945–1955.* New York.

Dow, E. 1924. *Principles of a note-system for historical studies.* London.

Freeman, D. 1983. *Margaret Mead and Samoa: The making and unmaking of an anthropological myth.* Cambridge, MA.

———. 1999. *The fateful hoaxing of Margaret Mead: A historical analysis of her Samoan research.* Boulder, CO.

Freeman, J. 2004. *At Berkeley in the sixties: The education of an activist, 1961–65.* Bloomington, IN.

Friedan, B. 1963. *The feminine mystique.* New York.

Gallagher, C., and S. Greenblatt. 2000. *Practicing new historicism.* Chicago.

Gardner, D. 1967. *The California oath controversy.* Berkeley, CA.

Geertz, C. 1974. "From the native's point of view": On the nature of anthropological understanding. In Geertz, *Local knowledge: Further essays in interpretive anthropology,* 55–70. New York [1983].

———. 1996. *After the fact: Two countries, four decades, one anthropologist.* Cambridge, MA.

Gluckman, M., and F. Eggan. 1963. *The relevance of models for social anthropology.* London.

Grafton, A. 1997. *The footnote: A curious history.* Cambridge, MA.

Grossman, V. [S. Wechsler] 2003. *Crossing the river: A memoir of the American left, the cold war and life in East Germany.* Amherst, MA.

Gupta, A., and J. Ferguson, eds. 1997. *Anthropological locations: Boundaries and grounds of a field science.* Berkeley, CA.

Handler, R. 2000. Boundaries and transitions. In Handler, ed., *Excluded ancestors, inventible traditions: Essays toward a more inclusive history of anthropology. History of Anthropology* 9:3–10. Madison, WI.

Handlin, O. 1957. What happened to race? In *Race and nationality in American life.* Boston.

Harris, M. 1968. *The rise of anthropological theory*. New York.

Heimann, J. 1998. *The most offending soul alive: Tom Harrisson and his remarkable life*. Honolulu.

Hymes, D. 1962. On studying the history of anthropology. *Items* 16(3):25–26.

———, ed. 1999. *Reinventing anthropology* [1972]. With new introduction. Ann Arbor, MI.

Kell, L., and J. Aldous. 1960. The relations between mothers' child-rearing ideologies and their children's perceptions of maternal control. *Child Development* 31:145–56.

Kerr, C. 2001. *The gold and the blue: A personal memoir of the University of California, 1949–67*, vol. 2, *Political turmoil*. Berkeley, CA.

Kluckhohn, C. 1944. *Navaho witchcraft*. Cambridge, MA.

———. 1949. *Mirror for man: Anthropology and modern life*. New York.

Koestler, A. 1941. *Darkness at noon*. London.

———. 1950. Arthur Koestler. In *The god that failed*, ed. R. Crossman, 13–75. New York.

Kroeber, A. 1915. Eighteen professions. *American Anthropologist* 17:283–88.

Kuhn. T. 1962. *The structure of scientific revolutions*. Chicago.

Lee, D., and R. Beck. 1954. The meaning of "historicism." *American Historical Review* 59:568–77.

Levenson, J. 1958. *Confucian China and its modern fate*, vol. 1, *The problem of intellectual continuity*. Berkeley, CA.

———. 1965. *Confucian China and its modern fate*, vol. 3, *The problem of historical significance*. Berkeley, CA.

Marcus, G. 1990. The production of European high culture in Los Angeles: The J. Paul Getty Trust as artificial curiosity. *Cultural Anthropology* 5:314–30.

Mead, M. 1970. Review of *Race, culture, and evolution*, by GS 1968a. *American Anthropologist* 72:378–79.

Munson, H. 1996. Review of GS 1995 in *Religion* 26:393–96.

Obama, B. 1995. *Dreams from my father: A story of race and inheritance*. New York.

———. 2006. *The audacity of hope: Thoughts on reclaiming the American dream*. New York.

Popkin, J. 2005. *History, historians, and autobiography*. Chicago.

Price, D. 2004. *Threatening anthropology: McCarthyism and the FBI's surveillance of activist anthropologists*. Durham, NC.

———. 2008. *Anthropological intelligence: The deployment and neglect of American anthropology in the Second World War*. Durham, NC.

Ragozin, L. 1997. J. Edgar Hoover made me do it. In Ragozin, *The odds must be crazy*, 3–18. New York.

Robertson, P. D., and R. L. Robertson. 1976. *Panhandle pilgrimage: Illustrated tales tracing history in the Texas Panhandle*. Canyon, TX.

Roe, A. 1953. *The making of a scientist*. New York.

Rostow, W. 1960. *The stages of economic growth: A non-Communist manifesto*. Cambridge, Eng.

Rutherford, M. 1994. *Institutions in economics: The old and the new institutionalism*. Cambridge, Eng.

Sayers, M., and A. Kahn. 1946. *The great conspiracy: The secret war against Soviet Russia*. Boston.

Schutz, A. 1944. The stranger: An essay in social psychology. *American Journal of Sociology* 49:499–507.

Segal, D., and S. Yanigisako. 2005. *Unwrapping the sacred bundle: Reflections on the disciplining of anthropology.* Durham, NC.

Stern, F. 1960. *The varieties of history from Voltaire to the present.* New York.

Stocking, C. H., and H. E. Stocking. 1981. *The Stocking ancestry.* Stillwater, OK.

Stocking, G. W. 1925. *The oil industry and the competitive system: A study in waste.* Cambridge, MA.

———. 1931. *The potash industry: A study in state control.* New York.

———. 1938. The Mexican oil problem. In *Arnold Foundation studies in public affairs.* 6:4.

———. 1954. *Basing point pricing and regional development: A case study of the iron and steel industry.* Chapel Hill, NC.

———. 1961. *Workable competition and antitrust policy.* Nashville.

———. 1970. *Middle East oil: A study in political and economic controversy.* Nashville.

Stocking, G. W., and M. W. Watkins. 1946. *Cartels in action.* New York.

———. 1948. *Cartels or competition.* New York.

———. 1951. *Monopoly and free enterprise.* New York.

Stocking, G. W., Jr. 1960a. American social scientists and race theory, 1890–1915. Doctoral dissertation, University of Pennsylvania. University Microfilms 60-3698.

———. 1960b. Franz Boas and the founding of the American Anthropological Association. *American Anthropologist* 62:1–17.

———. 1962. Lamarckianism in American social science: 1890–1915. In 1968a: 234–69.

———. 1963. Matthew Arnold, E. B. Tylor, and the uses of invention. In 1968a: 69–90.

———. 1964a. French anthropology in 1800. In 1968a:13–41.

———. 1964b. *The Negro in American history textbooks: A report of a study of the treatment of Negroes in American history textbooks used in grades five and eight and in the high schools of California's public schools* [prepared by a panel of University of California historians chaired by K. M. Stampp, esp. 9–12.] Sacramento: California State Department of Education.

———. 1965a. "Cultural Darwinism" and "philosophical idealism" in E. B. Tylor: A special plea for historicism in the history of anthropology. In 1968a: 91–109.

———. 1965b. From physics to ethnology: Franz Boas' Arctic expedition as a problem in the historiography of the behavioral sciences. In 1968a:133–60.

———. 1965c. On the limits of "presentism" and "historicism" in the historiography of the behavioral sciences. In 1968a:1–12.

———. 1966a. Franz Boas and the culture concept in historical perspective. In 1968a:195–233.

———. 1966b. The history of anthropology: Where, whence, whither. *Journal of the History of the Behavioral Sciences* 2:281–90.

———. 1968a. *Race, culture, and evolution: Essays in the history of anthropology.* New York.

———. 1968b. Empathy and antipathy in the heart of darkness: An essay review of Malinowski's field diaries. *Journal of the History of the Behavioral Sciences* 4:189–94.

———. 1968c. A historical brief for cultural materialism [review of M. Harris, *The rise of anthropological theory*]. *Science* 162(October 4):108–10.

———. 1968d. Tylor, Edward Burnett. *International Encyclopedia of the Social Sciences*, 10:170–77. New York.

———. 1971a. Animism in theory and practice: E. B. Tylor's unpublished "Notes on spiritualism." In 2001a:116–46.

———. 1971b. What's in a name? The origins of the Royal Anthropological Institute: 1837–1871. *Man* 6:369–90.

———. 1973. From chronology to ethnology: James Cowles Prichard and British anthropology, 1800–1850. Reprinted in Prichard, *Researches into the physical history of man*, ix–cx. Chicago.

———. 1974a. The Boas plan for the study of American Indian languages. In 1992:60–91.

———. 1974b. Some comments on history as a moral discipline: "Transcending textbook chronicles and apologetics." In *Studies in the history of linguistics: Traditions and paradigms*, ed. Dell Hymes, 511–19. Bloomington, IN.

———. 1974c. The basic assumptions of Boasian anthropology. In *The shaping of American anthropology, 1883–1911: A Franz Boas reader*, 1–20. Chicago.

———. 1975. Scotland as the model of mankind: Lord Kames's philosophical view of civilization. In 2001a:78–102.

———. 1976. Ideas and institutions in American anthropology: Thoughts toward a history of the interwar years. In 1992:114–77.

———. 1979a. Anthropology as Kulturkampf: Science and politics in the career of Franz Boas. In 1992:92–113.

———. 1979b. *Anthropology at Chicago: Tradition, discipline, department*. Chicago.

———. 1983. The ethnographer's magic: Fieldwork in British anthropology from Tylor to Malinowski. In 1992:12–59.

———. 1984a. Radcliffe-Brown and British social anthropology. *History of Anthropology* 2:131–91.

———. 1984b. Academician Bromley on Soviet ethnography. *History of Anthropology Newsletter* 11(2):6–10.

———. 1985. Philanthropoids and vanishing cultures: Rockefeller funding and the end of the museum era in Anglo-American anthropology. In 1992:178–211.

———. 1986. Anthropology and the science of the irrational: Malinowski's encounter with Freudian psychoanalysis. *History of Anthropology* 4:13–49.

———. 1987. *Victorian anthropology*. New York.

———. 1988. Guardians of the sacred bundle: The American Anthropological Association and the representation of holistic anthropology. In *Learned societies and the evolution of the disciplines*, 17–25. American Council of Learned Societies Occasional Paper 5. New York.

———. 1989. The ethnographic sensibility of the 1920s and the dualism of the anthropological tradition. In 1992:276–341.

———. 1991. Maclay, Kubary, Malinowski: Archetypes from the dreamtime of anthropology. In 1992:212–75.

———. 1992. *The ethnographer's magic and other essays in the history of anthropology*. Madison, WI.

———. 1993a. Reading the palimpsest of inquiry: *Notes and Queries* and the history of British social anthropology. In 2001a:164–206.

———. 1993b. *Granddaddy Stocking's Christmas Stockings*. Unpublished album (20 pages) for private circulation and eventual deposit in the Special Collections Research Center of the Regenstein Library.

———. 1995. *After Tylor: British social anthropology, 1888–1951*. Madison, WI.

———, ed. 1996. *Volksgeist as method and ethic: Essays on Boasian ethnography and the German anthropological tradition. History of Anthropology* 8. Madison, WI.

———. 1999. Presentism and historicism once again: The history of British anthropology as intellectual and personal history. *Journal of Victorian Culture* 4:328–35.

———. 2000. "Do good, young man": Sol Tax and the world mission of liberal democratic anthropology. In *History of Anthropology* 9:171–264.

———. 2001a. *Delimiting anthropology: Occasional essays and reflections*. Madison, WI.

———. 2001b. *California from Marin to Malibu: A haiku album*. Privately reproduced for deposit in the Special Collections Research Center of the Regenstein Library.

———. 2004: A. I. Hallowell's Boasian evolutionism: Human ir/rationality in cross-cultural, evolutionary, and personal context. In *History of Anthropology* 10:196–260.

———. 2006. Unfinished business: Robert Gelston Armstrong, the Federal Bureau of Investigation, and the history of anthropology at Chicago and in Nigeria. In *History of Anthropology* 11:99–247.

Stocking, H. 1980. "Stocking—A pioneer legend." *Clarendon Press*. August 21.

Stocking, R. L. 2000. *Bishops, councils, and consensus in the Visigothic Kingdom, 589–633*. Ann Arbor, MI.

Suzuki, P. T. 1959. The religious system and culture of the Nias, Indonesia. PhD dissertation, Leiden University.

———. 1976. The ethnolinguistics of Japanese Americans in the wartime camps. *Anthropological Linguistics* 18:416–27.

———. 1980. A retrospective analysis of a wartime "national character" study. *Dialectical Anthropology* 5(1):33–46.

———. 1981. Anthropologists in the wartime camps for Japanese Americans: A documentary study. *Dialectical Anthropology* 6(1):23–60.

———. 1986. The University of California Japanese Evacuation and Resettlement Study: A prolegomenon. *Dialectical Anthropology* 10(3):189–213.

———. 2009. Partially out of the closet: Coming to terms with American anthropology's unpleasant past. Paper presented at "The Activities of anthropologists during WWII in the Japanese internment camps" session of the American Anthropological Association Annual Meeting.

Watson, J. 1928. *Psychological care of infant and child*. New York.

Winkin, Y. 1986. George W. Stocking, Jr. et l'historie de l'anthropologie. *Actes de la recherche en sciences sociales*. 64:81–84.

Zelnik, R. 2002. "On the Side of the Angels: The Berkeley Faculty and the FSM." In *The Free Speech Movement: Reflections on Berkeley in the 1960s*, ed. R. Cohen and R. Zelnik, 264–338. Berkeley, CA.

Index

Page numbers in *italic* indicate illustrations.
GS in subheadings refers to George Stocking.

HISTORY OF ANTHROPOLOGY